BLACK

AND

GOLD

BLACK

AND

GOLD

ANTHONY SAMPSON

Pantheon Books New York

All rights reserved under International and Pan-American
Copyright Conventions.
Published in the United States by Pantheon Books,
a division of Random House, Inc., New York.
Originally published in Great Britain
by Hodder and Stoughton Ltd.

Library of Congress Cataloging-in-Publication Data

Sampson, Anthony.
Black and gold.
1. South Africa—Politics and government—
20th century. 2. South Africa—Foreign relations.
3. Industry—Social aspects—South Africa.
4. Investments, Foreign—South Africa. 5. Apartheid—
South Africa. I. Title.
DT770.S26   1987   323.1′0968   86-42978
ISBN 0-394-56053-1

Manufactured in the United States of America

First American Edition

Contents

Introduction

Oh I will sit me down and weep
For bones in Africa

A E Housman

No one can pretend to be wholly dispassionate about South Africa,
so it is wiser to declare interests beforehand. I felt pressed to write
this book from two very contrasted experiences. On the one side I
had been fascinated by the South African problem ever since I
worked for four years from 1951 as editor of the black magazine
Drum in Johannesburg. It was a job which provided an almost
unique opportunity to get to know black South Africans, including
such political leaders as Albert Luthuli, Nelson Mandela and Oliver
Tambo; and I was able to spend much of my time in Soweto,
Sophiatown and black shebeens at a time when there were few
bridges across the colour bar. After returning to London to work
on the *Observer* I took every excuse to report on South Africa,
including visits for the Treason Trials in 1957 (about which I wrote
a book *The Treason Cage*), for Macmillan's visit and the Sharpeville
emergency in 1960, for Mandela's trial in 1964, for the elections of
1970, for the Muldergate scandals of 1978. And in London I was
able to keep in touch with black politicians in exile.

But I have also had a long curiosity about the relationship
between corporations and politics, which may have originated in
my childhood when my father worked as a research chemist in ICI.
After studying the broader national power structure in my book
Anatomy of Britain in 1962 I became more intrigued by the political
involvements of multinational corporations, which I then explored
in a succession of books: about ITT, the oil companies, arms
companies and airlines. In each of them I came up against the
recurring problem of where corporate loyalties lie when confronted
with dictatorships or potential enemies; and when revisiting South
Africa I became more interested in business attitudes and dilemmas
over apartheid.

When the South African crisis became more acute two years ago

I was editing my own international newsletter which enabled me
to keep in touch through the telephone with South African friends
including Nadine Gordimer, Winnie Mandela, Gatsha Buthelezi,
Helen Suzman and Oliver Tambo. I found that international
direct-dialling could sometimes give easier access to a range of
information and opinions, including banned politicians, than communications inside South Africa. Through Tambo and other black
leaders I tried to learn more about the attitudes of the black
opposition; while at the same time businessmen both in London
and New York were becoming more concerned about their future
in a black South Africa, and I tried to ease the communications
between the two sides. As the crisis worsened I returned to South
Africa twice, at the beginning of each of the two emergencies, to
talk both to black leaders and to businessmen.

In this book I have tried to trace the erratic relationships between
these two groups of actors in the South African drama – the
international business leaders and the black politicians – since they
first encountered each other a century ago. I try to show how the
story developed from both sides, to explore some of the characters
and their motivations on the way, and to convey the flavour of
each period without hindsight. I do not attempt to analyse with the
same closeness the changing attitudes of Afrikaners and their
governments, except insofar as they affected the whole climate
and legislation of the country. But from 1978, when P W
Botha became prime minister, I look at the story in more detail, to
try to trace the stages towards the current tragic deadlock and to
show the viewpoint from America and Europe as well as South
Africa.

I have far too many debts and obligations, and too many discreet
or reluctant sources and helpers, to list. I am grateful to several
journalists in Johannesburg and London who have been generous
with their advice; I appreciate the trust and assistance of black
politicians; and I have had long talks partly in confidence with
many of the bankers and businessmen involved. I am grateful to
my American publisher Andre Schiffrin of Pantheon for invaluable
editorial suggestions; to my London publishers Hodder & Stoughton and my editor Ion Trewin for their continuing efficiency and
support; to my two agents Michael Sissons in London and Sterling Lord in New York; to Joe Bullman for useful research; to Bettie
du Toit for patiently listening, and advising on difficult chapters;
and to Carla Shimeld for helping through the last stages of
editing.

I hope this book may interest and help those who like me believe
that it is still possible to avert a catastrophe in that marvellous and

resilient country, and that businessmen, as well as politicians, can use their influence and foresight to prepare for a democratic future.

Anthony Sampson, *London, November 1986*

BLACK

AND

GOLD

1

Looking Across the Abyss

If we really want to lose everything, then we must hang on to everything now.

Donald Masson (retired president of the Afrikaner
Institute of Commerce), June 1986

In the big garden of Marlborough House in London in August 1986, seven Commonwealth prime ministers were attending a cocktail party before having a final argument about South Africa. It was a poignant setting, down the Mall from Buckingham Palace, in the former royal mansion which used to house only King George V's widow: it was now turned into the headquarters of the Commonwealth of forty-nine countries, run by its Guyanan Secretary-General, Sonny Ramphal, from Queen Mary's old bedroom. The South African fires six thousand miles away had rekindled all the smouldering emotions about black and white, about order and chaos, appeasement and confrontation. Marlborough House had become the central battleground: conservatives had been attacking Ramphal for trying to lure the Queen herself away from Britain's true interests, while across the street demonstrators had been yelling all day, 'Free Mandela!' Inside Marlborough House the prime ministers had spent two days arguing with Margaret Thatcher about the report of their 'eminent persons' who had warned them that unless they took effective measures South Africa could turn into 'the worst bloodbath since the Second World War'. They had had some of the most acrimonious exchanges they could remember: the room, said one participant, was 'flowing with vitriol'.

But at the garden party Ramphal was welcoming everyone with the same jolly laugh, and the multiracial Commonwealth still showed some life. Brian Mulroney from Canada, with his boyish chin, was joking with a lugubrious-looking Kenneth Kaunda from Zambia who was staring upwards with his horror-movie eyes. Robert Mugabe from Zimbabwe was gesturing intently at Bob Hawke from Australia. Malcolm Fraser, the former Australian prime minister, was restraining his emotional outbursts and beam-

ing down like a beacon. They were nearly all talking about sanctions
from the perspective of their own interests and oceans. Bob Hawke
was determined on stopping air traffic; but the Australian airline
Qantas had long ago stopped flying to South Africa. Mulroney was
pressing for wider sanctions, including minerals; but the Canadian
uranium producers would benefit. Rajiv Gandhi wanted to stop all
trade; India had (officially) stopped trading twenty years ago. They
all preferred to discuss the long term rather than the short term:
Mulroney insisted that the world must see 'the sweep of history';
Fraser explained that every country must be seen to be on the right
side in this historic crisis.

They were all gunning for Britain, which was by far the biggest
investor in South Africa; and the British isolation was very visible.
The senior officials stood round the edge of the lawn speculating
about the effects of a real Commonwealth split, while their prime
minister, looking for once exhausted, arrived late and kept her
distance. She listened patiently, with a puzzled expression, while
an Asian diplomat discussed a prize for Nelson Mandela, but before
long burst out against the hypocrisy of sanctions and the ignorance
of other prime ministers: 'They think that we could close down the
South African tourist office just like that . . . they don't understand
about bank loans . . . they don't realise there are 800,000 South
Africans with British passports.' The timing of this summit could
hardly be worse, she told me, just before Botha was due to make
another big speech to his people. She would have liked to talk to
him herself, but this was not the right time.

Everyone talked about national interests, but everyone had their
own emotional involvement; and few more than Mrs Thatcher. To
her, South Africa seemed partly like a nightmare caricature of the
dangers within Britain, from Brixton to Belfast, with terrorists
threatening to induce chaos, and rioters and strikers undermining
commercial stability. She sympathised with the embattled Afrikaners and their fighting spirit, encouraged by her husband Denis
– who had been back in South Africa in March – and by her
Afrikaner friend the writer Laurens van der Post: she saw them as
stubborn, ready to fight to the bitter end, thriving in isolation. As
she described them, she might be talking about herself; for at this
summit she seemed to gain new energy from being alone. But she
also believed that British voters were behind her: that they too were
fed up with being lectured by black autocrats who had made a mess
of their own countries and had locked up their opposition in jail.

At the conference inside Marlborough House she had slapped
down the black prime ministers, rubbing in their dependence on
British aid, and explaining how Botha was dismantling apartheid

and how South African blacks had higher standards of living and education than most others. When Mugabe protested, she replied: 'But weren't you educated in South Africa?' The prime ministers were predictably exasperated. Kaunda maintained that she 'cut a pathetic picture'. Gandhi complained that she had given up the moral leadership of the Commonwealth. Mugabe protested that 'Britain has let the people of South Africa down.' She seemed impervious to them all – except perhaps to General Obasanjo, the bulky former Nigerian president who had been co-chairman of the Commonwealth Group, who was heaving himself round the garden party in a genial mood. Thatcher held the general in unusual respect, and had exchanged friendly letters with him about the Afrikaner character in which the general had insisted that, though Afrikaners were stubborn, they would not commit suicide: but now he ended the correspondence with a despairing open letter to 'my dear Margaret': he was appalled, he wrote, by her ignorance of conditions inside South Africa, her absurd hopes of Botha's reforms, her apparent faith in his policy of dividing the tribes. 'Such was our discussion that I must ask: "Did you even read our report?"' He warned her that 'many people around the world view your continued opposition to sanctions as founded in instinct, not logic, and as displaying a misguided tribal loyalty and myopic political vision . . . Not only does the mental laager of the Boer seem to be mirrored in your own attitudes, but his fatal concessions of too little, too late, are paralleled in your actions.'*

But it was now Washington rather than London that was making the running, where the South African fires were arousing even higher emotions. President Reagan himself shared many of Mrs Thatcher's instincts, dreading revolution and terrorism and always hopeful that the Afrikaners would liberalise themselves; while his White House contained ideologues who naturally equated South Africa with Nicaragua, Iran or the Philippines, including his speech-writer Pat Buchanan who had hoped to be ambassador to South Africa. But the Congress, aroused by black protests and massive television coverage, had taken up the cause of black South Africans with rare bi-partisan unity; and when President Botha declared a second state of emergency the State Department under George Shultz was determined to send a strong signal of dis-approval to Pretoria. Then Reagan decided to make his first major speech about South Africa, which soon became a trial of strength among his advisers. Buchanan had already interested Reagan in an article in *Commentary* magazine by Paul Johnson, the British

* *Financial Times*, August 7, 1986

right-wing journalist whose books Buchanan admired (Johnson was
later told that Reagan had read the article three times). Johnson
had recently been to South Africa to write a book for Consolidated
Goldfields, and his article argued that blacks were better off in South
Africa than elsewhere in the continent and that disinvestment was
'a cruel absurdity'. The State Department prepared its own draft
for the President's speech, very critical of Botha and insisting on
more thorough reforms; but Buchanan got a look at it, complained
that it was 'relentless Boer-bashing', and quickly substituted his
own version, with several quotations from Paul Johnson about the
improvement of black conditions in South Africa compared to the
rest of Africa, and with lurid warnings against communism and
terrorism.* Many officials complained it would now only give
comfort to Botha, but Reagan went ahead to deliver his speech,
based on Buchanan's version, on July 22. It read like a catalogue
of doubts and hesitations about South Africa, swinging from but
to but, from however to nevertheless. The President agreed that
apartheid was morally wrong and politically unacceptable; but
agreed with Mrs Thatcher that punitive sanctions were also im-
moral and repugnant. Pretoria was not obliged to negotiate with
terrorists; but Mandela should be released, to participate in the
political process. The strongest allies of blacks, Reagan insisted,
were the Western businessmen who brought in their own ideas
of social justice: 'capitalism is the natural enemy of such feudal
institutions as apartheid.'

The speech rapidly achieved the opposite of what the State
Department had intended. President Botha welcomed it in support
of his anti-communist crusade, while black South Africans were
outraged. 'The West, for my part, can go to hell,' said Bishop Tutu
in Johannesburg. But it also appalled much of Washington. George
Shultz soon explained he was flexible about sanctions and wanted
to speak to black leaders, while Senators and Congressmen were
now determined to rescue America's reputation, as they saw it, by
pushing through a bill for sanctions. Three weeks after Reagan's
speech the Senators held an historic debate, re-stating their fears
about apartheid, and the Republican Senator Richard Lugar put
forward his bill for sanctions – against South African steel, coal,
airlines, textiles and new investment. 'We believe it is time to send
a blunt message to President P W Botha's government', said Lugar;
and his bill was passed with an emphatic majority. President Reagan
vetoed it, saying once again that sanctions would hurt blacks most
of all; but finally Congress used its two-thirds majority to override

* *New Republic*, September 15, 1986; are private information

the veto, by seventy-eight votes to twenty-one, in the biggest foreign policy reversal of Reagan's presidency.

In London Mrs Thatcher had also been compelled to modify her own stand under pressure from the Commonwealth and the European Community; and in September the twelve European nations had their own wrangle, with the Danes and the Dutch most determined on maximum sanctions and the Germans and Portuguese turning against a ban on South African coal. But by September 17 they had agreed to ban imports of iron, steel, gold coins or any new investment. The Western sanctions were much less biting and unambiguous than the complete mandatory sanctions which black South Africans had asked for. Yet they marked a tragic cross-roads: the end of a long open road of growing investment and trade, stretching back over a century, during which the Western billions had helped to transform the bottom of the continent into an industrial power-house. Sanctions ended the hopes that investment and wealth could in themselves undermine apartheid. But their economic consequences could prove less important than their signal that the West had finally dissociated itself from Pretoria, and begun to change sides.

The long Western debate about sanctions had highlighted all the conflicting images of South Africa, but without much relevance to the real inhabitants. To Western conservatives it stood for the disciplined white world in contrast to the chaos and disintegration in the black North: however awful the system, any revolutionary alternative must be more awful. Marxists saw South Africa as the ultimate case study of the class conflict, with workers painted black and capitalists white, whose origins had helped Lenin to form his theories about imperialism. To many American liberals it was the last replay of their own revolution, an assertion of inalienable human rights: to American blacks it was an extension of the civil rights campaign. To ageing European liberals it was the last of the liberation epics, the bottom line after all the false accountings through Africa, which called for an agonising reappraisal of what kind of freedom the early liberations had really achieved.

South Africa seemed not so much a real country as a map of the mind in which anyone could find his own place. The blacks, who had so often since Rousseau's Noble Savage been receptacles for liberal imaginations, now appeared as the last of the underdogs, fighting battles which had long ago been won elsewhere. Idealists could still find reassurance in their half-biblical world, where words like crucifixion and persecution still had a literal meaning, and where protest still had a kind of innocence, uncorrupted by power. Many Western conservatives, like Mrs Thatcher, identified them-

selves with the Afrikaners as the extreme exponents of will-power
and survival in a world threatened by chaos; while others saw them
as the reincarnations of Nazis, bringing back the horrors of racialism
and genocide.

White South Africans heard the Western theorising with wry
smiles. They noticed that while Americans enjoyed self-righteously
attacking the brutalities of apartheid, they preferred not to consider
the consequences of a black majority as in the rest of Africa. They
noticed the ignorance of their critics, explaining: 'We know the
Bantu'. But behind that confident singular did they really know
him – or them? Most whites had never been inside a black township;
few had talked to any of them except as servants. It was a country
of dialogues of the deaf, of leaders who had never met each other:
the censored television and newspapers gave South Africans less
news of key events in their own country than could be gained by a
casual TV viewer in the West; and many foreign correspondents
knew far more about black politics than South African members of
parliament. Was South Africa really a nation at all? Some British
politicians speculated whether they could not rescind the Act of
Union which created it 75 years ago; and even the Pretoria government had its doubts. 'We are not really one nation,' the ambassador
to London, Denis Worrall, told British MPs: 'and do not have a
single perceived history or one single set of shared heroes.'*

Behind all these black-and-white images South Africa was always
a much greyer area than the theorists described: far more industrialised and detribalised than the rest of the continent. For over a
century – before the nation had been invented – the mills of industry
round Johannesburg and elsewhere had been grinding away at the
old tribal structures, drawing still more people into its disciplines
and motivations. Sowetans had as little in common with Ugandans
as British factory workers had with Polish peasants, and the rural
myths of the Afrikaners had more to do with their reaction against
the harsh facts of industrialisation than with their enduring charac-
teristics. The makers of this modern state were as much the industrialists, miners and bankers as the politicians and tribal chiefs,
whether Afrikaners and blacks. And while Western politicians were
arguing about interests, ideologies and strategic importance, the
businessmen were contending with much more practical worries
about who they could do business with in the future, and whether
their companies could survive.

                    *   *   *

* Evidence to Foreign Affairs Committee Report on South Africa, June 30,
1986

Down in South Africa, the view was much more detailed, but much more fragmented, like a cracked telescope. Johannesburg, its commercial hub, had always been a city of money and business, or nothing, and had transformed everyone it had drawn into its field – white, black and brown. Unlike other African cities it had been started from scratch, built up on a bleak landscape 400 miles from the sea, with no river or trees, with no tribal or rural traditions to modify its intense urban character, and gold as its only reason for existence. It was soon driven by its gold-wealth and ambition, until it became the biggest industrial complex in the continent. Now in its centenary year its glittering white suburbs stretched twenty miles to the north, linked by a brand-new freeway system which seemed to promise indefinite expansion; while some of the palatial old mansions, complete with white-suited black servants, seemed to be competing as sets for *Gone with the Wind*. Their peace and security was still undisturbed by black dwellings which had been largely contained in the vast township of Soweto in the south, where the houses were a quarter of the size. Every day the white executives drove to work from the north, while the black workers poured in by train or bus from the South, combining their energies which had built up the city's prosperity. Every evening they all separated out again, like unravelled knitting, to their opposite areas.

But by June 1986, Johannesburg and its hidden twin Soweto were at the core of the crisis, the immediate cause of the state of emergency which President Botha had declared, just before the planned celebrations of the tenth anniversary of the Soweto uprising. I had flown out there just beforehand, to see again the magnetic city where thirty years ago I had moved without much difficulty between the black and white worlds. Now it seemed almost as if war had been declared between them. On the Monday of the anniversary the city centre was like a ghost-town, with shut shops, empty streets and young blue-capped police reservists fingering their rifles: only a gun-shop was doing much business. Newspaper and television news offered government propaganda and extended sports coverage. The *Financial Times* arrived from London with its front-page story blacked out. All the roads to Soweto, only ten miles away, were blocked by police who searched every car, while the telephone lines to Soweto went dead, 'for technical reasons'. The only journalists admitted were flown in by helicopter, and driven briefly round in a barred van. It seemed more remote from white Johannesburg than East Berlin from the West. President Botha had just declared apartheid outdated: but in the geographical sense it had never been so effective.

The state had mobilised its resources to enforce the most thorough

clampdown in South Africa's history, with the strongest army in
Africa to reinforce the police: they had been given almost limitless
powers of arrest and detention, and were deliberately trying to
terrify the blacks by making people disappear; what they called 'the
Argentine option'. 'I can't find out about my black clients', said an
Indian defence lawyer: 'whether they're detained, or are hiding, or
have left the country – or are dead.' 'That's the worst part of it,'
said a young Sowetan writer, 'not knowing what's happened to your
friends.' There was no legal means of public protest: only a special
service at the cathedral where Bishop Tutu warned that there would
be 'greater and greater repression with smaller and smaller results'.
At dinner at his house next evening I found the bishop subdued
and depressed by a talk with President Botha who seemed as
committed as ever to his apartheid policy of homelands; but he
talked with the same passion in private as in public: 'Why don't
people understand the pain in our hearts? How many more thousands must be killed?'

Yet with all the government's show of strength the blacks seemed
almost absurdly uncowed and confident of victory. I was reminded
of the words of the Afrikaner political scientist, Hermann Giliomee:
'The most serious failing is the inability of each side to assess the
other's real strength.' The Afrikaners put their confidence in money
and guns; the blacks in ideas and world opinion. Each had tragically
underestimated the other, in this ultimate non-meeting of minds.

Certainly the blacks had some reason to question the power of the
state. Their oldest black political organisation, the African National
Congress, had been banned since 1960, its members exiled or imprisoned; yet its leader, Nelson Mandela, was far more famous than
when he was jailed twenty-four years ago, and the ANC never had more
support. The more the government denounced its exiled president
Oliver Tambo the more he was admired in the townships. The
government had just distributed 70,000 copies of a free booklet about
the ANC, to warn the whites about its communist influences; but the
blacks gobbled it up in the townships, quoted the speeches and pinned
up Mandela's photograph (the next edition left out the photograph).
At the weekend before June 16 a car-bomb had exploded on the
Golden Mile beachfront in Durban, close to popular nightspots such
as Magoos and the Why Not bar, killing three white women. The
police immediately blamed it on the ANC, and the whites were united
in horror: the government called it 'despicable and cowardly'; the
opposition leader Colin Eglin said it was 'cowardly and despicable'.
But most blacks preferred not to comment on it.

Ironically the only black political leaders who were easily access-
ible were twenty-two who were already in prison, being tried for

treason in the small town of Delmas, forty miles east of Johannes-burg. When I went out there with their defence attorney we found the accused waiting behind bars in the cells below the courtroom, where they had been on trial for months and could face life imprison-ment. Yet they seemed more exuberant and optimistic than most people outside, and they were preparing for a wedding of one of the accused in the courtroom next day: I began to understand why white liberals who visited black prisoners often found they needed the visits to revive their own spirits. The prisoners were full of questions about Western politics: would Mrs Thatcher agree to a coalition? Would Chester Crocker keep his job in the State Department? The thirty-four-year-old activist Popo Molefe was one of the generation who had been politicised by the Soweto revolt ten years before, who had become the general secretary of the United Democratic Front: 'it was the voice,' he insisted, 'to say that there was still a chance to bring about change without great loss of life. Now the state of emergency can't contain the anger of the people.' But he still put much hope on international pressure. 'This is a moment of truth for the West: they've run out of excuses. We don't expect countries to ignore their self-interest. We know we won't get complete sanctions. But they can be selective, to show they mean business. What are the interests you have in this minority govern-ment? You know, we're aware of these things.'

Talking to black journalists, I found them all the more convinced of their strength by the government's reaction. 'The emergency was a deadly mistake,' said Percy Qoboza of City Press, 'the leadership is already regrouping, and the jungle telegrams are still working.' 'If Botha had reformed from a position of strength the black people might have been grateful,' said Stanley Motjuwadi, the editor of *Drum* magazine: 'but they know that it's pressure that made him move . . . The more people he detains, the greater the armies of his enemies.'

But to a white lunch-party in northern Johannesburg, on a brown lawn under that marvellous bright winter sun, this black confidence seemed merely pathetic; and the turmoil in Soweto seemed as distant as another continent. How could this solid material city, with all its Western technology and communications, protected by the massed police and defence forces, be seriously threatened by incompetent terrorists, still riddled with informers, instructed by a bunch of out-of-touch exiles in Zambia six hundred miles north? Was it more improbable, I ventured, than the confidence of the Ayatollah Khomeini, confronting the military might of the Shah with only a mad idea? Or even of the Afrikaners themselves when they took on the might of the British Empire eighty years earlier? But

the Shah's army had none of the determination of the Afrikaners, I
was told, and the blacks in South Africa had none of the fanatical
unity of either the Islamic fundamentalists or the old Boers.

Yet the English-speaking whites were clearly less confident about
everything than they had been when I last visited Johannesburg a
year earlier. Whatever new unity they might have found from the
emergency and the threat of sanctions, they had no convincing
future to look to: the government's policy had shown no real
consistency, and no serious new political blueprint to take the place
of the grand apartheid of the past, with its homelands and elaborate
demarcations: the next homeland due to be declared independent,
KwaNdebele, was already in open revolt, while the new three-
chamber parliament, which was President Botha's special creation,
had been overridden and discredited by the emergency. Whatever
the temporary boom the record numbers of emigrants (3,000 a
month, according to British Airways) told their own story, as they
took the 'chicken-run' to escape from conscription and the prospect
of a future civil war. Each batch of emigrants made the eventual
conflict look harsher and more uncompromising.

And many people on both sides, black and white, were now
talking not so much about winning or losing, but about chaos: a
continuing loss of control from both sides, as black and white
violence fed on each other while relative moderates, including both
Mandela and Botha, were pushed out of the way. In the townships
the 'necklace' – the tyre filled with petrol and set alight round the
victim's neck – had become the instrument of retribution from the
young 'comrades' providing their own counter-terrorism to stamp
out informers and collaborators. The rubber necklace had become
the symbol of anarchic power, the subject of dark threats and jokes:
'You can have your choice, Goodyear or Firestone.' Two months
earlier Winnie Mandela, the wife of the ANC leader who was now a
politician in her own right, had sent shivers down many white
spines by calling for blacks to go into the white suburbs, armed
with their necklaces and matchboxes. Tambo and the ANC leaders
had told her to keep quiet: she was incommunicado for a few weeks
and then modified her remark, while Tambo later emphasised that
the ANC disapproved of necklaces – 'you can take a hint.' But the
ANC's 'Radio Freedom' still made bloodthirsty broadcasts, and the
necklace remained the image of black fury. To Western leaders it
was the portent of chaos: 'a barbaric atrocity', Reagan called it.
But to many radical young blacks it was their only demonstration
of power, which had to be extended into the white world. I asked
a group of young Sowetans, whether they and their friends were
worried by the implications of Winnie's outburst. 'They didn't bat

an eyelid,' said one of them. 'They know in their heart of hearts that they must go into the white suburbs – which epitomise all our problems', said another: 'They take the necklaces for granted.' The only way to avoid far worse violence, they all insisted, was sanctions: 'The right question isn't: do you support sanctions? It's "Do you want to destroy apartheid? If so, do you prefer sanctions or violence?" But we know that the Iron Lady and the Cowboy will be on the side of the Boers in the end. Violence will be our only weapon.'

Both sides were making their own parallels with the horrors of the Algerian War thirty years earlier. Was South Africa, too, moving into a civil war in which another million could be killed? Was it now like Algiers in early 1958, when the rebels had lost the battle but won international support? Would the Afrikaners, like the French colonists, continue to give too little, too late, and to lock up the only rebels they could negotiate with? Would the Afrikaners fight to the bitter end, because they had nowhere else to go? Or was it because the French did have somewhere to go that they fought so ferociously; while the Afrikaners, who had to stay, knew that in the end they would have to do a deal?

Facing this vortex of violence, how could the businessmen who had built up this unique industrial society protect their own interests? Everyone was now looking towards them, whether as villains or potential saviours. 'There can be no real change until business takes the side of freedom,' Winnie Mandela had said to me with careful emphasis. 'At present we regard them as the government's allies. If they want real change with stability, they must identify themselves with the aspirations of our people.' 'Botha retains his power because of big business,' said Popo Molefe. And President Reagan said in his August speech that the Western business community should be the 'agents of change and progress and growth'; while Henry Kissinger had told the tycoon Harry Oppenheimer that 'business in South Africa may have a decisive role to play, because it can set an example and do unilaterally what would be very difficult for the political process to originate.'*

The business leaders in Johannesburg, in their sunny palaces surrounded by greenery, still have the confident, open-air style of men who are accustomed to developing half a continent; but they heard these conflicting messages with growing unease. They could not yet afford to get too caught up in ideologies and mythologies like the politicians: they had to be prepared in the end to do business

* HFO: some personal perspectives. Privately printed for the Anglo-American Corporation, Johannesburg 1985

with anyone. They longed for stability; yet they knew that they had
to be prepared for unprecedented changes – perhaps even some
kind of revolution. The giant Anglo-American Corporation which
controlled half the gold mines and half the Johannesburg stock
exchange was now openly divided. The bluff chairman Gavin Relly,
who had earlier talked with the ANC revolutionaries, was now wary:
'Frankly, the uncertainty is driving some people bonkers.' But his
more political director Zach de Beer was outspoken against Botha's
policies and the emergency: 'I'm extremely disappointed that it
should be thought necessary . . . It's vital for the government now
to negotiate with legitimate black leaders.' Gordon Waddell, the
hearty chairman of Anglo's subsidiary, Johannesburg Consolidated
Investments, explained with his impenetrable bonhomie: 'Most
businessmen think that the government had to restore law
and order. But the trouble is that business never really changes
until it feels the impact. Let's face it, we're not much good at
politics.'

Botha, like Hitler in 1933, was confident that he could rally
businessmen to his side against the threatened 'communist onslaught'. On the first morning of the emergency he had summoned
eighteen of his favoured conservative businessmen, including Julian
Ogilvie Thompson, the head of Anglo's sister-company De Beers,
to explain the need for tough measures. Most businessmen agreed
about the necessity. 'Both the internal and external image of the
country is one of being out of control,' said Fred du Plessis, the
chairman of the Afrikaner conglomerate Sanlam who also presides
over the SA Foundation, a major spokesman for business: 'The
state of emergency was therefore a necessary step.' 'Drastic security
action was necessary,' said the chief executive of Trust Bank, Chris
van Wyk, 'but it must be accompanied by an ambitious, bold,
imaginative and accelerated programme of reform.'

A few younger businessmen resisted all Botha's pressures, and
even talked openly about the ANC eventually coming to power. Tony
Bloom, the young entrepreneur who runs the Premier group of
mills, bakeries and stores, insisted in his last chairman's report that
'Negotiations with the ANC are an historic inevitability. The question
is not whether, but rather when such negotiations will take place.'
Chris Ball, the forty-four-year-old managing director of Barclays
National, the biggest bank, maintained that most so-called extremists were 'decent people wanting the same as the rest of us' and was
on friendly terms with Winnie Mandela. 'The only way to get away
from a perpetual state of emergency,' he told me, 'is to extend the
process of conciliation rather than restrict it.' The supermarket-
owners and retailers who depended both on black customers and

black trade unionists were openly outraged by the arrest of union leaders with whom they were negotiating. The most outspoken business critic of all was Bob Tucker, the young chief executive of the SA Permanent Building Society, who was exposed to black conditions as legal adviser to the Urban Foundation. 'It's tragic that business has been able to stay so aloof from the blacks,' he said to me. 'South African capitalism is the greediest, the most acquisitive, the most short-term, in the world. We may be substituting economic domination for racial discrimination – which could be even more pernicious.'

The emergency and the threat of sanctions had given Botha most of the business support he had hoped for, in his determination to stamp out the black revolt. In the next two months the police detained over eight thousand suspected black activists; the army moved into schools and surrounded whole townships; while the press was forbidden to report them. The military leaders and hawks in the cabinet who had advised Botha to defy world opinion had made their point, and many businessmen looked with relief towards a new period of calm. Yet few had much confidence that the military offensive could provide any lasting solution. They knew that each new crackdown would radicalise the blacks further. 'Blacks regard capitalism and the government as almost synonymous,' said Robin Plumbridge, the conservative head of Gold Fields. 'Most of them haven't really got into the system: they're terribly exposed to home-grown socialism.' Clive Menell, the elegant and liberal vice-chairman of the Anglo-Vaal group, had said that 'the vast majority of black South Africans regard business, the government, apartheid, the *status quo* and the devil as one.' 'We dare not allow the baby of free enterprise,' said Zach de Beer, 'to be thrown out with the bathwater of apartheid.' But many young blacks looked forward to both baby and bathwater flooding out; while anti-capitalist feeling in the townships was running higher than ever. 'The experience of the working class dictates that it is too late to save the free enterprise system in this country,' said the leader of the black mineworkers Cyril Ramaphosa. 'The alliance between big business and the apartheid regime has gone on too long and is soaked with the blood of workers . . .'

The businessmen knew they were approaching an abyss, and that they must find some way round it: but they could not bring themselves to look down it for long. They knew that they could not run their factories and mines for long without the consent of the black workers, and that black political ambitions could not be suppressed indefinitely. Many even agreed that there could be a black government in ten years time. But they could

not visualise any likely transition between now and then. They
were prepared to offer blacks almost anything except the one thing
they demanded: one man, one vote. Most found it impossible to
contemplate majority rule, or to deal with the blacks who were
likely to command it.

Back in London the multinational executives, whose companies
had invested in South Africa for most of the century, were now
anxiously trying to rethink their policies towards Pretoria; with
more detachment than their Johannesburg counterparts, but still
with some dread. 'Businessmen are supposed to be trained to work
with uncertainty', said one of them at the Commonwealth garden
party, 'but we hate it.' The British Industry Committee on South
Africa had just announced that 'South Africa is approaching the
edge of an abyss . . . unless apartheid is ended soon South Africa
could be plunged into even greater chaos.' The British, like the
South Africans, were very unsure how to get round the abyss, but
they were beginning to wonder more seriously: was there really no
alternative to Botha? Might they not be able to work with a black
government in the future?

Three weeks after the emergency was declared a group of international businessmen sat down for lunch with the African National
Congress, at the Connaught Rooms in London. It was a surprisingly
relaxed encounter between capitalists and revolutionaries who could
never see each other inside South Africa, meeting in the solidly
respectable Masonic building dedicated to business lunches. Some
bombs had exploded that morning in central Johannesburg, but
there was little sense of a tense confrontation. Tambo had brought
with him several members of the ANC executive including Thabo
Mbeki, the director of information, and Mac Maharaj, who had
spent several years in jail on Robben Island. They sat between the
bankers and businessmen cheerfully discussing how they might
more effectively undermine apartheid and achieve something
together. At the head was Oliver Tambo, the sixty-eight-year-old
President of the ANC who looked less like a terrorist than a reverend
(which he nearly was) or like a kindly uncle with his grey side-
whiskers and questioning eyes. Tambo was still desperately hoping
that sanctions and world pressure could avert a far more serious
bloodbath, by making apartheid unworkable: 'as the price for
maintaining the apartheid system rises' he had said the day before,
'so will it be clear to many of these White South Africans that the
time for change has come.'* He looked to Britain as the defender
of freedom which had stood out against Hitler and racialism; and

* Speech to the Royal Commonwealth Society, June 23, 1986

he looked to businessmen to bring their own pressure on both the South African and foreign governments.

The bankers and businessmen each came with their own perspectives and worries, as they tried to peer over the abyss from their different viewpoints. The chairman of the two biggest banks in South Africa, Lord Barber of Standard and Sir Timothy Bevan of Barclays, were both now at odds with their own prime minister and determined to keep in touch with the black opposition. They took turns to talk privately to Tambo ('do they *both* want to be bankers to the ANC?', asked one observer). Barclays had lent over a billion dollars to South Africa and had come under fire for supporting apartheid; but Bevan had been persuaded that they could not jeopardise their interests elsewhere, and he was now much more openly confronting Pretoria: Barclays would not lend a penny more, he insisted, until the bankrupt system of apartheid had been abolished. Lord Barber was a former conservative Chancellor of the Exchequer, and his bank had lent $1.5 billion, even more than Barclays, to South Africa;* but he had also been a member of the Commonwealth group reporting on South Africa, and had boldly stated that it was unreasonable to expect the ANC to renounce violence unconditionally.

The industrialists, stuck with their immovable assets on South African soil, were more cautious than the bankers. The two oil giants, Shell and BP, had built up refineries and chemical plants which had fuelled South African industry and defence over the last fifty years. BP were becoming much more concerned about Botha's policies, and had already made some contacts with the ANC. Shell was more cautious, but vulnerable, since the ANC had called for a boycott of all their filling-stations in America and Europe until they pulled out of South Africa. Only one percent of their profits came from there, against 25 percent from the United States: but Shell were proud of being able to do business in almost every country. They had been approached by a South African group to sell their interests, and were quite tempted; but they decided they should stay and 'keep chipping away' at apartheid. Shell was always reluctant to take political sides: 'We will always serve under the government, whatever it is,' said one of its top men. 'There's one thing you must never ask a multinational to do: to choose.'

Other companies at the lunch faced still more agonising choices. Consolidated Goldfields, Cecil Rhodes' old company, had been

---

* For details *see* John E Lind & Diane V Espaldon, *South Africa's Debt at the Time of Crisis*. San Francisco: California-Nevada Interfaith Committee on Corporate Responsibility, April 1986. *See also* next chapter

making profits for a century from its subsidiary Gold Fields of South
Africa, which had friendly links with Pretoria: but the London
parent had been extending its interests round the world and was
now even interested in China: it had to take a longer perspective,
wondering who might rule South Africa in ten years' time. The
textile multinational Courtaulds had invested heavily in a wood-
pulp plant to supply other Courtauld plants round the world; but
it was a joint venture with the Pretoria government. Unilever, the
soap-and-food group, preferred to stay aloof and take the lowest
possible profile, conscious of their huge investments in black Africa
and hoping that protesters would not notice their wide spread in
South Africa. The Anglo-American Corporation, the most influential of all, was also lying very low; but the two most outspoken
business leaders from Johannesburg, Tony Bloom of Premier and
Chris Ball of Barclays National, had come to London to talk to the
ANC, and to sense the British reaction.

At lunch Tambo talked quietly about the extremity of the crisis:
he reminded them of President Botha's threat that he had not used
a tenth of his forces, but he warned that the ANC had not, either.
He explained how he and others had realised, when the first
apartheid government came to power in 1948, that they were treated
as foreigners in their own country. He described how they had
tried to protest through passive resistance and strikes until the
government used troops to break them up, and how they reluctantly
decided that they could only respond with violence. But for thirty
years they had been asking for sanctions to bring pressure to
prevent a total confrontation. Unless the international community
intervened, they would have to fight it out themselves. The businessmen must decide: would they serve apartheid, or serve the whole
country?

The businessmen discussed with the ANC leaders what they might
do: the two from South Africa looked to the British to help them,
while the British looked to the South Africans. They asked whether
the ANC could make common cause with other black leaders, particularly with the Zulu Chief Buthelezi. Lord Barber told Tambo about
his talks with Mandela in jail, who had convinced him that he
could bring black unity: Tambo, who had been Mandela's closest
colleague in the 'fifties, interrupted him: 'Do you realise that you're
the only person in this room who has met Mandela for twenty-five
years?' The businessmen were clearly relieved that the revolutionaries were prepared to discuss their country's economic future
calmly with Western capitalists. They all agreed that they wanted
further meetings and issued a public statement saying they should
all 'contribute what they can to help ensure that South Africa

becomes a democratic and peaceful country.' The ANC leaders were still sceptical about the extent of the capitalists' change of heart: 'They always go running back to Botha in the end,' said one of them. But they recognised that it had been businessmen, more effectively than diplomats, who had opened up the bridge to the West; and during the lunch Tambo had arranged to see Lynda Chalker, the conservative minister in charge of Africa at the Foreign Office, later that day. It was a diplomatic breakthrough – the first time a British minister had talked with the ANC – and a few days later the State Department announced that it too was planning closer contacts. Three months later, Tambo was talking to both Sir Geoffrey Howe, the Foreign Secretary, and Chester Crocker from the State Department. It was the end of a quarter-century period when Britain and America had left the ANC out in the cold.

Across the Atlantic the big American corporations and banks were engaged in a more fundamental debate. They were under much heavier pressure from their shareholders to show that they were fighting apartheid, and to prove that capitalism was on the side of democracy and justice. South Africa had become the new testing-ground for all the old arguments about the social responsibility of corporations. Mobil, the biggest investor, was bombarding Pretoria with statements and advertisements – its favourite artillery – and had offered a multi-million-dollar fund for black education. Coca-Cola, from its black stronghold in Atlanta, had promised another $10 million in trust funds for black welfare. General Motors, the biggest employer, had been losing money in South Africa for four years; but its chairman Roger Smith seemed committed to stick it out and show his company's concern for its black employees. But more and more corporations were giving up the two-way battle against both Afrikaners and shareholders, selling up and getting out.

Would the blacks begin to see capitalism as on the side of their freedom and democracy in this final showdown? Or would communists find the proof they had been looking for, to show that apartheid had always been the tool of the capitalists? It was a hundred-billion-dollar question, which could settle the future of half a continent. But it could not be answered in simple ideological or economic terms; for it had as much to do with people and perceptions as with hard statistics; and the story was full of twists and surprises. For years the Left had depicted the American bankers as the arch-villains who lent money to Pretoria for each new military build-up of apartheid; but it was the bankers who had made decisions, a year before Botha's crackdown, which had undermined South Africa's economic future much more drastically than any government's pressures, and as the banking crisis had unfolded it threw light on the whole relationship between South African money and politics.

2

Pulling the Plug

The nationalist leader who is frightened of violence is wrong if he imagines that colonialism is going to 'massacre all of us'. The military will of course go on playing with tin soldiers which date from the time of the conquest, but higher finance will soon bring the truth home to them.

Frantz Fanon, *The Wretched of the Earth*, 1961

In the Chase Manhattan Plaza just off Wall Street the chairman of the Chase, Willard Butcher, was an unlikely choice to be the arch-enemy of apartheid in July 1985. It had, after all, been the Chase under David Rockefeller, the personification of capitalism, which had been reviled by black South Africans when it had begun lending to the Pretoria government after Sharpeville two decades earlier, when protesters had chanted 'apartheid has a friend in Chase Manhattan'. And when Butcher had taken over from Rockefeller in 1981 he was seen as a more conservative and technical chairman, with none of his predecessor's princely style. Bland and long-winded, he bored many fellow bankers with his slow sporting clichés and saw himself as 'an evangelist for the free market system'. He was dedicated to catching up with Citibank, Chase's old rival; and after the Mexican debt crisis of 1983 he was much preoccupied with Chase's shaky loans to Latin America.

By comparison, the Chase's loans to South Africa of $500 million, and their Johannesburg office with eighteen people, were much less important than the Latin exposure. And for Butcher and his board they were providing tiresome complications: withdrawals and share-holders' motions were damaging their business in Manhattan. Morgan Guaranty, the most aloof and discreet of all the New York banks, was already rapidly 'managing down' its South African exposure; and all the big banks were becoming more weary with the 'hassle factor' over apartheid. The Chase was the quintessential New York bank with a high visibility: South Africa accounted for less than half a percent of its total assets of $87 billion, and it was not worth the hassle.

Already by the end of 1984, as violence was building up in the black townships, the Chase was reducing its exposure to South

Africa. When President Botha declared his first state of emergency
on July 20 it was the last straw. The rand was already falling as
investors pulled out; and New Yorkers were protesting more angrily.
On July 31, the French government announced a ban on investment
in South Africa: it was a hollow gesture, since the French had
scarcely invested anything since the arms embargo had limited their
chief exports. But on the same day Butcher and his chief executive
Thomas Lebrecque decided to stop rolling over the loans to South
African companies – so that they would recall credits as they came
due – and to freeze all the unused lines of credit. The South Africans
would thus have to repay a few hundred million dollars over the
next year; and 85 percent of the American banks' loans were
short-term, due to be repaid within a year.*

It was a deadly decision. 'There is no country in the world that
can repay all its short-term debts, even when the proportion of
short-term debts is much lower,' said the Swiss banker Fritz Leutwiler afterwards. 'That is absolutely impossible. And if one bank,
such as a big American bank, starts the process then a chain reaction
is almost inevitable . . . South Africa is much less important to the
big US banks than a South American country. A US bank would
have considered the matter many times before withdrawing from a
big Latin American country.'†

It was Butcher's decision, and David Rockefeller himself (who
was still chairman of the bank's advisory committee) was against
it. He was concerned about apartheid, and had even talked to Oliver
Tambo; but he was worried about the implications of withdrawal.
Butcher's decision was taken on strictly technical grounds, with no
indication of moral motives. The bank always insisted that public
condemnations of foreign governments raised impossible precedents
and parallels: what about loans to Russia, or Chile? South African
businessmen quickly assumed that the pull-out was influenced by
Hughlyn Fierce, the black banker at the Chase (whose brother
worked for the Ford Foundation) who had recently been put
in charge of Africa and the Middle East. But Fierce later assured
them that he had nothing to do with it. Butcher continued to maintain a deadpan and technical posture; but soon afterwards he received a letter written on tattered toilet paper by a black political
prisoner in South Africa, thanking the Chase. The sheets were
carefully pieced together and Xeroxed, to be circulated round the
bank.

When the news of the Chase's withdrawal appeared in the *Wall*

* Lind and Espaldon: *Ibid*
† Interview with *Leadership* magazine, Johannesburg, Vol. 5, 1986

Street Journal the bank never publicly confirmed, denied or explained it. While it had marched into South Africa a quarter-century earlier with a roll of drums, it now retreated in silence. But all South African businessmen knew what Butcher had done, and realised the implications: they called him the Butcher of the Rand. The currency, the Rand, immediately began falling; and the Chase's decision had a snowball effect. Security Pacific followed suit immediately; other big banks, including Bankers Trust, Manufacturers Hanover and Bank of America, planned a 'phased reduction'. One big American bank dropped South Africa's credit-rating from B to D without stopping at C (E is bottom). The other New York banks, particularly Citibank, the biggest lenders, were furious with the Chase for 'pulling the plug' without warning. By getting out first the Chase had caused a stampede; 'they got their money', said a Citibank man, 'but at our expense. Everyone knew they could have done it gradually.' It was a bankers' saying that 'when everyone runs for the door, no one gets out.' But in the course of August the American banks withdrew about $400 million from South Africa – about a tenth of their loans.* The immediate impact was partly offset, it was thought, by Japanese banks who made short-term loans†; but the American withdrawal marked a massive loss of confidence.

American bankers were partly motivated by depositors and shareholders threatening to pull out, and by the danger of Washington imposing sanctions that could cripple their South African clients. Their worries had been compounded by the riots, raids and whippings in the townships which were being shown almost every night on the TV screens; while their children, wives and friends were adding to the chorus of protest, forcing them to talk and think about the connections between money and politics. Many politicians – particularly those opposed to government sanctions, including Reagan and Thatcher – would later point to the bankers' withdrawal as part of the wisdom of the market-place making its own judgment on apartheid. But that was a misreading of what happened. It was not the simple calculations of profit or loss, risk and reward, which had finally warned off the banks. It was the careful intervention of churches, foundations and shareholders' pressure groups which insisted, not that apartheid was unprofitable, but that it was morally intolerable. It may well have been in the banks' long-term commercial interest to withdraw: but it was the hassle, more than the numbers, which forced their decisions.

* Lind and Espaldon, p. 3
† *New York Times*, August 1, 1985

At the South African Reserve Bank at Pretoria, the donnish governor Gerhard de Kock was appalled. He rang up Butcher in New York, who seemed surprised by the furore he had caused and explained that it was part of the routine monthly revision of credit risks round the world. De Kock, he said later, 'tried to ride the storm.'* The European banks stayed in, and a few Swiss and Germans increased their loans at very high interest rates – as much as 4 percent above the normal interbank rate (LIBOR), a higher rate than Zaire. There were hopes that the falling currency would produce bargains which would attract foreign buyers back again: but they now seemed to be so worried about the political instability that they would not come back at any price. The South African banks began desperately buying dollars to repay the loans as they came due, which pushed down the rand further and made the loans more expensive; while the country's foreign currency reserves, including its gold, were falling perilously. Two years earlier Governor de Kock had been hailed as the great liberaliser of South Africa's financial markets, opening the windows to the world. Now the windows were letting in an icy gale.

As the rand fell further the South African bankers and businessmen put their faith in the promised speech of President Botha – who had so carefully cultivated them since 1979 – who was to address the opening of the National Party Congress in Durban on August 15. Rumours were circulated, and not denied, that he would make spectacular concessions including releasing Nelson Mandela. An American team, including Reagan's national security adviser Robert McFarlane and his African expert Chester Crocker, met beforehand with the South African foreign minister Pik Botha in Vienna and came away reassured and expectant. And the speech was transmitted live by satellite round the world, while brokers and exchange dealers listened to every word.

It was a historic anti-climax, a harangue designed to reassure his Afrikaner supporters rather than black South Africans or the rest of the world. 'I am not prepared to lead white South Africans and other minority groups on a road to abdication and suicide,' said the President; and he reached a climax of finger-wagging by saying: 'Don't push us too far! Don't push us too far!' He talked about his country's economic health as if nothing was wrong: overspending eliminated, money supply under control, balance of payments in surplus, interest rates down, gold reserves up. He blamed the unrest on 'barbaric communist agitators' and on the foreign media, and slammed the door on Mandela.

* To Charles Grant, in *Euromoney*, December 1985

To black South Africans the speech was an insult: 'I felt truly ashamed of being dominated and oppressed by a man of such poor quality,' Winnie Mandela complained to me afterwards. 'Can any human being imagine himself a separate entity from the rest of the world, to threaten everyone including the West? He has pushed *us* too far.' But to international bankers and businessmen the speech was equally exasperating, and the Mandelas seemed suddenly on the same side as the bankers. Overnight the speech caused a massive loss of confidence and a flight of capital; and the rand fell with a record drop.

The crunch did not come until some days after the speech on 'Black Tuesday', August 27. That morning de Kock had published his annual statement which explained how well the economy was doing: the current account surplus of R400 million (about $140 million at the morning's rate) could repay all foreign loans and other capital outflow. 'In several fundamental respects the underlying state of the economy is sounder than it was a year ago.' But during that Tuesday the Cape leader Allan Boesak had been arrested, more riots had broken out and confidence was fading further. It was impossible now to separate economic from political judgments.

That afternoon I happened by chance to be in the Johannesburg stock exchange, watching the white brokers dealing and screaming on the floor, while three black men on a platform chalked up the share-prices as the rand was falling still faster. The most furious trading was in gold-shares, which South Africans were buying to protect themselves against the devalued currency, and which were breaking new records. But my stockbroker companion explained: 'The share values reflect what South Africans are thinking: that everything is OK. The rand reflects what the world thinks, and it's saying God Help You.' By the close of trading on that Tuesday, the rand was worth half its value against sterling compared to a year before. I asked three stockbrokers just afterwards: how would the rand react if the government were to release Mandela? One said it would make no difference, the others insisted it would rapidly increase confidence: 'Even the Afrikaner brokers want him out.'

In Pretoria, while the rand was collapsing, Governor de Kock was talking with the minister of finance Barend du Plessis. They agreed there was only one solution: to close the markets. 'We had to protect our banks,' de Kock explained later. 'They did not know how many loans they would have to repay. The German and Swiss banks were loyally standing by us, but did not want to be the last in the queue for repayment.' Just after trading stopped at the stock exchange the government announced that all dealing would be suspended for four days.

On the Sunday, September 1, du Plessis made the announcement
that already seemed inevitable. South Africa would freeze repay-
ments on its foreign debts until the end of the year, while still paying
interest. The strict exchange controls which Pretoria had only
recently abandoned with relief would be reintroduced, with the
'financial rand' – through which shares were bought and sold –
selling at a discount compared to the 'commercial rand' for trade
and domestic transactions. South Africa, in spite of all its economic
prospects, gold exports and industrial resources, was now suddenly
in a state of virtual default like the most unreliable Latin American
debtor, with a credit-rating near the bottom of the league. The
President's confident claims two weeks earlier were meaningless.
From now on, the Republic had lost nearly all its charms to foreign
investors. 'The unrest is now so serious,' wrote the cold-blooded
Lex in the *Financial Times* on September 2, 'that decisions to lend
to, or invest in, South Africa are not just based on moral scruples:
they are hard to justify by any measure of risk and reward.'

De Kock immediately set off on a thirteen-day tour of America
and Europe, visiting nineteen bank chairmen, four central banks
and the IMF and the State Department in Washington, to negotiate
an emergency loan, falling back on gold reserves to provide extra
credit. The spectacle of the central banker rushing round Western
capitals cap in hand hardly accorded with the proud Afrikaner
legend of defying foreign critics by retreating 'back to the laager'.
And the worries in Pretoria about the economic collapse were
already undermining the recurring arguments that sanctions would
have no effect, or would simply compel South Africa to become
self-sufficient. 'We will always need foreign capital,' said Clive
Menell the vice-chairman of Anglo-Vaal, 'and the technology that
it brings with it.' 'It's the lack of capital which really hurts us,' said
Mike Rosholt the chairman of Barlow Rand. The 'capital boycott'
by foreign bankers was soon proving more devastating and fast-
acting than anything Western governments were planning: even
Afrikaner capitalists could not ignore this harsh equation between
politics and money.

It was a double irony. 'Those whom the far Left would call
apartheid's best friends, the pillars of its financial entrenchment,
have hit us where it hurts most,' said Nigel Bruce, the editor of the
conservative *Business Day*: 'In our ability to finance immediate
economic growth consistent with a rapidly rising black birth rate.'*
And campaigners against apartheid were surprised to find that their
old capitalist enemies were now their best allies. 'Who would have

* Nigel Bruce, *Leadership*, 1985

thought,' said the editor of *International Reports*, Andrew Hilton, giving evidence to the UN in New York, 'that decisions taken – probably in haste – by two US banks not to roll over trade lines would have forced the South African government on the defensive in a way that decades of pressure by this institution had failed to achieve?'*

On his world tour, de Kock soon painfully discovered how rapidly his country had become a bankers' pariah. In New York he first called on Citibank in Park Avenue on August 30, where he regarded Bill Rhodes, their tireless master-negotiator and rescheduler of debts, as his 'mentor and teacher'. But Citibank's chairman John Reed was wary of any public association: he himself, when he was running Citibank's consumer division under his right-wing predecessor Walter Wriston, had resisted pressure to expand in South Africa. Citibank was furious with Chase for having pulled the plug and started the whole panic; but as the biggest American lender to South Africa and the only bank which took local deposits it felt yet more vulnerable to New Yorkers' protests. The last thing Citibankers wanted was to be seen to help Pretoria out of its fix. 'We told him Pretoria must change its politics first,' said one of them; and soon afterwards two senior Citibankers, Hans Angermuller and Bill Koplowitz, went out to visit South Africa and came back more worried.

Nearly everywhere de Kock was treated as if he had the plague. In Washington de Larosiere of the IMF said that they were short of liquidity, and they could only lend for balance-of-payments problems. Even the Swiss cold-shouldered him: Pierre Languetin of the Swiss National Bank went to the extraordinary length of officially denying a report that he had seen him. In London no banker wanted to be seen at a meeting with him, and Rothschild's (whose chairman Evelyn de Rothschild was a director of De Beers) only met him very discreetly. The governor of the Bank of England, Robin Leigh-Pemberton, would not see him and the British government made it known that he had received no help. 'De Kock seemed to have been pole-axed,' said one senior Bank of England director. 'We thought he was quite internationally-minded when he was a director of the IMF. But he never seemed to have realised how isolated Pretoria had become.' And whenever de Kock or any South African officials were asked what kind of concessions the West wanted, the same words came back: release Mandela, release Mandela. It was a weird equation: the man who had been in jail for a

* United Nations, New York: public hearings on the activities of Transnational Corporations in South Africa and Namibia, September 16, 1985

quarter-century, whose party, writings and photograph were
banned in the Republic, who was condemned by the State President
as a terrorist and a communist, was now seen as the only key to
unlock the billions on which the state depended for its future
expansion.

On the face of it South Africa was in a far healthier state than
most developing countries in debt: it had a current-account surplus
of $2 billion a year, and its debts were not out of scale with its
exports – half of them gold. But this performance was totally
overshadowed by the political hazards for the bankers, both in the
Republic and at home. 'Last year our political situation was good,'
complained the finance minister du Plessis, 'but the economy was
completely overheated . . . Yet in one morning I could borrow a
billion dollars. This year it's just the opposite.'*

Back in Pretoria, de Kock faced many recriminations as the crisis
revealed how inadequate were the central banks' controls and
information. Two years before he had encouraged South African
companies to borrow short-term in dollars abroad, at lower interest
rates than locally: now the short-term debts were coming due, and
proved bigger than he thought – $14 billion instead of $12 billion
– while the dollars were far more expensive to repay. De Kock had
been praised for liberalising the financial markets; but now all the
liberalisation had turned against him. The foreign branches of
South African banks (as the Bank of England had warned him a
year before) turned out to be raising loans for their headquarters
banks, thus increasing the exposure. 'Ripples from the rest of the
world,' said Chris van Wyk of Trust Bank, 'are tidal waves when
they hit Johannesburg.' 'It's hard to find a banker in Johannesburg',
wrote Charles Grant of *Euromoney*, visiting South Africa after the
crash, 'who doesn't blame this fervent advocate of free enterprise
markets for at least some of the debt crisis.' Nedbank, the biggest
Afrikaner bank which a year before was admired as 'South Africa's
international bank', was now in severe difficulties with its over-
adventurous foreign branches. It had rashly banked on the rand
recovering, to the point of reaching parity with the dollar; and
as the rand sank further de Kock had to write a 'letter of comfort' promising that the Reserve Bank stood behind its branches –
which meant providing more dollars. Nedbank never really
recovered from the loss of confidence: its share-price collapsed,
and its chief executive Rob Abrahamsen eventually resigned in
March 1986.

De Kock was now desperate to find a respected negotiator who

* *Wall Street Journal*, October 22, 1985

could mediate between his government and the twenty-nine main creditor banks, who were refusing to join any committee to deal directly with the South Africans. After an anxious search the Union Bank of Switzerland, which was much involved in gold deals with South Africa, proposed Fritz Leutwiler, the former president of the Swiss National Bank who had become chairman of the Swiss engineering group Brown Boveri. Leutwiler liked South Africa which he had first visited seven years before, and had become friendly with the former finance minister Owen Horwood. He asked the President of Switzerland, whom he knew well, whether negotiating for South Africa would damage his country; he said no, and Leutwiler agreed. Pretoria would pay expenses for him and two assistants, and for the accountants, Price Waterhouse in London; and he would expect a fee from the bankers.

Leutwiler was well-known as a very sound central banker: his first job at the age of twenty-four had been as secretary for the Association for a Sound Currency. But his experience was limited to high finance, and he was not politically sophisticated. He faced an appalling assignment which he only accepted, said de Kock, 'out of a sense of responsibility for the international banking system.' The tensions between the bankers were hard enough: the Europeans were furious with the Chase and other Americans for beginning the panic; the Swiss and Germans criticised the British for political bias, while the Swiss were blamed as usual for making money out of the crisis. The Swiss were delicately but profitably placed. They were insistently neutral, refusing to talk the language of morality, not wanting to favour any one nation. But they were the biggest lenders to South Africa per head of their population; and their three biggest banks had lent one percent of their assets to South Africa – as high a ratio as Barclays in Britain.* The Swiss also profited from laundering South African funds illegally leaving the country, thus easing the capital flight which was a major part of Pretoria's problem. They could make money both from the hole in the bucket, and from filling it up. But even the Swiss were now forced to make some political linkage; and Max Kuhne, managing director of the Swiss Bank Corporation, said that the banks were eager for genuine political reform in return for a rescheduling agreement.† Nor was Leutwiler himself altogether politically immune: the Brown Boveri Company had important contracts in developing countries including China; and Beijing had politely made clear that they had noticed that the chairman was involving himself with white South Africa.

* Lind and Espaldon, *op. cit.*, p. 16
† *International Herald Tribune*, November 16, 1985

Pretoria was now taking a high moral line. At the annual IMF
meeting in Seoul, South Korea, in October officials explained that
the West had a duty to continue lending, for the sake of the blacks,
and half of Africa was dependent on them: 'There is no way in
which sub-Saharan Africa can develop in the next ten years,' warned
de Kock, 'unless the Republic of South Africa is part and parcel of
the action.' The finance minister du Plessis warned about 'the threat
to the integrity of the present international financial system', and
stressed the need for South Africa to develop.

If ever there was a time when man's morality should match his
technology, it is now. If ever his compassion was to be equal to
his skills in material goods and wealth, the time is now. The
challenge to those who have lies in caring sufficiently to share
their knowledge and other resources and to materially assist
developing nations on the road to sustainable economic growth,
with due regard to their dignity and self-respect.

Leutwiler was soon in a hornet's nest. His first task was to try to
call a meeting of the twenty-nine main creditor banks – who
remained fearful even to be seen with a South African – which he
eventually fixed in London on October 23. The anti-apartheid
protesters were now beginning to see their old villains the bankers
as potential allies who could be lobbied individually. From London
Father Trevor Huddleston, as president of the Anti-Apartheid
Movement, wrote personally from his office in Mandela Street to
the British banks to warn them that there could be no peace and
stability until apartheid was abolished, and to ask them not to
attend the meeting. From Johannesburg Bishop Tutu and Beyers
Naude of the South African Council of Churches asked the bankers
hopefully to 'make rescheduling of South Africa's debt conditional
upon the resignation of the present regime and its replacement by
an interim government responsive to the needs of all South Africa's
people.' The bank chairmen all politely agreed with Huddleston
about the evils of apartheid, and several explained how they were
working for peaceful change. But they turned up to Leutwiler's
meeting.
    The bankers officially said nothing about politics, but in fact they
made clear to Leutwiler that they 'expected some positive political
signals from Pretoria' and he knew he could not evade politics.*
The South African team headed by the Afrikaner Chris Stahls
stressed that exporting capital would make the blacks poorer, and

* *Leadership*, p. 14

explained the impossibility of repaying $14.3 billion within a year. But the bankers could reach no agreement, and postponed any decision. 'Looking at this as an economist you'd say there's no problem,' de Kock said the next week in Pretoria. 'But because of political considerations it was a very difficult meeting to handle. The banks can't be seen as helping South Africa because it would be seen as propping up apartheid.'*

The bankers were now in a critical position. They had asserted their formidable negative power, by withdrawing support from the apartheid regime; could they go further and assert a positive power by encouraging a non-racial alternative? Some opponents of apartheid now thought they had a unique opportunity. 'Should they not say,' asked Robert McNamara, the former President of the World Bank, 'today we are very reluctant to put new funds at risk in that country, but we would take a quite different attitude were the government to move towards a more stable situation by beginning to negotiate with the blacks for their participation in the political process?'† All eyes were on Leutwiler, who now appeared to have more political leverage on Pretoria than all the world's governments and do-gooders; for he controlled the one thing that President Botha really needed – money. And Botha himself said that 'debt is our only problem', though he was still amazingly ignorant of the laws of economics. (When in October one economic journalist asked him how he explained the collapse of the rand he explained it was because of the strength of the dollar – even though the dollar had just suffered a precipitate decline.)

Leutwiler certainly seemed to be trying to bring his own pressure with an outspokenness unusual for a Swiss banker. On Swiss television he complained on November 15 that Pretoria's repression was 'the very opposite of what I had hoped for' and that restricting the media was 'the most stupid thing the government could have done.'‡ There was no prospect of an agreement, he told a Swiss newspaper, unless there was a 'positive statement at the highest level . . . If South Africa delays much longer certain clients, particularly those of American, British and other banks, will say they will be satisfied only by the principle of one man, one vote.'§ And the bankers' pressure seemed to be taking some effect: in Johannesburg de Kock for the first time made a direct link between the financial and political crisis, telling a banquet of businessmen that foreign bankers were viewing South Africa as in the throes of 'an Iranian-

* To Steve Mufson of the *Wall Street Journal*, October 30, 1985
† Interview with author, October 1985
‡ *International Herald Tribune*, November 16, 1985
§ Zurich: *Tages Anzeiger*, November 14, 1985

type, pre-revolutionary situation', and warned that 'unless improvements are effected, South Africa may have to remain a
capital-exporting country for some time'. De Kock was now vigorously defending the open international economy against Afrikaners
who seemed prepared for South Africa to retreat into autarchy. 'All
the measures that will contribute to South Africa's isolation and
tend to turn it into a siege economy,' said de Kock, 'should be
opposed.' The rand was falling again, but the South African team
of bankers still hopefully put forward a proposal for a 'multi-year
rescheduling', which meant that they would not repay any money
until 1990. Leutwiler passed on their plan to the bankers in New
York, who were appalled by the South Africans' arrogance and
cross with Leutwiler for even lending his name to the proposal. By
the beginning of December the rand was down to thirty-five cents,
close to its bottom on Black Tuesday: and Pretoria had to introduce
new rules by which the Reserve Bank would pay the gold mines in
rand, not dollars.

In the New Year Leutwiler went out to South Africa to discuss
his new proposals with President Botha, the finance minister and
the bankers' team. He insisted that Pretoria must repay some money
quickly to show goodwill and must offer a generous interest rate of
one percent above the existing high rate – particularly to satisfy the
American banks – in view of the political risk. 'I could not run the
risk of a refusal of my proposal by the banks,' he said later. He
talked at length with the President who assured him that his next
major speech, at the opening of parliament at the end of January,
would propose much more definite reforms than his August 'Rubicon' speech. South African businessmen were once again waiting
in hope for Botha, and the tobacco king Anton Rupert publicly
pleaded with him, quoting the Swiss theologian-soldier Zwingli:
'For God's sake, do something brave.'

Leutwiler was now visibly turning. He said that Botha's reforms
– which he had seen in a draft of the speech – were 'a helluva
programme'. He had stopped warning Pretoria and was now trying
to reassure his banker-clients. In South Africa he talked to twenty
people chosen by de Kock, including the Zulu leader Chief Buthelezi
whom he had already met in Switzerland. Leutwiler had some
criticisms of apartheid, particularly of the long journeys which
blacks had to make to get to the factories; but he refused to meet
Oliver Tambo or any members of the African National Congress,
arguing that they had admitted receiving arms from the Soviet
Union, 'which doesn't make gifts for nothing'. 'I'm reluctant to
shake hands with a communist without counting my fingers afterwards,' he said. 'I don't trust them. My impression of the ANC is

that it does not represent the blacks.'* It was a surprising refusal, in the light of the insistence by many bankers, and even by Thatcher and Reagan, that releasing the leader of the ANC was a pre-condition for a peaceful settlement. Leutwiler even claimed that the businessmen who visited the ANC in Lusaka now regretted their visit, though one of them, Tony Bloom of Premier, promptly contradicted him: 'The talks were not a mistake, and the door remains open for future meetings.'

Leutwiler left South Africa convinced, he said, 'that positive signals will be given in the not-too-distant future', and he prepared optimistically for a further meeting of the creditor banks in February. He appeared now to have discarded his leverage and to have reversed the previous insistence of political reforms first, money afterwards. 'The world needs South Africa,' he explained, 'and South Africa needs a healthy economy as a prerequisite of further political reforms.'

Botha's speech to parliament in January was totally different in tone to his provocative harangue five months before: it might have been written for the bankers, and it confirmed some hopes for genuine reforms, including abolishing the hated pass-laws. The contrast between the two speeches in itself appeared a tribute to the power of the bankers. But it soon turned out to be much less promising and specific than Leutwiler had suggested, and it was followed by an open row with the foreign minister Pik Botha which made it look still less promising. Leutwiler was disappointed, particularly after the leader of the opposition Van Zyl Slabbert had precipitately resigned in despair of the white parliament. But he partly blamed the media: 'One thing is clear. South Africa should improve its PR.' He prepared new proposals for the next meeting in London on February 20 with the bankers, who were now anxious to settle and receive at least some money up front; and he sent the proposals to them ten days beforehand saying 'take it or leave it'. The South African political atmosphere was still explosive, while the Johannesburg township of Alexandra was becoming a new and bloody battlefield: and before the meeting the churchmen Tutu and Naude, together with Allan Boesak, stepped up their terms for the bankers: they now wanted not only the white government's resignation, but the seizing of South Africa's assets abroad, including aircraft and ships.

Leutwiler faced a nerve-racking meeting. The Americans wanted more money up front, and many bankers wanted more than five percent on the interest rate. Leutwiler insisted that South Africa could not afford more: he would walk out if the proposals were not

* *Leadership*, p. 14

accepted. He had warned the South Africans that if they defied the
banks and tried to be self-sufficient 'there would be a lot of court
cases: South African aircraft would be attached, likewise ships. The
lawyers would be happy and extremely busy.'* Eventually the
bankers agreed to Leutwiler's plan. Pretoria would repay $500
million over the next year, while the other 95 percent of the frozen
debt would be 'rolled over' pending a reassessment after twelve
months – a stipulation on which Leutwiler insisted, which was to
hang over Pretoria like a black cloud. Leutwiler issued a statement
that the banks had reached a 'broad consensus', and later sounded
confident that the banks would keep up the political pressure.
'Within these twelve months something must happen,' he said on
British television the following Sunday. 'Promises must be delivered
and implemented.' And he warned Botha: 'If he does not deliver
reforms, my patience is limited and so I think is the bankers'
patience.'†

The deal was agreed, but far from settled: American banks
quickly complained that there was no such 'broad consensus', and
that they had been steamrollered: they dreaded the next round of
annual meetings, where the protesting shareholders, having tasted
political blood, would step up their attacks. The bankers, as the
Financial Times warned, now had to live with a new fact of life: 'This
reality is the unexpected emergence of the banking system as a
conduit for the US public's attitude towards the situation in South
Africa. It has allowed shareholders, depositors and the public
directly to impose an economic sanction without having to persuade
their government to do so.'‡

Leutwiler himself lay low, but he was soon further disillusioned
by Botha and told him (it was rumoured) that he must get down
to talking to the black leaders. In July 1986 a banker colleague
announced that Leutwiler had given up his mandate because of his
disappointment at the new state of emergency: Leutwiler promptly
denied it but did not offer any reassurance to Pretoria and did not
attend the next bankers' meeting. In the meantime South Africa's
prospects of repaying her debts looked more doubtful with sanctions
overhanging them; and confidence was not increased when the
ambassador to London Denis Worrall warned that South Africa
might renege on its debts if sanctions were imposed.

*   *   *

Even Barclays Bank in London – which half-owned Barclays

---

* TV Channel 4, London: Business Programme, February 23, 1986
† *Ibid.*
‡ *Financial Times*, February 19, 1986

National, the biggest bank in South Africa, and which had so long stonewalled against shareholders' complaints – was now rapidly changing ground. Its chairman Sir Timothy Bevan was cautious and conservative, but he was fed up with losing student accounts and personally outraged by Botha's policy. By the middle of 1985 he and his board, including his future successor as chairman John Quinton, were doubtful whether their South African business was worth the odium: they were longing to remove their name from the blue signs in South African branches, and were still more embarrassed when Barclays National advertised in Britain for computer specialists with the slogan: 'Fill in your passport to a lifestyle of your dreams.'*

Barclays became bolder in their contacts with black leaders, and after talking with Tambo were more reassured about the prospects under a future black government. By November 1985 Sir Timothy had become more open, explaining that Barclays had talked to the ANC and attacking apartheid as 'repugnant, wrong, unchristian and unworkable'. Then in March 1986, just after Leutwiler's last meeting, Sir Timothy produced his annual report with the comment at the end:

> Our policy on further lendings to South Africa is quite simple: we shall commit no new money to that country nor shall we be party to any formal debt rescheduling until South Africa has demonstrated its ability to reduce its indebtedness and meet its obligations and until there are changes which confirm an end to the bankrupt policy of institutionalised racial discrimination.
>
> But the present moratorium does mean that the probability of South Africa receiving the benefit of foreign capital inflow is virtually non-existent and without inflow it will be increasingly difficult for South Africa to promote economic growth to employ the ever-growing non-white population.

It was the nearest any bank had come to spelling out the total connection between politics and money, including the terrible bankers' word '*bankrupt*'. They would not lend a penny more unless the policy was changed; and without new money, South Africa was facing catastrophe.

Would the blacks, then, come to see capitalism as on the side of their freedom in South Africa? Certainly the world's bankers had travelled far since the seventies, when they had encouraged invest-

* See 'Barclays Shadow Report 1986', published by End Loans to South Africa, P.O. Box 686 London NW5

ment and repeatedly disowned political or moral responsibility. The long collaboration between international finance and apartheid, which had its first roots in the diamond and gold fields a century earlier, had now come to a very dead end. The financial world appeared to have experienced a very sudden disillusion; and President Reagan claimed in his speech in August 1986 that 'the market-place has been sending unmistakable signals of its own' about the wrongness of apartheid. South African businessmen, for their part, were appalled by what they depicted as the irresponsibility of the bankers. 'More by accident, it seems, than by design,' said Gavin Relly, the new chairman of Anglo-American, 'the international banking community may itself be in the process of bringing about the economic wasteland of South Africa.'* Many ironies remained after the bankers' turnabout: while Pretoria was accusing the ANC of being communists, the ANC was looking to the capitalists to exert pressure and avert a bloodbath; and as sanctions moved forward, President Botha began to sound even more hostile to Western capitalists than to Eastern communists.

It was another matter to persuade the young 'Comrades' and schoolboys in the black townships that capitalism was on their side; and the market-place was never as consistent or as logical as Reagan suggested. As the South African crisis worsened through 1986 the markets made new twists. Within South Africa, the less confidence investors had in the future of industry, and the higher the inflation, the more they put money in the stock market which reached new peaks; while new doubts about the world economy – together with the fears about South Africa itself – helped to push up the price of gold, which in turn pushed up the currency and im-proved Pretoria's prospects of repaying her debts. Gold which had so suddenly created the country's wealth a century ago, and which still made up half its exports, still had some new surprises up its sleeve.

And behind many of the bankers' calculations there was, in truth, a fearful pessimism. They had pulled the plug and turned off the taps but they could not bring themselves to support any alternative solution or power; privately they talked only about chaos and bloodshed. Three months after Leutwiler's agreement, before a new state of emergency, old Lex in the *Financial Times* uttered a devastating analysis of how the 'banking parlours will comme-morate a decade in which the South African experiment well and truly fell to bits'. It concluded 'the numbers are suggesting that the

* *Guardian*, October 7, 1985

financial community will sit on its hands, with its capital written off, until South Africa and half a continent slide away.'*

Had the South African experiment totally collapsed? Were the bankers now dealing with a nation, or only with an accidental combination of peoples and forces which had never really coalesced? Since its union in 1910, South Africa had always had an uncertain identity, like so many subsequent African states. Its three main components were always at odds. The English-speaking capitalists who first developed its gold and diamonds had little contact with either the Afrikaner settlers or with the black tribesmen whom they lured into their mines. The Afrikaners had remained a separate tribe, more separate than the Zulus or Xhosas; while the blacks who made up the vast majority were kept outside the democratic system, without votes or rights.

The generation of older leaders from these three components, whose lives had spanned most of their country's history, had little contact with each other. President Botha, whose father fought in the Boer War, had little in common with Harry Oppenheimer, whose father had emigrated from London to build up Anglo-American, the biggest corporation in the country. Oliver Tambo, who had run the ANC for the last quarter-century, had never met either Botha or Oppenheimer. Individuals from the different groups were more likely to see each other in New York or London than in their own country. It was like an atlas where the roads only met off the map. Each of these three men could look back on their own proud journey, but with no certainty that their paths would eventually meet.

* *Financial Times*, June 2, 1986

3

Capitalists against Nationalists

Nowhere in the world has there ever existed so concentrated a form
of capitalism as that represented by the financial power of the mining
houses in South Africa, and nowhere else does that power so completely realise and enforce the need of controlling politics.

J A Hobson, *The Evolution of Modern Capitalism*, 1930

Few existing multinational corporations can claim more extraordinary origins than the Anglo-American Corporation and its sister
company De Beers which was founded twenty-two years before
South Africa itself. Few businesses have been so dominated by
single individuals – first by Cecil Rhodes, later by Ernest Oppenheimer and his son Harry. The Oppenheimers were chairmen of
Anglo-American for sixty-five years. Today Harry Oppenheimer
can look back on a country which is only two years older than
himself, which has grown up in uneasy partnership with the corporation that controls a large slice of its wealth.

Among all the social transformations wrought by capital and
industry in the nineteenth century, none was so abrupt, with such
extremes of poverty and wealth, as the discovery of diamonds and
gold in South Africa. Up till 1867 the white colonies and republics at
the bottom of the continent were predominantly rural communities,
clustered round the ports like Cape Town and Durban, with a few
isolated towns like Pretoria or Bloemfontein: only sixty-five miles
of railway ventured inland from the coast. The Republic of the
Transvaal had only a few thousand Afrikaners, who had trekked
up from the coast to escape British liberalism, subduing black tribes
on the way. Most of the black farmers had never seen white men.
The settlements of Southern Africa were far less prosperous than
the rich lands of Australia and New Zealand; and the chief importance of Cape Town, before the opening of the Suez Canal, was as
a coaling station on the way to India.

But the discovery of diamonds in 1867 in 'New Rush' – soon to
be renamed Kimberley – 500 miles inland from Cape Town, brought
a stampede of adventurers and international money which transformed the tiny settlement and the surrounding black tribes. (It
was two years after the American civil war had ended, and a year

after the Civil Rights Bill for black Americans had passed through Congress.) The corrugated-iron diamond town became one of the new wonders of the world. 'A city in the desert,' as the geographer Morton described it in 1877, 'dropped, as it were, from the clouds, so detached does it seem from all the ordinary surroundings of civilised communities. A city of tent-cloth and corrugated iron, and here and there substantial brick.'*

It was an essentially white city. The diggers were determined to exclude blacks from the digging, complaining that they stole the stones. They burnt their tents, flogged them if they tried to dig and imposed a system of passes to keep them out of the fields, against protests from the Colonial Office in London. Soon blacks were only allowed to work on the fields as labourers or servants, and the colour bar was built into the diggers' society. But the diggers still needed thousands of workers and began to lure blacks from surrounding tribes, who were encouraged by their chiefs to work in Kimberley to earn money to buy guns. The diamond fields soon gave European travellers a very different glimpse of Africa from the pastoral accounts of missionaries and explorers. When Anthony Trollope visited Kimberley in 1878, he was fascinated by the transformation. 'This black man, whose body is only partially and most grotesquely clad, and who is what we mean when we speak of a Savage, earns more than the average rural labourer in England.' He was struck by the capacity of the blacks to work and to become part of a disciplined and civilised society: unlike savages elsewhere in the British Empire they were not 'perishing while we have been considering how we might best deal with them. Here, in South Africa, a healthy nation remains and assures us by its prolific tendency that when protected from self-destruction by our fostering care it will spread and increase beneath our hands.' But Trollope ridiculed the idea that blacks, or 'Kafirs', would soon become entitled to vote under the liberal franchise of the Cape Colony. 'The suggestion that the "Kafir" should have a vote,' wrote Trollope, 'is received by Europeans in South Africa simply with a smile.'†

It was this abrupt conjunction of peoples which provided the origins of the first major international corporation in Southern Africa, when in 1888 the rival miners and dealers were amalgamated into a single diamond monopoly, De Beers Consolidated Mines, which for the next century would remain one of the most successful cartels in the world. It was the creation of the most famous of all

* Morton: South African Diamond Fields, Proceedings of the American Geographical Society, 1877

† Anthony Trollope, *South Africa*, London, Chapman and Hall 1878, pp. 158–89

imperial entrepreneurs, Cecil Rhodes, who saw it from the beginning as an instrument to extend British domination over the whole
continent. The character of Rhodes – with his combination of
shrewdness and adolescence, romanticism and ruthlessness, imagination and vulgarity – has eluded all his biographers. As Geoffrey
Wheatcroft describes it: 'The looming gap between his deeds and
his unfathomable personality remains.'* But the myth of Rhodes
remained potent for both admirers and haters, and he came to
personify the capitalist imperialism of the late nineteenth century.
He was part of the intricate financial mechanism which channelled
the surplus capital of the late Victorians to develop vast tracts of
territory, and turned the savings of small investors into 'red on the
map'. 'Every man has his foible,' said Lord Milner. 'Rhodes' foible
was size.'

In purely financial terms De Beers was small compared to Rockefeller's Standard Oil Trust formed in 1882, six years before the De
Beers monopoly. But De Beers was far richer and more powerful
compared to the country which it helped to transform. Fifteen years
after diamonds were discovered South Africa had 1,620 miles of
railway connecting Kimberley to the ports of Cape Town and Port
Elizabeth. Finance was closely interlocked with politics and military
force: De Beers' original trust deed gave Rhodes the ability to invade
the territories to the North which soon bore his name; while by
1890 he was also prime minister of the Cape Colony.

Kimberley itself set a pattern for total segregation which few
visitors challenged. The whites had their own village called Kenil-
worth, which Rhodes had planned as his special hobby, planted with
eucalyptus trees, shrubs and vines and equipped with a club-house,
billiard-rooms and reading-rooms. The black workers lived in the
compounds, specially devised to prevent diamond smuggling with
the help of elaborate inspections. Lord Randolph Churchill who
visited the diamond fields in 1891 described how 'stark naked, they
then proceed to the searching room, where their mouths, their hair,
their toes, their armpits, and every portion of their body are subject
to an elaborate examination. White men would never submit to
such a process, but the native sustains the indignity with cheerful
equanimity, considering only the high wages which he earns.'†

Ten years after the discovery of diamonds a prospector, George
Harrison, had made a far more important discovery of gold on the
Witwatersrand or 'ridge of the white waters' near Johannesburg,

* Geoffrey Wheatcroft, *The Randlords*, London, Weidenfeld & Nicolson, 1985,
p. 283
† Lord Randolph Churchill, *Men, Mines, and Animals in South Africa*, London,
Sampson Low, 1893, pp. 45ff

250 miles from Kimberley. In the subsequent gold-rush prospectors and entrepreneurs raced to Johannesburg, buying up farms and staking out claims. Three years later, just when the gold seemed to be running out, the discovery of deep-level gold opened up limitless prospects. The gold-rush on the Witwatersrand (or 'The Rand') unlike Klondyke or Yukon, had come to stay; and gold, unlike diamonds, could be mined indefinitely without depressing the price. Johannesburg was at first largely financed from Kimberley, but the deep-level mining required a continuing flow of capital from the rest of the world. Two great finance houses straddled both diamonds and gold. Cecil Rhodes was chairman both of De Beers and of Consolidated Gold Fields which produced about a tenth of the gold. But the real gold giant was the partnership of the two Germans, Julius Wernher and Alfred Beit, with their Johannesburg partner Hermann Eckstein, working through their partnership Wernher, Beit, which became known as the 'Corner House'. Beit, who had already helped to put together De Beers, was the financial genius who foresaw the full prospects of the Rand, raised money through Rothschilds in Germany and France and put together the new company Rand Mines which boldly bought up land in anticipation of the deep levels. It was Beit who dealt Rhodes into his company, thus setting a pattern of interlocking ownerships ('Rhodes' brains are not to be despised,' he wrote, 'and if we had interests apart from theirs there would always be friction'). The Corner House and Rand Mines, which later merged into Central Mining, became the central engine of South African capital, with its own intelligence system, its political nominees, and its newspaper the *Star*.*

The gold millionaires in Johannesburg acquired fortunes which, if not on the scale of Rockefeller or Vanderbilt, brought a new stimulus to European stockmarkets. Their London offices attracted the same kind of excitement as railway shares forty years earlier – with far less knowledge of the underlying conditions; the word *Kaffirs* was soon used to describe the shares rather than the people who worked behind them ('Tintos climbed to $12\frac{1}{4}$ and even Kaffirs raised their sickly head' 1889). The mine-owners brought an ostentatious new wealth to London as well as Johannesburg, acquiring Park Lane mansions, racehorses and country houses, and even penetrating the 'Marlborough House Circle' of the Prince of Wales which in the 1890s was 'galvanized by a spectacular infusion of new wealth from the gold and diamond mines of South Africa.'† In 1902

* A P Cartwright, *The Corner House*, London, Macdonald, 1965, pp. 61–131
† Philip Magnus, *King Edward the Seventh*, London, John Murray, 1964, p. 245–6

a popular new musical in London *The Girl Kays* featured a vulgar
South African mine magnate called Hoggenheimer of Park Lane
who was to take his own nasty place in Afrikaner mythology.*

The mine-owners needed far more black workers on the Rand
than in Kimberley, particularly in the deep-level mines. They
naturally wanted to use the cheapest workers available and they
had no interest in protecting the jobs of the more expensive white
miners. When the white miners pressed for a colour bar the Chamber
of Mines opposed it, but they could not prevent the Transvaal
passing the first statutory colour bar in 1893.† Thus from the
beginning, the mine-owners were not necessarily in favour of discrimination, as Merle Lipton points out in her analysis of capitalism
and apartheid. But they did impose rigid segregation through the
compound system they had devised in Kimberley to accommodate
migrant workers, which helped to conceal the 'native problem'.
John Hays Hammond, Rhodes' American engineer, objected to the
dependence on migrant workers: 'In order to ensure a permanent
supply of efficient miners, I suggested to Rhodes we establish native
villages near the mines, where boys could live with their wives and
families'.‡ But the other mine-owners did not approve, and it was
many years before they were to face the political consequences of
the workforce they had created.

The mine magnates soon found that doing business in Johannesburg had one fundamental difference from Kimberley; they were
not now in the British Cape Colony, but in the Transvaal Republic,
ruled by 50,000 Afrikaners who had little connection or sympathy
with the booming new industry. The British had briefly annexed
the Transvaal in 1877 but after bitter fighting in the First Boer War
they gave it back four years later to the Afrikaners, who were all
the more determined to resist British influences. The rugged biblical
figure of their leader Paul Kruger, with his top hat and wide
beard, became a symbol of stubborn intransigence, a much more
formidable tribal chief than any black leader. Kruger saw himself
in the Old Testament, leading a chosen people who were facing
ungodly invaders. To Barney Barnato, the most flamboyant of
the mine-owners, the Transvaal government was 'an unlimited
company of some 20,000 shareholders'.§ To Kruger the mine-
owners were representatives of the devil. 'Every ounce of gold taken

* *Standard Encyclopaedia of Southern Africa*, Vol. V, pp. 559–60
† Merle Lipton, *Capitalism and Apartheid*, London, Gower Temple Smith, 1985,
p. 112
‡ The autobiography of John Hays Hammond, New York, Farrar and Reinhart,
1936, Vol. 1, p. 304
§ Paul Emden, *Randlords*, Hodder & Stoughton, 1935, p. 142

from the bowels of our soil,' he said, 'will yet have to be weighed against rivers of tears.' Yet Kruger was quite content to exploit them, and well aware of the importance of capital: in 1890 he encouraged the setting up of the National Bank in Pretoria to conduct the banking business of the Transvaal government: Kruger himself laid the foundation stone and was photographed surrounded by the early staff.*

The contrast between the foreigners or Uitlanders in Johannesburg – English, German, American, Jewish – and the Afrikaners in their capital in Pretoria thirty miles north was obvious to every visitor, as it has been ever since. The millionaires who had been largely unrestricted in Kimberley found it intolerable to be subject to taxes, monopolies, delays and obstruction from a backward foreign people; and most British visitors agreed with them. When Randolph Churchill arrived in Johannesburg he was fascinated by the manifestation of the power of money (all the more, no doubt, because he was a shareholder in gold mines): 'one is confirmed in the belief that there is nothing that money cannot do.' But he complained that 'if this country had been in the hands of the English or the Americans it would probably now be peopled by some millions of Europeans . . . but Providence has cursed it with the rule of 50,000 Boers, and for a time, but I expect only for a time, it is destined still to languish.'†

By the 1890s the tension between Pretoria and Johannesburg was reaching breaking point after Kruger had introduced a new law which required foreigners to wait fourteen years before getting the vote. In 1895 the mine-owners plotted – in the office of Rhodes' Consolidated Goldfields – to take the law into their own hands, with tacit encouragement from the Colonial Secretary in London, Joe Chamberlain. Rhodes, Beit and the other mine-owners financed an armed raid to capture Johannesburg, led by Dr Leander Jameson. The raid was foiled and the Afrikaners captured its leaders, imposing heavy fines and sending them to London for a spectacular trial, after which Rhodes and his colleagues were briefly disgraced. The Jameson Raid was seen by British liberals as an unforgivable blunder – while later liberals speculated whether South Africa might have had a more peaceful future if it had succeeded.

The Afrikaners were still more distrustful of the mine-owners: they imported weapons from Germany and France and built forts round Pretoria against a new threat. But the mine-owners became

* Barclays International: A Banking Centenary, 1938
† Churchill, pp. 58–91

still more impatient as the financial importance of Johannesburg increased. By 1899 the Transvaal had overtaken Russia, Australia and America as the greatest gold power in the world. Their new opportunity came with the arrival in 1897 of the new British High Commissioner, Sir Alfred Milner, who shared their interest in a new showdown with the Afrikaners, as the prelude to his vision of a united Southern Africa. Milner began to see war as the only solution; and while Rhodes was wary, Alfred Beit was prepared to sacrifice the short-term losses of earnings from gold if war broke out. His firm eventually guaranteed a loan of £50 million. As the historian of the Boer War Thomas Pakenham has shown: 'the gold-bugs, contrary to the accepted view of later historians, were thus active partners with Milner in the making of the war.'*

Milner was determined that Britain would annex the Transvaal and establish 'a self-governing White Community, supported by well-treated and justly governed black labour from Cape Town to the Zambezi.' He achieved his immediate object in 1899 when Kruger refused to give way, thus provoking the Boer War; but the blacks soon proved the chief losers. When the British captured Johannesburg they were cheered by blacks on the pavements; but they soon enforced colour-bar laws more strictly than the Afrikaners: 'The laws that made Africans into the helots,' says Pakenham, 'were now to be applied with an efficiency that the Boers had never been able to muster.'† The young Oxford graduates from New College whom Milner brought in as his 'kindergarten' to reconstruct South Africa had their own insulation and arrogance. Lionel Curtis, the 'prophet' of the kindergarten who became town clerk of Johannesburg (and who later wrote a memorandum which was the first step to the Union) described the situation in 1900:

> The very presence of black men in large numbers makes the white minority indolent and incompetent. The relative proportions of black and white are such that I am not hopeful of the ultimate future of the country. It would be a blessed thing for us if the negro like the Red Indian tended to die out before us, for he acts like decay among teeth. The tendency of Trade Unions to exclude coloured labour should be fostered by all patriotic men in Australia and America.‡

* Thomas Pakenham, *The Boer War*, London, Weidenfeld & Nicolson, 1979, p. 89
† Pakenham, *op. cit.*, p. 554
‡ Lionel Curtis, *With Milner in South Africa*, Oxford, Basil Blackwell, 1951, p. 226

It was a revealing and confused complaint, for much of the wealth of the country now depended on black workers without whom the deep-level gold-mines would be unworkable. As the historian de Kiewiet wrote: 'What an abundance of rain and grass was to New Zealand mutton, what a plenty of cheap grazing land was to Australian wool, what the fertile prairie acres were to Canadian wheat, cheap native labour was to South African mining and industrial enterprise.'* And the white workers with their unions were soon to cause more difficulties for the mine-owners than the blacks without unions.

The Boer War was won by the British at an expense of over £250 million, with 400,000 British soldiers in South Africa at one time. But the treaty at Vereeniging that ended the war soon proved a victory for the Afrikaners. The English-speaking whites had gained the franchise; but they soon lost their hope that a flow of British immigrants would outvote the Afrikaners who, as Pakenham puts it, 'had a secret weapon in the shape of the cradle' (President Kruger alone had 156 living children, grandchildren and great-grandchildren).† In South Africa, demographics were to make their own logic. The irony of the war was not lost on contemporaries: 'The British colonials know quite well,' said 'Indicus' visiting South Africa from India in 1903, 'that unless they can disenfranchise or in some way gerrymander the Dutch, power must pass . . . into Dutch hands.'‡ Four years after the end of the war the Afrikaner leader Louis Botha, leading his populist party Het Volk, won the election in the Transvaal.

The mine-owners could return to expansive conditions. Wernher and Beit, who controlled a third of South Africa's gold, were among the richest men in the world. When Beit died in 1906, even in the midst of a new slump, he left £8 million – the biggest will to be proved in Somerset House. But the gold millionaires could never connect their wealth with political power and many anyway loosened their links with South Africa. Wernher retired to Luton Hoo, his huge country seat north of London, which his son Harold took over, marrying Lady Zia, the daughter of a Russian grand-duke: two of their grandchildren married English Dukes (Westminster and Abercorn). Beit's nephew, Sir Alfred, still lives in the great Irish mansion Russborough; (his nephew and heir Theodore Bull married a Zambian princess and took part of the Beit fortune back to Africa).

* C W de Kiewiet, *A History of South Africa*, Oxford University Press. 1941, p. 96
† Pakenham, *op. cit.*, p. 259
‡ '*Indicus*': *Labour and Other Questions in South Africa*, London, 1903, p. 130.

The Boer War was soon seen by Marxists as a prime example of
the power of international capitalism. 'The South African war,
openly fomented by gold speculators for their private purposes,'
wrote the Manchester economist J A Hobson in his famous book
*Imperialism** in 1902, 'will rank in history as a leading case of this
usurpation of nationalism.' But he also foresaw that 'a South African
federation of self-governing states . . . will demand a political career
of its own, and will insist upon its own brand of empire, not that of
the British government, in the control of the lower races in South
Africa.' Hobson in turn much influenced Lenin when he wrote
his own book on Imperialism in 1916† in which he inaccurately
described Cecil Rhodes as 'the man who was mainly responsible
for the Anglo-Boer War' – while Lenin's theories in turn heavily
influenced Third World governments after independence. Contemporary Marxists still see the Boer War, in the words of Jack
and Ray Simons, as 'a classic example of imperialist aggression
prompted by capitalist greed'.

Hobson and later Marxists had reason to suspect that the mine-
owners had fomented the war; but were the war-mongers really
acting in their own long-term interests? When Sir Norman Angell
wrote his popular book *The Great Illusion* in 1910, arguing that
aggression does not pay economically and that groups do not
necessarily act in their own interests, he pointed out how the British
government could not capture any of South Africa's wealth as a
result of the war, and that 'the *political* control of the area containing
one of the great sources of the world's gold is in process of passing
out of the hands of Britain.'‡

The real victory of the Afrikaners was to come in 1910 with the
creation of the Union of South Africa, which united the two colonies,
the Cape and Natal, with the two Afrikaner republics, the Transvaal
and the Orange Free State, to form an independent state within the
British Empire. It was to remain an uneasy combination of Afrikaner rulers, international capitalists and voteless blacks of whom
little notice was taken. It was at the cost of any further black
advancement, and the superseding of the old liberal Cape constitution which had allowed some blacks the vote. For the blacks, the
outcome of the Boer War was the opposite of the American civil
war forty years earlier.

And the First World War hastened the development of South

* J A Hobson, *Imperialism*, London, Allen & Unwin (3rd edition), 1938,
pp. 127, 346
    † V Lenin: *Imperialism*, Moscow, Progress Publishers, 1978, p. 75
    ‡ Sir Norman Angell, *The Great Illusion, 1908–1914*, 1933 edition, London,
Heinemann, p. 194–5

Africa's 'own brand of empire'. Facing perilous sea-lanes the mining companies had to become less dependent on Britain, and soon found they could extend to other industries, producing many manufactures more cheaply than imports; while the mines were becoming less dependent on foreign capital and the second-generation South Africans no longer saw themselves as expatriates. After the war, high tariffs continued to encourage local manufacturers, while Western corporations and banks were beginning to look to South African investments inside the tariff walls. Ford had arrived in 1923, and the next year General Motors set up a car-assembly plant in Port Elizabeth. In 1925 the National, Kruger's old bank, was bought out by Barclays in London.

Central Mining, the legacy of Wernher and Beit, remained the dominant group; Rhodes' old company Consolidated Goldfields rapidly acquired other industrial companies. But it was a new group founded by Ernest Oppenheimer in 1917, with the grand name of the Anglo-American Corporation, which was to become the cornerstone of the new South African capitalism and which developed into the biggest concentration of financial power in the continent.

Ernest Oppenheimer provided a bridge between the early diamond days and the new intricate gold-mining empires. The son of a German cigar merchant, he had become a clerk in the London diamond firm of Dunkelsbuhler and went out to Kimberley to represent it, mastering the finances of diamonds and becoming Mayor of Kimberley. The war was a setback for men with German-sounding names, and Oppenheimer retreated back to London; but he soon returned to Johannesburg to investigate the potential of very deep-level gold-mines which needed still larger investments to develop them. He was convinced of the prospects, but his company had the difficulty, in the middle of the First World War, of being one-third owned by German shareholders;* so Oppenheimer raised funds to form his own mining company which would be doubly unique: it would be based not in London but in Johannesburg; while it would raise most of its capital not in London – where the war restricted investment – but in New York. Oppenheimer made many American connections through his mining engineer William Honnold, including the 'great engineer' Herbert Hoover, the Newmont mining corporation, and the banker J P Morgan. He first wanted to call his company the African American Corporation, but Honnold cabled back: AFRICAN-AMERICAN WOULD SUGGEST ON THIS

* Duncan Innes, *Anglo-American and the Rise of Modern South Africa*, Johannesburg, Ravan Press, 1984, p. 91

SIDE OUR DARK-SKINNED FELLOW COUNTRYMEN AND POSSIBLY RESULT
IN RIDICULE . . .* And Oppenheimer eventually agreed to call it the
Anglo-American Corporation of South Africa, thus embracing all
three continents. The chief advantage of a South African base was
the lower taxation; but Oppenheimer from the beginning stressed
his company's patriotism, and he and his family were much more
thoroughly committed to the country than the earlier mine-owners.

With himself as chairman and permanent director, Oppenheimer
formed the Anglo-American Corporation in 1917, and soon used all
his ingenuity to extend his interests in the new very deep-level gold-
mines: already by 1918 his group controlled four of the eleven mining
companies on the East Rand. He was already preparing a bold strategy to move into diamonds, and began stealthily to encircle De Beers
by gaining control of the new diamond fields that had opened up
independently of the Kimberley monopoly; first the fields in South
West Africa which had lost their German control after the war; then
fields in Lichtenburg and Namaqualand; then in West Africa. He
played his cards with extraordinary patience and skill – until by 1929
De Beers were compelled to accept him as chairman, as the only
means to impose order. Soon afterwards the depression provided the
opportunity to integrate the diamond business more thoroughly, and
to reinforce the De Beers monopoly. He was now king of diamonds as
well as gold. He was also moving into South African manufacturing
industry, and beginning his partnership with the British explosives
and chemical combine ICI (*see* page 94). And he could also use his
financial and technical base to develop resources elsewhere in Africa,
particularly in the British colony of Northern Rhodesia (now Zambia) where he developed lucrative copper mines in competition with
the American group of Chester Beatty. Anglo-American's expansion
was increasingly self-financing, and after the Second World War,
when Oppenheimer gained control of new goldfields near Welkom
in the Orange Free State, he was able to finance their development
largely with the profits from De Beers.

Oppenheimer was soon the new personification of the South
African capitalist; an updated version of Cecil Rhodes as hero and
villain. He had none of the territorial ambitions of Rhodes, and his
style was low-key: but he was more single-minded in his pursuit of
financial power. His admiring biographer, Sir Theodore Gregory,
saw him as an indispensable entrepreneur who could mobilise
capital with a decisiveness and direction which dramatically
speeded up African development. The Afrikaner nationalists saw

* Sir Theodore Gregory, *Ernest Oppenheimer and the Economic Development of Southern
Africa*, Oxford University Press, 1962, p. 88

him as the reincarnation of Hoggenheimer, the Jewish exploiter. The Marxists insisted that his own personality was largely irrelevant: Anglo-American, wrote its chronicler Duncan Innes, 'was responding to the underlying tendencies of concentration and centralization of production and capital which characterize monopoly capitalism . . . Oppenheimer's "genius" lay in the fact that he correctly perceived the fundamental tendencies of the time.'*

Certainly Anglo-American, as it expanded and interlocked with other groups, showed some signs of monopoly capitalism as described by Hobson and Lenin, with a concentration of money, power and technology which towered over the Pretoria government and employed the biggest black labour-force in the continent. But South Africa was hardly a perfect model of a Marxist state. The Afrikaner governments were less and less like 'the executive committee of the bourgeoisie'. The mine-owners were far from certain where their true interests lay as they confronted both black and white workers; while the sudden impact of capital and industry was soon countered by two successive nationalisms, Afrikaner and African, which increasingly challenged them for control of the wealth of the young nation.

One of Oppenheimer's last public acts was in 1957 when the slight, unobtrusive old man opened the splendid new offices of De Beers, at the end of London's 'diamond street' of Hatton Garden, now sharing the same building as Anglo-American, formally marrying diamonds to gold. It was a monument to South Africa's own capitalism: by the time of Oppenheimer's death six months later his company was producing not only all of South Africa's diamonds, but 30 percent of its gold, 44 percent of its coal, and more than half Northern Rhodesia's copper.† His political legacy in South Africa was less certain: he was astute in handling Afrikaners, but like the other mine-owners he remained insulated from the huge black workforce which he had helped to build up; and his official biography records no black individual. When in 1955 Sir Ernest read the bestselling book *Naught for your Comfort* by Father Trevor Huddleston, which described the full miseries of black South Africans, he maintained (according to his son Harry) that it was biased and unfair; but he decided to look again at the conditions of blacks in Soweto, and soon afterwards he persuaded the mining houses to lend £3 million for black housing.‡

* Innes, *op. cit.*, p. 111

† Edward Jessup, *Ernest Oppenheimer: A Study in Power*, London, Rex Collings, 1979, p. 317

‡ Speech on March 11, 1958, unveiling his father's memorial tower (Gregory, p. 580)

Already in 1933 Ernest's son Harry was sitting in on his father's meetings, and over the next twenty-five years he was groomed as the successor. Harry had none of the rough schooling of a self-made entrepreneur: he was educated in England, at Charterhouse school and Christ Church, Oxford. He seemed overshadowed: he was shy and self-effacing with embarrassingly good manners, sidling sideways into a room, listening patiently to bores and seeing guests out to the front door. He admired the English tradition, was brought up an Anglican, married a very English South African, recruited many public-school men. Yet, like his father, he was as hard as a diamond in business deals. He was always aloof from English influences, contemptuous of the sleepy old boy network of the City of London; and he became a rare example of a son inheriting both a genius and a drive for business, and vastly extending his inheritance. 'When you are brought up in the purple,' he once said to me, 'the only thing worth doing is to be some kind of an artist. I found I couldn't be that; so there was nothing to do but business.' He became an artist in that.

He was intensely aware of his political vulnerability ever since, as MP for Kimberley, he had come up against the Afrikaner fanatics of the National Party clamouring to nationalise Anglo-American. He did not shirk political commitment: in the 'fifties he financed the 'Torch Commando' of war veterans who defended the constitution against the Nationalist government, and he went on to subsidise liberal politicians including his friend Helen Suzman. He considered his own political career a failure, though he was much more far-sighted and imaginative than other mine-owners or even his father.

But he faced far more testing political problems than his father after the coming to power of the Afrikaner nationalists in 1948. The very dominating success of Anglo-American – like the monopoly of IG Farben in Germany in the 'thirties – could be exploited by the state to make it more dependent. And the immediate need to conciliate Afrikaner nationalists could easily obscure the long-term need to come to terms with black nationalists who would provide a much more serious threat to the future of his corporation.

4

Afrikaners against Blacks

We are not a nation of jellyfish.

P W Botha, July, 1986

Pieter Willem Botha, who was born six years after the union of South Africa, could look back on a far more heroic and military version of history than that of the Oppenheimers and mine-owners. His father had been one of the 'bitter-enders' who fought to the end of the Boer War; his mother had been in a British concentration camp where she lost two of her children; and eighty years after that war Botha still continually reminded his audiences that his people 'nearly brought the British empire to its knees'. From his youth on his father's farm through his first career as a National Party organiser he was imbued with the belief that the future of South Africa depended on the unique qualities and endurance of the Afrikaners.

When South Africa became a nation in 1910 it was already dominated by Afrikaner leaders, with one war-hero Louis Botha as prime minister and another, Jan Smuts, as his minister of interior, mines and defence. The old dreams of a British South Africa as conceived by Rhodes or Milner were already modified, and Afrikaans had official equality with English. The first government was conciliatory towards the British, and many Afrikaners fought on their side in the First World War. But by 1914 another hero of the Boer War, General Hertzog, had already formed his more extreme National Party; and two years later a group of nationalists formed the Broederbond, the secret society which countered the English-men's power establishment with its own network dedicated to Afrikanerdom.

The Union was one of the most disparate and fragmented nations in the world. It was not only that the blacks were thoroughly segregated from the whites. The Indians in Natal never mixed with the blacks or the whites; the coloureds (of mixed blood) in the Cape were shunned by their white cousins, and looked down on the blacks; and the two dominant white groups – the English-speaking businessmen and the Afrikaner politicians – went their separate ways with a legacy of distrust. When the English talked about 'the racial question' they usually meant the Afrikaners, not the blacks. Afrikaner politicians were to remain obsessed by the injustices and sufferings of the Boer War, rightly proud of their wartime resistance: 'The first of the freedom fighters,' as they would depict themselves afterwards. Successive British governments on their side would treat Pretoria with a mixture of awe, guilt and contempt which made normal communication impossible, while English writers and publicists from John Buchan to Baden-Powell would invest rural Afrikaners with an enduring romanticism and their language would be infused with the vocabulary of treks, spoors, laagers and sjamboks.

But the Afrikaners were themselves becoming industrialised: as their many children left the farms for the cities they faced the full discipline of the gold-mines and factories, with scarcely better qualifications than the blacks; and there began a new kind of revolt. In the first years after the First World War, the mine-owners in Johannesburg had a brief honeymoon with the government under Smuts, who knew that profitable gold-mines were crucial to development. But a sudden fall in the gold price precipitated their first major clash with white workers in the 'red revolt' of 1922, a more brutal showdown between capital and labour than any in Europe or America. The Chamber of Mines insisted on using more black miners until the white miners' protest escalated into a general strike under the famous slogan: 'Workers of the World unite for a White South Africa.' It was more like a war than a strike, and Smuts eventually won it with troops and artillery: over 250 people were killed, and the leaders were hanged. (P W Botha would speak with some jealousy about Smuts, who was so ruthless at home yet preserved his high-minded reputation abroad.) The mine-owners pressed ahead with sacking whites and employing more blacks, and in 1924 they declared record profits. But it was a Pyrrhic victory; for in the same year Smuts was defeated by a coalition of nationalist Afrikaners and white labour unionists under General Hertzog, united in championing white labour. Hertzog's Afrikaner supporters were soon dominant, and determined to protect white workers, farmers and local manufacturers against international industry and finance: they established nationalised industries including the extravagant state-owned steelworks Iscor, to provide secure jobs. The young urban Afrikaners, with the help of the Dutch Reformed Church, resisted the integrating forces of industry and cities.

The Afrikaner nationalism amidst which P W Botha grew up was already semi-socialist, with bitter experiences of capitalism as well as imperialism. The mine-owners still had some clout: during the depression Hertzog tried but failed to prevent Ernest Oppenheimer from closing diamond mines; and he dared not embark on large-scale nationalisation.* But by the 'thirties the Afrikaners were already seriously limiting the profits and expansion of the capitalists, who blamed them for inhibiting economic progress. 'A basic cause of the low average income of the inhabitants of the Union,' Professor Herbert Frankel, who was also Oppenheimer's economic adviser, wrote in 1938, 'is the lack of "economic mobility" of its workers – both black and white.'†

The depression forced Hertzog into a coalition with Smuts and English-speaking voters to produce a fused 'United Party', which still favoured farmers and manufacturers against the mine-owners. The more militant Afrikaner nationalists were still more implacable, augmented by the growing number of poor whites and the Afrikaner-based industries which felt damaged by the British connection. In 1934 they formed the new 'purified' Afrikaner National party under Dr Daniel Malan – which young P W Botha was to join as an organiser two years later – which would change the face of South Africa. It was pledged to establish a genuine Afrikaner state, supported by a powerful religious and patriotic lobby, and it had a strong nationalist socialist element, influenced by Nazi Germany. One of their most powerful intellectuals, Dr Nico Diedrichs who later became State President, studied Nazi politics and economics in Germany and back in South Africa was closely involved in setting up Afrikaner financial institutions including the bank Volkskas, the 'people's bank' which provided an important financial base. Many of the National Party leaders, including Albert Hertzog the son of the General, called for wholesale nationalisation of industry including the gold-mines. The combination of ethnic and economic appeal was irresistible; and in 1938, when the nationalists re-enacted their Great Trek into the interior a century earlier, the wave of nostalgic nationalism revealed the full force of the Afrikaner pride.

During the war, while Smuts again supported the British, many of the National Party leaders openly sided with Hitler and some attempted sabotage, through a new right-wing group the Ossewabrandwag: the future prime minister John Vorster was imprisoned together with his future intelligence chief Hendrik van den Bergh. When Hitler started losing, the future appeal of the National Party seemed more doubtful, and Smuts emerged after the war as an international statesman; but most English-speakers had underestimated the power and organisation of Afrikaner nationalism.

* Lipton, *op. cit.*, p. 266

† Sally Herbert Frankel, *Capital Investment in Africa*, Oxford University Press, 1938, p. 143

Then in 1948 the general election brought Dr Malan into power with a new infusion of National Party MPs, including P W Botha. 'For the first time since Union,' said Malan in his triumph, 'South Africa is our own, and may God grant that it will always remain our own.' It was the beginning of a virtual Afrikaner monopoly of power over the next four decades. The historian Arthur Keppel-Jones *had* predicted the nationalist victory in a prophetic book published eighteen months before the election called *When Smuts Goes*: it forecast that the Nationalists would introduce authoritarian laws, leave the Commonwealth, provoke a black revolt and go to war with Britain in 1977, after which South Africa would eventually revert to barbarism. Keppel-Jones' own moral was 'that the salvation of the country can lie only in a reversal of historic tendencies, a reversal so thorough as to constitute a revolution.'* In the years after 1948 his readers would anxiously watch his predictions coming true.

The National Party had conflicting economic ambitions. Most of the dominant leaders wanted to take over the existing industrial system, replacing English-speakers with Afrikaners and building up nationalised bodies to counterbalance the Anglophone strongholds. They saw the Industrial Development Corporation, run by H J Van Eck, partly as a 'bulwark against the Anglo-American Corporation'.† Others with trade union support still wanted to nationalise much of the economy. But they were united in their determination to build up Afrikanerdom and to enforce the new policy called apartheid which the National Party had been formulating over the previous years.

There was nothing fundamentally new about apartheid: thorough segregation had been advocated by the white Labour Party as well as Afrikaner Nationalists in the 'thirties, and Smuts himself sternly defended segregation. As P W Botha later explained with only some exaggeration: 'Apartheid as we understand it existed in South Africa from previous centuries under British rule . . . Colonial paternalism had a racial connotation and whites for some four hundred years had governed blacks all over the world. South Africa inherited colonial paternalism and this entailed the governing of blacks by whites.'‡ But the unique characteristic of apartheid was to institutionalise both segregation and racialism just when the Western world was repelled by it at the end of the war against Hitler, with a more ruthless division than anything that the British or

* Arthur Keppel-Jones, *When Smuts Goes*, Pietermaritzburg, Shuter and Shooter, 1950, p. *xii*
  † Andries Wassenaar, *The Assault on Private Enterprise*, Cape Town, 1977, p. 123
  ‡ Interview with Bruce London, *The Times*, London, August 23, 1986

Smuts had attempted. Within two years of 1948 the National government had passed the two bedrock laws which enforced discrimination: the Population Registration Act ensured the purity of the white race – with the help of a Board which could examine skin, hair and nails – while the Group Areas Act enforced separate residential areas. There followed a quick succession of laws to enforce segregation in schools, universities, local government and political systems. It was the total opposite to the trend in the United States. In the early 'fifties the conditions of many blacks in the Southern States could be compared to those in South Africa. But by 1954 the Supreme Court in Washington had dismissed the old doctrine of 'separate but equal' and declared that segregation in public schools must end – the year after the Bantu Education Act in South Africa had enforced separate education, with a built-in inequality.

The implementation of apartheid – particularly the inferior education – was also clearly damaging to long-term industrial expansion; for white workers were already in short supply. But the English-speaking opposition in the United Party, which represented most business interests, was reluctant to oppose the new apartheid laws, and felt vulnerable to attack for encouraging a black flood. 'It is not always useful,' as de Kiewiet put it in 1956, 'to distinguish between the English and the Afrikaner in racial matters.'* The British Labour government in London had few illusions about the racial dangers of apartheid, and the British High Commissioner, Sir Evelyn Baring, frequently compared the Nationalist government to the Nazis. In his farewell despatch (which impressed his Prime Minister, Attlee), he warned that 'to despise or ignore the strong and expanding force of South African Nationalism in 1951 would be as unwise as it was to decry in March 1933 the power of Hitler to do harm . . . Nationalist fanatics control a strong and important country.' But he also warned that 'it will be useless to attempt to draw a complete *cordon sanitaire* round South Africa and to cut ourselves and our African dependencies off from that country.'† The Labour government in London, anxious to secure uranium and to reach a new gold agreement, was easily bullied by Pretoria, and timid in challenging apartheid in the British protectorates on its frontiers which they feared South Africa would take over; when Seretse Khama, the chief of the Bamangwato tribe in Bechuanaland (later Botswana) married a white woman, Ruth Williams, in 1949, they refused to recognise him for five years.

* De Kiewiet, *op. cit.*, p. 32
† Charles Douglas-Home, *Evelyn Baring, The Last Proconsul*, London, Collins, 1978, p. 214

But the early apartheid of Dr Malan and his successor, Hans Strijdom, was relatively modest compared to the ambitious 'grand apartheid' of the third nationalist prime minister, Dr Hendrik Verwoerd. A professor of both psychology and theology, with little interest in economics, he had been educated largely in Germany and acquired a total confidence in his Calvinist view of the world, which radiated from his innocent face and beatific smile. He was a religious leader as much as a political one: speaking, he clasped his hands and looked upwards as if for inspiration. He took apartheid much more literally than his predecessors, and was prepared to make genuine sacrifices. His fellow ministers including P W Botha were easily silenced by his confidence which took apartheid to its logical limits. As secretary for native affairs, Verwoerd had already been the architect of the new Bantu 'homelands' and Bantu education and had constructed a system which saw no role for the blacks, except as servants, in the white men's cities.

Verwoerd's theory of apartheid stressed above all that the blacks were not part of the South African nation, but a group of separate tribal nations – Zulu, Xhosa or Sotho – which would gain dignity and self-respect outside the white man's world. 'The Bantu is neither a backward black Englishman, nor a backward black Afrikaner,' as Schalk Pienaar, one of his most articulate intellectual supporters, put it in 1960. 'He is not even a backward black Bantu. He is a Zulu or a Xhosa or a Sotho or what you will. A nation in his own right.'* Pienaar and many other Afrikaners projected the blacks in their own image, as proud tribes that did not wish to be assimilated: 'We will not deny the Bantu what we have claimed for ourselves.' And as black Africa moved towards independence they saw a new justification: 'The black nations of South Africa can become free even as Ghana is today.' Much of the Afrikaner intellectual confidence was based on ignorance of urban black society; and while the Afrikaners were determined to preserve their tribe – even at the cost of economic and industrial development – most political blacks were determined to escape from tribalism, and to become a single nation.

But Afrikaner students could see Verwoerd's apartheid as much purer and more acceptable than the cruder version of Dr Malan. 'I remember the excitement, even thrill, some experienced when it was explained for the first time,' wrote the liberal Afrikaner politician Van Zyl Slabbert, recalling his time as a student at the Afrikaans university of Stellenbosch. 'Any aware young Afrikaner

* S Pienaar and Anthony Sampson, *South Africa, Two Views of Separate Development*, Oxford University Press, 1960, pp. 9–15 and p. 56

knew instinctively and with a pervading sense of doom that apartheid until then was a holding action, that a solution to living with
the blacks still had to be found. Here, some sensed, was the
beginning of one. It made logical sense and addressed very prickly
moral issues. The beauty of it was the audacity of its most basic
assumptions: "You don't have to find a solution to living with
blacks, because there are no blacks, only ethnic groups who cannot
really tolerate one another anyway . . ."*

Western governments never recognised the supposed independence of the homelands; and the extravagant costs and suffering
involved in the territorial separation were soon very apparent, with
forced removals, shack villages and endless bus-journeys to carry
workers to the white factories. But Afrikaner politicians including
Botha could never abandon the idea, for it enabled them to think
in terms of black minorities rather than a single black majority.
And many multinationals as well as local companies at first propagated the idea that the homelands were beneficial to both blacks
and industry. 'The South African government's policy is to encourage and assist the Bantu to develop their territories into self-
governing national homelands,' reported Roy Hill, the local general
manager of Colgate Palmolive in 1966. 'Decentralisation of white
territories and the establishment of industries in border areas near
the national homelands, calculated to ensure a more equitable
distribution of wealth and contribute to the economic development
of the homelands, are firm matters of government policy.'†

But the extremism of Verwoerd's grand apartheid was becoming
an embarrassment to Britain, which was still by far the biggest
foreign investor but also had growing interests in black Africa, which
was moving rapidly towards independence. Verwoerd's fanaticism
soon came face-to-face with British pragmatism. At the beginning
of 1960 the Conservative prime minister Harold Macmillan made
a historic tour of the continent, flying from newly-independent
Ghana via Nigeria and Rhodesia to South Africa. He was preparing
a major speech to the parliament which was celebrating its fifty-year
jubilee. When he reached Cape Town he stayed with Dr and Mrs
Verwoerd, where he was amazed by their Calvinist zeal: there were
no black servants, only Afrikaners including a doddering butler. 'I
began to realise to the full extent,' Macmillan wrote afterwards,
'the degree of obstinacy, amounting really to fanaticism, which Dr

* Frederik Van Zyl Slabbert, *The Last White Parliament*, London, Sidgwick &
Jackson, 1986, p. 76
    † Jerome Blood (editor), *Management looks at Africa*, American Management
Association, 1966

Verwoerd brought to the consideration of his policies.'* Macmillan
was more worried by the dogmatism of apartheid than its economic
consequences: 'If they didn't make an ideology of it they would
almost certainly succeed in getting the results they seek with a
minimum of concession,' he told his press secretary Harold Evans.
'Economic differences between black and white would alone be
sufficient to achieve practical separation . . .'† But when he finally
revised his speech (the British High Commissioner Sir John Maud
complained privately), he left out some criticisms, including a
reference to Lord Melbourne's dictum that: 'Nobody ever did
anything very foolish except from some high principle.'

Macmillan's eventual speech brilliantly summed up the
Afrikaner's predicament. He began with his own tactful historical
analysis, stressing how South Africa had built up its strong economy
with much help from British capital. But he continued with a
warning about the growth of African Nationalism: 'The wind of
change is blowing through this continent, and, whether we like it
or not, this growth of national consciousness is a political fact'. He
went on 'to soften the impact' (as he explained afterwards):

> Of course you understand this better than anyone. You are
> sprung from Europe, the home of nationalism, and here in Africa
> you have yourselves created a new nation. Indeed in the history
> of our times, yours will be recorded as the first of the African
> nationalisms . . .

But his concluding message was unambiguous. However much
Britain wanted to give support and encouragement to another
Commonwealth member, 'there are some aspects of your policies
which make it impossible for us to do this without being false to
our own deep convictions about the political destinies of free men
to which in our own territories we are trying to give effect.'

The speech was received in parliament (where I watched it from
the press gallery) with a slow double-take: the members were so
dazed by its range and eloquence that they took some time to realise,
after reading British comments, that Macmillan was beginning to
back black Africa at the expense of white. 'We have our last chance
of contact with Europe – which is drifting away,' the then editor of
Die Burger, Piet Cillie, said to me before the speech. 'Isolation leads
to insanity.' But the speech made South Africans much more aware,

---

* Harold Macmillan, *Pointing the Way*, London, Macmillan, 1972, pp. 150–60
† Sir Harold Evans, *Downing Street Diary*, London, Hodder & Stoughton, 1981,
p. 102

as the *Cape Times* put it, that 'our isolation is practically total'.

Three months later, after the Belgian Congo had collapsed into independence and chaos, the 'Wind of Change' already looked more menacing: Macmillan had to explain that it was 'not the same thing as a howling tempest which would blow away the whole of the new developing civilisation.'* Inside South Africa the Sharpeville massacre (*see* next chapter) led to a sudden wave of protest and reprisals which further antagonised world opinion. Verwoerd was determined to turn South Africa into a republic, for which he won a referendum by a narrow margin in October 1960: but he still wanted South Africa to remain within the Commonwealth, to which South Africa had to re-apply at the conference of prime ministers in March 1961. Macmillan also hoped to keep the Republic inside the Commonwealth, while the Treasury was fearful about its gold leaving the Sterling Area. But Verwoerd, said Macmillan, 'seemed to have no understanding that anyone could consider the political and social position of the vast majority of the population of South Africa was not a purely "domestic" question.' Verwoerd refused any concession to the non-white members of the Commonwealth, and insisted that any black diplomats visiting South Africa would have to stay in a separate non-white hotel. It was a comic irony that this social aversion should be the breaking-point – when only a few years later Pretoria would be welcoming black diplomats from neighbouring states to multi-racial hotels. On March 13 Macmillan formally told parliament that 'the Commonwealth ties with South Africa, which have endured for fifty years, are shortly to be severed . . .' Diplomats continued to argue whether Britain might have better influenced the Republic if it had remained inside the Commonwealth, while many black politicians insisted that *their* people had never left it.

As a republic the Afrikaner government had finally achieved their longed-for independence from the British and they were soon rewarded with striking economic success. While the Labour government in London after 1964 would hurl more words against apartheid, the Afrikaners knew that British companies were becoming still more eager to invest and trade; and by the time P W Botha became minister of defence in 1966 he was well able to channel European investment and technology into his expanding military machine. But Botha and his colleagues who had so triumphantly established their own nationalism were now coming up more sharply against another nationalism which they had helped to provoke, as

* Anthony Sampson, *Macmillan*, London, Allen Lane, The Penguin Press, 1967, p. 190

the British had provoked theirs. And however much they hoped to divide and control the black tribes by separating them into smaller units, the facts of industrialisation and cities were now pushing the blacks harder into the opposite direction, towards a single nation.

5

Blacks against Apartheid

The truest optimism in South Africa is in the crowded, disease-ridden and crime-infested urban locations. They represent the black man's acceptance of the new life of the western world, his willingness to endure a harsh schooling and an equal apprenticeship in its ways.

C W de Kiewiet, *The Anatomy of South African Misery*,
Oxford University Press, 1956, p. 37

The leaders of the African National Congress, Oliver Tambo and his jailed colleague Nelson Mandela, could look back in January 1986 on seventy-five years of their organisation's history: the ANC was two years older than Botha's National Party and only two years younger than South Africa. From the beginning the blacks had associated the Union with diminishing rights, with a political system from which they were shut out, and with white leaders they never met. But they insisted that they were South African patriots, loyal to the new nation rather than the tribe. 'Under apartheid one of us must be the foreigners in South Africa,' said Tambo: 'It will not be us.'

And they saw themselves as an integral part of the industrial society that had been created long before the nation. Already when De Beers was established in Kimberley in the 1880s an urban black population was developing outside the compounds: about 20,000 blacks were working in four 'locations' as servants or employees of traders and contractors. A few were the 'educated natives', mostly Xhosas or Mfengu, who came from mission schools, particularly from Lovedale in the Eastern Cape, for whom the sudden Kimberley boom provided some modest openings for young blacks. The post office could not persuade whites to deliver telegrams, so it took on black school-leavers who were content to take lowly jobs. 'We are just emerging from barbarism,' wrote the black writer John Knox Bokwe in 1894, 'and have to find our way, and by degrees gain their (whites') confidence.'* Among the black telegraph-boys was the young Sol Plaatje who later became secretary of the African National Congress. And among the 'savages' described by Trollope

* Brian Willan, *Sol Plaatje: South African Nationalist*, London, Heinemann, 1984, p. 30

in the diamond mines was Peter Matthews, a Christian from the
Barolong tribe who worked in the mines until his leg was run over
by a mining-truck, when he opened a small tea-and-buns café in a
township. Matthews instilled into his six children that education,
as much as guns, had been the weapon with which the white men
had conquered his people. Four of them became teachers: one of
them was to become Professor Z K Matthews, a prominent leader
of the ANC in the 'fifties and the first ambassador of Botswana to
the United Nations.*

It was the Union in 1910 which directly precipitated the founding
of the Congress in 1912. The blacks had already seen clearly that
Afrikaner dominance would reduce their hopes, and after the Boer
War they had set up black 'vigilance associations' to protect their
rights and land. In 1909 a delegation of blacks sailed for London
to protest against the 'colour-bar clause' in the proposed union
which threatened to disenfranchise the blacks and (said the black
educationalist D D T Jabavu) 'struck the death-knell of Native
confidence in what used to be called British fair play. The cow of
Great Britain had gone dry, they said, and they must look to
themselves for salvation'.†

In the same year as the Union, an ambitious young Zulu lawyer
returned to South Africa from London. Dr Pixley ka Izaka Seme
(named after an American pastor) was one of the much-mocked
'School Kaffirs'; but he had a strong sense of black dignity: a
contemporary photograph shows him in a top hat, morning coat
and spats and he was related to the Zulu royal family (one of his
nephews was to become Chief Buthelezi, the present Zulu leader).
Seme was appalled to see his people in the Transvaal being pushed
off pavements, dodging cars, kicked and knocked and herded into
cattle-trucks. He was determined to unify the black tribes into a
common nation which could defend itself against the new white
state. He collected three black lawyer friends from different tribes
– Mangena, Montsioa and Msimang – and wrote a manifesto: 'We
are one people: these divisions, these jealousies, are the cause of all
our woes and of all our backwardness and ignorance today.' His
agitations led to a conference of black leaders at Bloemfontein two
years after the union. 'It was a gathering of tribes that had never
met before except on the battle fields,' Seme's follower Richard
Selope-Thema later described it.‡ Seme addressed them eloquently:

* Z K Matthews, *Freedom for My People*, Cape Town, David Philip, 1983,
pp. 8–14. *See also* Anthony Sampson, *The Treason Cage*, London, Heinemann, 1958,
pp. 118–20
† D D T Jabavu, *The Black Problem*, Lovedale, 1920
‡ *How Congress Began*, *Drum* magazine, Johannesburg, July 1953

Chiefs of royal blood and gentlemen of our race, we have gathered together to consider and discuss a scheme which my colleagues and I have decided to place before you. We have discovered that in the land of their birth, Africans are treated as hewers of wood and drawers of water. The white people of this country have formed what is known as the Union of South Africa – a union in which we have no voice in the making of the laws and no part in the administration.

They agreed to form a 'South African Native National Congress' – vaguely modelled on the American Congress, on the British parliament and chiefly on traditions – with an upper house of chiefs who sat behind the office-bearers and pronounced verdicts separately from the elected lower house. A sergeant of arms presided in a strange regalia, with a military tunic, breeches and gaiters, a skin shield, knobkerry and axe. Its first leaders all came from the small black professional class or aristocracy, including Dr Seme as Treasurer and Sol Plaatje as secretary, with the Zulu teacher Dr John Dube as president. It was the first occasion where blacks had dropped tribal loyalties – anywhere in the continent – to accept a common nation. It was not nationalist in the sense of being anti-white, militant or revolutionary: it was heavily influenced by Christian teaching, not at all by socialism, and pathetically hopeful of white allies. But it marked the birth of African nationalism in the sense of giving loyalty to the nation rather than the tribe.

The next year Congress saw its worst fears borne out, when the new Union government passed the Native Land Act which forbade the black three-quarters of the population to own land anywhere outside the 'reserves' which covered only one-thirteenth of the country. 'The South African Native found himself not actually a slave,' wrote Plaatje, 'but a pariah in the land of his birth.'* After the First World War, when blacks loyally supported British troops as non-combatants, Congress sent a delegation to London, who saw the British prime minister David Lloyd George. He was visibly moved and later wrote forcefully to Smuts advising him to talk to the Congress leaders. 'You have in Africa men who can speak for native opinion and make themselves felt . . . if they do suffer under disabilities and if they have no effective mode of expression it is obvious that sooner or later serious results must ensue.' Smuts responded that Congress was not representative and that Pretoria was working on 'improved machinery for voicing the needs of

* Sol. T Plaatje, *Native Life in South Africa*, London, P S King, 1916, p. 17

and interests of the Natives.'* It was the beginning of a long
non-dialogue.

There were some political stirrings from the harsher new world
of black factories and urban slums; and in the twenties a brilliant
black demagogue, Clements Kadalie, set up a high-sounding 'Industrial and Commercial Workers' Union' (ICU). But Kadalie was
deflected from his militancy by white patrons, and his movement
split, crumbled into corruption and left a trail of bitterness.

The emerging black intellectuals were too fascinated by Western
culture to look far back into their own cultural roots. They were
steeped in the Bible and in English literature. 'I discovered that
Shakespeare had things to say not only to his England or to the
Western men who have read him since, but also to me, a twentieth
century African,' said the young Z K Matthews, the son of the
Kimberley mineworker, who in 1924 became the first black to take
a South African degree. 'I was a new specimen in the zoo of South
African mankind,' he wrote afterwards. 'In the public service there
was not a single post anywhere as yet provided for such a one as I.'†

The First World War and the Russian revolution had helped to
make blacks more politically conscious, which worried some white
employers. In January 1918, in Kimberley, Sol Plaatje had asked
De Beers to donate an old tram shed as an assembly hall for the
blacks (which he had already suggested to Ernest Oppenheimer).
De Beers agreed, conscious of the wave of black unrest and realising
(as their director Sir David Harris explained) that the gift might
enhance 'their loyalty to De Beers as a generous employer of
labour'.‡ It was the only recorded case of De Beers subsidising
Congress. When the Communist Party of South Africa was set up
in 1921 it held little promise for blacks. All its delegates and
executives were white, and the Rand Revolt the next year brought
out all the racialism of white workers: the white martyrs who sang
the Red Flag on the scaffold after the mine strike had little interest
in their black brothers. But by the mid-'twenties the communists
turned more emphatically to the blacks, trying to build up trades
unions in factories and townships, and a small band of white
communists spread their political education among blacks through
night-schools and meetings: for the next thirty years the SACP would
be the only interracial political party. But the communists faced
bitter quarrels as they tried vainly to reconcile white and black
workers, and in 1927 the Comintern in Moscow adopted a new

* Willan, p. 244
† Matthews, *op. cit.*, pp. 54, 82, 130ff
‡ Willan, *op. cit.*, p. 220

policy of a 'native republic' for South Africa which antagonised many white communists and black leaders.

The black chiefs and professional men in Congress were fearful of the idea of equality. In 1927 Congress elected a radical new president James Gumede who was fêted in the Soviet Union (he said) as if he were the prime minister. Congress briefly swung to the left: and the communists began a national pass-burning campaign. But the government stamped it out and the black communists antagonised the conservatives in Congress. 'The Tsar was a great man in his country,' said one chief, 'of royal blood like us chiefs, and where is he now?'* By 1930 Congress turned back to its staid co-founder Dr Seme who was autocratic in his dealings with blacks and sycophantic towards the government.

The lowest ebb of Congress came in 1935, the jubilee of union, when the coalition of Hertzog and Smuts gained the necessary two-thirds majority to deprive all blacks of their remaining votes. The ANC attended a convention of five hundred who appointed a delegation to see Hertzog; but they were divided and placated by being allowed to elect their own 'native representatives' and 'native representative council' which soon proved to be a 'toy telephone'. The persistent hopes of Congress leaders in front of so many slamming doors continued to exasperate their critics, including the communists. Certainly the ANC was less ready for martyrdom than the Indian Congress or other liberation movements in Asia. But black South Africans were both less confident of their own roots, and faced a far more formidable power structure and industrial system.

The Second World War gave far more serious grounds for hope. Hitler's racialism, while it was supported by the Afrikaner extremists, generated a strong anti-racialism among many whites; while the need for black support – particularly when the Japanese might invade – induced the government to promise better conditions, even the abolition of the pass laws. The blacks identified themselves with the fight against tyranny, and the President for nine years from 1940, Dr Alfred Xuma, was a pillar of black respectability who had married a black American. The end of the war produced a surge of optimism, as the idealism of the UN and the Atlantic Charter swept into South Africa with returning troops; and Congress drafted its own Bill of Rights based on the Charter, which they took very literally. But the first hopes were soon shattered when 70,000 black miners went on strike in the gold-mines in 1946. Smuts and the mining companies were united: police with bayonets charged into

* Roux, *op. cit.*, p. 219

the compounds to force them back into the mines, and after five
days nine blacks were killed and hundreds wounded.

But the most permanent change from the war was in the character
of the cities. It brought a new surge of blacks escaping from drought
and starvation to work in the booming new industries. By 1943 manufactures had overtaken mining in their share of the gross national
product, calling for more sophisticated and settled black workers,
including women: the government even briefly suspended influx control. The migration produced the same kind of chaos and squalor as
existed round the edges of São Paulo or Mexico City, but further out
of sight, and out of mind. The cluster of townships to the south-west
of Johannesburg which came to be called 'Soweto' was already one of
the biggest cities in Africa; but few white Johannesburgers had ever
been inside it, and the maps did not even show it. On the wrong side
of the mine-dumps, where the wind blew the gold-dust, Soweto was
made up of tens of thousands of tiny box houses without electricity,
dominated by the police stations, with only hoardings breaking the
skyline. It looked uniformly proletarian; but it pressed together black
teachers, small businessmen, clerks, gangsters and layabouts, who
all piled every day into the packed trains or buses which shuttled
them to work in the white city. By the 'fifties many Sowetans were
the third or fourth generation of town-dwellers – grandchildren or
great-grandchildren of the first miners and other migrants to the gold
and diamond mines – who had never seen a homeland. In the evenings
the townships came to life with a vigour and confidence, vibrating
with jazz, jive and American slang, which defied any notion of tempo-
rariness or tribalism, or any lingering white hopes that the blacks like
Red Indians would destroy themselves with drink and despair. As de
Kiewiet wrote: 'The great Bantu race refused to follow what one
Australian governor called the "natural progress of the aboriginal
race towards extinction".'*

In fact they were beginning to establish a more urban culture
than the Afrikaners who were so determined to keep them tribalised.
'. . . It was only when our labour was needed that a deliberate drive
was made to haul us from our tribal havens to come out to work,'
as the black writer Can Themba reflected in 1957. 'And when
tribalism did not help to demonstrate the dignity of labour, tribalism
had to be smashed. They were so bloody successful that now they
fear they have drawn too many of us into the fields of urban industry
and have sired themselves a problem'.† Or as Ezekiel Mphahlele
described the predicament of the urban black in 1962:

* De Kiewiet *op. cit.*, p. 179
† Can Themba, 'The Bottom of the Bottle', from *The Will to Die*, Heinemann,
London, 1972

He drifts to the towns to seek work so that he may pay his taxes and levies and feed his dependants who remain scratching for a living on poor soil in the reserves. He must understand his employer's instructions in English or Afrikaans, read names of streets and shops. He feels utterly inadequate in this respect, and he begins to realize how vital education is to the needs of his kind. 'You must go to college, my son, and come and look after me and your brother and sister. They must also go to school'. So said my mother when I went to high school. This kind of 'pep talk' has launched thousands of Africans into the uncharted seas of an insecure education in an insecure life.*

It was this intensely urbanised world which was the background to the new generation of more militant black politicians, who included Nelson Mandela and Oliver Tambo who had been fellow-students at Fort Hare, the black university college. They both came from the rural background of the Transkei: Mandela came from a royal family, with a tall commanding presence, while Tambo was a peasant's son – still with his ritual tribal scars on his cheeks – who was quieter and more introverted and taught mathematics before becoming a lawyer. They were both founder-members of the Youth League that was set up inside the ANC in 1944, inspired by an austere Zulu catholic, Anton Lembede, who was appalled by the moral degradation of the urban black slums. Lembede mocked the fatuous petitions of the 'Old Guard' and their preoccupation with Western culture: 'A pair of boots,' he said, 'is better than all the plays of Shakespeare.'† The Youth Leaguers saw themselves as pure black nationalists who could appeal to the industrialised blacks; and they called for boycotts, mass organisation, mass education. The most influential was Walter Sisulu, a self-taught former ploughboy and miner who by 1949 was the ANC's secretary-general – its only full-time official. It was he who found a job in a law office for Nelson Mandela. The Youth Leaguers were at first fiercely anti-communist, and wanted to expel communists from Congress. But the Suppression of Communism Act in 1950 ironically helped to bring communists closer to the ANC leaders, to whom they could offer an opening into a wider world: only the Communist Party was committed to one man, one vote. As Mandela later said: 'For many decades the communists were the only political group in South Africa who were prepared to treat Africans as human beings and

* Ezekiel Mphahlele, *The African Image*, London, Faber & Faber, 1962, p. 56
† Profile in *Drum* magazine, Johannesburg, January 1954; and Lodge *op. cit.*, pp. 21–2

their equals; who were prepared to eat with us; talk with us, live with us, and work with us.'* The law firm of Mandela and Tambo was a hive of left-wing multi-racial activity in the early 'fifties, in an old building near the centre of Johannesburg; but it had no links with the white business world or the great stone fortress of Anglo-American round the corner.

After the victory of the Afrikaner nationalists in 1948 the Congress leaders still followed a cautious path for a time. Dr Xuma was ousted from the presidency, but replaced by Dr James Moroka who was scarcely more militant: a landowner and doctor with a ponderous style. But the Youth League and the threat of apartheid soon gave Congress a sharper edge; and at its conference in Bloemfontein in 1951 the ANC took the boldest step in its history. It was still little known: when I arrived to report it the only other whites were two bored local journalists, the communist journalist Ruth First and a small clergyman with a wispy beard, Arthur Blaxall. Many delegates had never been photographed before, and some objected. The meeting began three hours late and rambled on for three days under hot corrugated iron, sounding more like a prayer-meeting than a political conference. But behind the scenes the Youth Leaguers including Sisulu and Mandela had been pushing forward their 'programme of action' against apartheid; and later in the meeting a joint planning council including the Indian Congress produced a report calling for the repeal of 'six unjust laws' – failing which they proposed a defiance campaign to challenge the laws. It was the first step on the road to total confrontation.

In June 1952 the Congress launched the defiance campaign with a discipline and control which took whites by surprise: a small group of Africans and Indians entered a location at Boksburg, near Johannesburg, without permits and were arrested and sentenced to short terms of imprisonment. In the bleak dusty township this challenge to the state seemed eerily calm and anti-climactic. But over six months more than eight thousand went to jail. They owed something to Gandhi, who had first experimented with passive resistance forty-five years before in South Africa, and whose son Manilal still lived on his father's old ashram in Natal. But the ANC was more pragmatic and less spiritual than the Gandhis: and they knew they were dealing with a much more determined government, and a more industrialised society. It was the Eastern Cape which produced 71 percent of the volunteers, centring on Port Elizabeth which had been rapidly industrialised in the 'forties, with car and tyre factories including Ford, Volkswagen and General Motors.

* Statement to the court, Pretoria, April 20, 1964

The workers had wretched conditions and were nearly all from one tribe, the Xhosa, with a long Christian tradition. It was a forewarning that the factories of the Eastern Cape would provide the most fertile seed-bed for future revolt.*

The ANC could not maintain the momentum of defiance, and the apartheid government soon showed itself far tougher than the British in India. After riots and the murder of a white nun they passed two drastic laws – supported by the white opposition – which made it an offence to encourage blacks to resist the law. They arrested twenty leaders, including Dr Moroka, and charged them under the Suppression of Communism Act: the judge convicted them all of 'statutory communism' – which he explained had nothing to do with communism as usually recognised – and gave them suspended sentences. The campaign fizzled out with recriminations: Dr Moroka disowned his own role and the young 'kingmakers' of Congress, including Sisulu, Mandela and Tambo, replaced Moroka with another traditional leader, the Zulu chief Albert Luthuli. But Luthuli was a much more courageous leader: he had just been sacked from his chieftaincy for taking part in the campaign, and after his election he eloquently summed up the disillusion of his generation: 'Who will deny that thirty years of my life have been spent knocking in vain, patiently, moderately and modestly, at a closed and barred door?'

Professor Matthews, one of the most conservative Congress leaders, first proposed the next step: a 'Congress of the People' to point the way to a new society for all South Africans. It was held on a football field outside Johannesburg eighteen months later in 1955, where the ANC proclaimed its new bill of rights, the 'Freedom Charter' which had been painfully agreed in the previous months. It was the nearest they ever got to a serious manifesto. Sounding more like a psalm than a policy, full of deliberate vagueness, it included two contentious sentences which resounded across future decades: 'South Africa belongs to all who live in it, black and white,' and 'the mineral wealth beneath the soil, the banks and monopoly industry shall be transferred to the ownership of the people as a whole.' The Freedom Charter was soon to be pickled in history, endlessly reinterpreted after its authors were jailed and the organisations banned. It would often be depicted as Marxist, though it was hardly more radical than the contemporary Labour Party manifesto in Britain which likewise called for nationalising all the means of production; and it was actually less socialist than the

* Tom Lodge, *Black Politics in South Africa since 1945*, London, Longman, 1983, pp. 45–60, analyses the causes of militancy in the Eastern Cape

wartime programme of Malan's National Party. Nelson Mandela
wrote that the Charter 'strikes a fatal blow at the financial and
gold-mining monopolies and farming interests,' but went on to
explain optimistically that breaking them up 'will open up fresh
fields for the development of a non-European bourgeois class.'*

The police were soon raiding and searching the houses of anyone
involved with the Freedom Charter and in December 1956 they
arrested and charged 156 of them with 'high treason' – including
Luthuli, Matthews, Mandela and Tambo as well as Indians, whites
and coloureds. In the subsequent 'Treason Trial' the prosecutor
argued that the Charter was a prelude to revolution which aimed
to set up a communist state: it would drag on for five years before
the last accused, including Mandela, were acquitted in March 1961.
Like subsequent trials it had achieved its main object: to put any
effective black leadership out of action.

But the Freedom Charter had itself precipitated a serious breakaway from Congress by 'Africanists' who rejected its idea of a
multi-racial society, and who soon briefly proved a greater threat to
the government. They were led by a thirty-three-year-old university
lecturer, Robert Sobukwe, who left the ANC in 1959 to set up the
new Pan Africanist Congress (PAC) which identified strongly with
the newly-independent states to the North. The concept of Africa
as a single entity was now rapidly impinging on both black and
white South Africans. The Mau Mau rebellion in Kenya and the
transformation of the colonial Gold Coast into independent Ghana
had reverberated through the townships, and small boys called
themselves Jomo or Kwame. The map of Africa was looking different
as air-routes took over from sea-routes, opening up new links
between countries. The independent black states further alarmed
the whites in the South, and added to the frustration of the blacks
who thought they were much more westernised than the 'peasants'
to the North. In fact South Africa remained a totally separate case;
not only because it had far more whites, but because its dynamic
industrial machine was pressing whites and blacks alike into a new
mould.

Sobukwe called for a purer black nationalism, as had the Youth
League ten years earlier. 'In a country where everyone says white
is beautiful we *have* to say that black is beautiful,' he once said to
me. 'The government doesn't want us to be proud of being black:
that would make them worried.' He and his followers – including
many young intellectuals – were courageous and impatient; and
they planned to defy the pass-laws in March 1960 with remarkable

* *Liberation* (Johannesburg) June 1956 quoted in Lodge, *op. cit.*, p. 73

optimism and lack of planning. The atmosphere seemed full of revolution: Macmillan had proclaimed the wind of change two months before, and the Congo was suddenly independent. The ANC were planning their own anti-pass campaign, but it was the PAC who got in first. Sobukwe himself led his followers to a police station in Soweto and was promptly arrested – never to be a free man again. But it was the black township of Sharpeville, fifty miles south of Johannesburg near the state steel mills of Iscor, which brought the situation to a flashpoint, with its background of unemployment, rent increases and rigid influx control. Thousands of blacks gathered outside the police station. The police panicked, shot sixty-seven blacks dead, and prepared the way for a revolt which soon seemed close to revolution. After more shootings in Langa outside Cape Town a twenty-three-year-old disciple of Sobukwe, Philip Kgosana, led a procession of 20,000 blacks towards Parliament Square. The police stopped them and their commander promised Kgosana that the minister of justice would see him if he dispersed the crowd. Kgosana, determined to remain non-violent, told the huge procession to go home quietly – which they did. When Kgosana returned to see the minister, he was arrested.* With this strange anti-climax the revolt collapsed, and with it most black confidence in non-violent protest. The police cordoned off Langa and moved in with armoured cars, batons, crowbars and guns, arresting 1,500 people and forcing the rest back to work.

Would South African history have been different had Kgosana not dismissed the crowd? Recriminations continued. Certainly for a few weeks after Sharpeville many blacks believed they could be on the verge of liberation like the movements in the north. The ANC in Johannesburg had already made its own plans to defy the pass laws: it organised a successful one-day strike and a pass-burning campaign; Chief Luthuli himself burnt his pass. International protests were inhibiting the government, and the police were ordered not to arrest blacks without passes. The expectations were enhanced by the attempted assassination of Dr Verwoerd by an eccentric English-speaking farmer, David Pratt. The blacks wondered if their white masters might be driving each other mad. The acting Prime Minister Paul Sauer promised that: 'The old book of South African history was closed at Sharpeville.'

When I visited Soweto at that time there was heady talk, expecting a real revolution: 'This is *it*.' 'We never dreamt it could come

* For the account by Kgosana, now in Sri Lanka, *see* Joseph Lelyveld, *Move Your Shadow*, London, Michael Joseph, 1985. New York, Times Books, 1985, pp. 315–27

so soon', said a Congress leader. 'The police are so polite, *it hurts*', said a messenger boy. 'Jeez a cop even called me *meneer*.' I found Mandela touchy about the PAC's initiative, but cautiously confident about the prospects of the ANC: 'We've got to have the machinery, the organisation.' His colleague Duma Nokwe reckoned that 6,000 people had already burnt their passes: 'We'll have them roasted . . . This country is in a pre-rev . . .' (he stopped himself). No one then would have imagined that another sixteen years would follow before the next serious confrontation with government.

But it was a short honeymoon. In April 1960 parliament voted by 128 to sixteen to declare both the ANC and the PAC 'unlawful organisations': and after forty-eight years, Congress ceased to have an official existence inside South Africa. Immediately hundreds were detained. A month after Sharpeville the government had totally regained control. Saracen tanks patrolled the townships, protesters and strikers were beaten into submission. The pass-laws were reimposed still more strictly. Verwoerd recovered and Paul Sauer soon disappeared from political view. 'This isn't *It*,' said the black writer Can Themba, gazing into a brandy glass. 'They seemed to think that *It* was just round the corner. It never seemed to occur to them that the wind might be only a breeze.' 'The 'mopping up' continued for months afterwards, with hundreds of ANC and PAC supporters tried under the Suppression of Communism Act.

The banned leaders knew that they were coming to the end of the road of peaceful protest, and prepared for violence. The PAC was the most ruthless, contemptuous of the ANC's restraint: 'They think sabotage will frighten the white men. But you couldn't frighten Hitler,' Zeph Mothopeng who was its acting leader told me in 1962. 'Essentially the struggle is here: the world won't help: it backs the winning horse.' The PAC formed its own underground terrorist movement called Poqo (meaning 'pure') which was dedicated to a black revolution with reckless terrorism. By 1964 202 Poqo members had been convicted of murder.* But the PAC leadership had become increasingly disorganised and vulnerable to infiltration by South African spies. It moved from Lesotho to Tanzania, and later to Zambia, but increasingly riven by dissidents and deserters; and after Poqo was crushed it produced no very effective action inside South Africa.

The ANC was now led underground by Nelson Mandela, who first tried secretly to organise a three-day stay-at-home strike which was suppressed by the army, and was then convinced that only more

* Lodge, *op. cit.*, p. 241

violent tactics could influence white opinion. By June 1961 a handful of ANC leaders had decided, as Mandela said, that 'it would be unrealistic and wrong for African leaders to continue preaching peace and non-violence at a time when the government met our peaceful demands with force'. Already in 1961 the first recruits had been sent abroad for guerilla training. But Mandela still hoped to confine the attacks to sabotage, which 'did not involve loss of life, and offered the best hope for future race relations'. Their targets for sabotage were chosen carefully with an eye on international opinion: 'We believed that South Africa depended to a large extent on foreign capital and foreign trade,' Mandela explained. 'We felt that planned destruction of power plants, and interference with rail and telephone communications, would tend to scare away capital from the country.'* It would be another quarter-century before the internal violence began to have that effect – in a far less disciplined context than Mandela had planned.

The armed struggle was entrusted to a military wing, called Umkhonto we Sizwe, 'the Spear of the Nation', with Mandela as its commander-in-chief, and a high command and structure copied from the Jewish Irgun organisation set up in Palestine in 1944. It soon announced itself with remarkable haste. On two days in December 1961 a succession of explosions hit public buildings and installations in Durban, Johannesburg and especially Port Elizabeth, while Umkhonto leaflets optimistically explained: 'We hope we will bring the government and its supporters to their senses before it is too late . . .' Mandela was smuggled out of South Africa early in 1962 to visit African states: he then realised, he said, that nearly every black movement before independence had received aid from socialist countries, and he later urged the ANC to send a mission to the East. But he also looked to Britain, where he talked with Labour Party leaders including Hugh Gaitskell and Denis Healey, and the Liberal leader Jo Grimond.

Mandela was already a minor legend. Back in South Africa as the 'black pimpernel' he was hunted by the police while he and other revolutionaries with aliases and disguises were preparing a new wave of sabotage on a farm at Rivonia, outside Johannesburg. It was a foolhardy venture: the police had been infiltrating Umkhonto and breaking its secrets with the help of torture and informers. Mandela was caught in Natal in August 1962 (with the help of CIA information, it was later alleged) and was tried two

* Nelson Mandela, statement to court at the Rivonia Trial, April 20, 1964. Republished in *The Struggle is My Life*, London, International Defence and Aid Fund, 1978

months later, charged with incitement to strike and sentenced to five years. But the police in the meantime were tracking down the other conspirators and in July 1963 they swooped on Rivonia and arrested several of them, together with piles of documents.

Three months later the conspirators, including Mandela, were charged with sabotage and seeking to overthrow the government by violent revolution. It was a tense and dramatic trial, bristling with police (watching it one day, when I gave a signal of recognition to Mandela I was immediately taken out for questioning). The state prosecutor Percy Yutar had an easy task in proving sabotage and revolutionary intent. In his long final speech, carefully prepared with the help of his fellow-prisoners and lawyers, Mandela recounted his political development, how he had turned to sabotage and guerillas but cherished the ideal of a democratic and free society. 'If needs be, it is an ideal for which I am prepared to die.' He and seven others were sentenced to life imprisonment and were sent to Robben Island, South Africa's Alcatraz, off the coast of Cape Town.

But the state could not prove the most serious charge, that they were part of an international communist conspiracy. It had produced documents in Mandela's handwriting including one which began with the incriminating words: 'We communist party members are the most advanced revolutionaries in modern history,' and continued '. . . the enemy must be completely crushed and wiped out from the face of the earth before a communist world can be realised.' Twenty years later President Botha was to quote it as evidence that Mandela was a dangerous communist. But as Mandela explained to the court he had copied it out (he copied out many very contrasting documents) from a Chinese pamphlet by Liu Shao-chi called 'How to be a good communist'.*

Mandela's relationship with communism would stir up constant argument a quarter-century later. In his final speech he insisted that 'The ANC has never at any period of its history advocated a revolutionary change in the economic structure of the country, nor has it, to the best of my recollection, ever condemned capitalist society.' He explained that: 'The communist party sought to emphasise class distinctions whilst the ANC seeks to harmonise them.' He admitted that he had been influenced by Marxist thought, like Gandhi or Nasser, but explained that, unlike Marxists, he admired the Western parliamentary system, the impartiality of British judges and the American separation of powers. He compared the ANC's

---

* See the transcript provided by the CIA to Senator Jesse Helms in the Senate debate on sanctions, Washington, August 14, 1986

co-operation with communists with the Western wartime alliance with Stalin:

> It is perhaps difficult for white South Africans, with an ingrained prejudice against communism, to understand why experienced African politicians so readily accept communists as their friends. But to us the reason is obvious. Theoretical differences amongst those fighting against oppression is a luxury we cannot afford at this stage.

With Mandela and his colleagues on Robben Island, and the Poqo terrorists convicted, the black opposition was crushed. Many went into exile. Mandela's friend and colleague Oliver Tambo had already been designated by Luthuli to lead the ANC in exile, and after Sharpeville had slipped out of the country. He first based himself in London, and toured the United States and Western Europe, vainly seeking financial support and boycotts of South African goods. Then the ANC established its headquarters first in Tanzania, later in Zambia, where it gradually built up its military and diplomatic force. Tambo looked for friends where he could; Mandela had already forged a link with the FLN army in Algeria, which helped to train Umkhonto and provided some financial help, and Tambo later travelled with an Algerian passport. The Organisation of African Unity (OAU) which was formed in 1963, gave some help, but never enough; while in western Europe only the Scandinavians and Dutch gave money. But when Tambo went in 1963 to the Soviet Union he was promised a supply of weapons free of charge.* And the ANC thereafter looked increasingly to Russia and East Germany, not only for weapons, but for funds, training and jobs.

To most white South Africans the ANC now appeared finally broken. The police became more brutal in their use of torture, and more sophisticated in their intelligence and control with the help of training in Europe and computers from IBM or ICL. The sporadic sabotage was ineffective and provided pretexts for further reprisals. Mandela was out of sight and out of mind. And the way was clear for the biggest boom in South Africa's history since the first gold-rush.

* Evidence to the Foreign Affairs Committee of the House of Commons, October 29, 1985

6

The Apartheid Boom

I have seen the wicked in great power,
And spreading himself like a green bay tree.

Psalm 37, verse 35

Each trade agreement, each bank loan, each new investment is another
brick in the wall of our continued existence.

John Vorster, 1972

When the Afrikaners came to power in 1948 they had been determined permanently to separate the races just when industrial pressures were moving in an opposite direction. 'The perverse economics
of apartheid,' as de Kiewiet put it, 'sees alien invaders instead
of needed immigrants, and over-population where there is really
under-population.'* By 1951 manufacturing industry already
accounted for 22 percent of South Africa's national income, while
gold-mining contributed only eleven percent; and factories called
for a more stable and skilled black workforce than the migrants in
the mines. The numbers of blacks employed in private manufacturing had doubled in ten years to over 300,000 in 1947–8 – increasing
much faster than white employees. The very visible surge of blacks
into the towns blatantly contradicted the apartheid theory that they
had no permanent place in the white man's world. Many observers
insisted that these economic pressures were bound to prevail over
the dogma of apartheid. 'It is the irresistible force of economic
integration which wins and must win,' wrote Basil Davidson of the
New Statesman in 1952, 'however hatefully the majority of whites
may resist its pressure.'†

But businessmen remained ambivalent. They wanted stable and
more skilled black labour, but they shared many of the Afrikaner
government's fears about the black flood, and some of their racial
prejudices. They wanted both to have their blacks and contain
them. Much of the segregation within corporations – whether in

* De Kiewiet, *op. cit.*, p. 67
† Basil Davidson, *Report on Southern Africa*, London, Jonathan Cape, 1952,
pp. 109–14

canteens, toilets or sports grounds – turned out, on investigation, to
be customary rather than statutory. Hardly any white businessmen,
whether South African or expatriate, had any social contact with
black people except as servants or as a labour-force: they were
totally cut off from the black politicians and intellectuals who were
already shaping the character of the opposition. Only a very few
Western businessmen asserted themselves to promote black workers
against the pressures of apartheid. One of them was Wayne Freder-
icks, a young executive who had come out in 1948 to set up a
cornflakes plant near Johannesburg for the Kellogg company of
Battle Creek, Michigan. 'I always believed there was a measure of
sovereignty behind the factory gates,' he said afterwards; and he
later maintained his opposition to apartheid in the State Department and the Ford Company. But most American expatriates
reckoned that if they wanted to be promoted when they returned
home they should not rock the boat.

The South African industrialists were still overwhelmingly
English-speaking and their lives in the suburbs had little contact
with the Afrikaner suburbs. The contrast under Kruger was now
more complete, between the Afrikaners who controlled politics in
Pretoria and the English and other later immigrants who controlled
the wealth in Johannesburg. The Anglophones were now decisively
in a minority, as they had never been in Australia, New Zealand
or Canada, and they were bitter about their exclusion from power.
But there was a tacit assumption which suited many: they were left
to make money, while the Afrikaners made politics. And as politics
became rougher the bargain had its advantages: the Anglophone
businessman could blame the brutality of apartheid and Afrikaner
police, while offering no real alternative. To white immigrants,
particularly to Englishmen escaping from winter, austerity and
rationing, the opportunities and luxury of South Africa seemed
magical. Apartheid might in the end be damaging for business, but
it also meant no unions, low taxes and cheap and obedient servants.

Was capitalism fundamentally on the side of apartheid? Many
Marxists, seeing the Afrikaners in the image of Nazi Germany,
could now argue their case with added moral conviction, branding
capitalists as racists. In fact the crude charge could not be upheld:
as Merle Lipton wrote in her study of capitalism and apartheid,
the Afrikaners' policies clearly showed that they were acting against
the interests of urban capitalists, and in 1948 they precipitated a
flight of capital and of skilled and professional whites out of the
country.* But there were more sophisticated arguments which will

* Lipton, *op. cit.*, p. 284

recur: that business interests, including American and British, were
far too easily seduced by the apartheid government into conniving
with their system, much as Hitler manipulated German industrialists after 1933; and that businessmen never seriously tried to dissociate themselves from apartheid or to identify with black
aspirations until violent opposition compelled them, too late. It is
an argument which cannot be purely economic; for the question
is not only whether businessmen were condoning apartheid, but
whether they were seen to do so by the emerging black political
class. And in a country of almost unique financial concentration
the answer lay with individuals as much as economic forces.

The argument became more virulent after Sharpeville, when the
repression of the black opposition was more ruthless and evident.
For a few months after Sharpeville Western investors appeared to
have voted with their wallets, making their own decisive judgment
about South Africa's future under apartheid. South African shares
plummeted and £48 million left the country almost immediately.
International capitalism appeared to be decisively dissociating
itself from apartheid. The flight of capital ran down the foreign exchange reserves to only £77 million by May 1961, while economic
growth was down to zero. The government quickly had to impose
controls on imports, foreign exchange and hire-purchase to stem
the flow.

But the capital flight proved short-lived and less fundamental
than it looked. Most of it came from foreign investors selling their
shares, and as the crisis subsided shrewd investors – including
Anglo-American and the British financier Isaac Wolfson – began
buying at the bottom of the market. The direct investment by
British multinationals remained committed, and even in 1961 £9
million flowed into the country. Anglo-American took the lead in
restoring confidence, both by buying up shares and by obtaining a
record loan of $30 million in 1961, guaranteed by Barclays in
London after heavy pressure from Oppenheimer in person. But
South Africa also received welcome endorsement from one of the
high-priests of international capital, David Rockefeller, the chairman of the Chase Manhattan Bank. After visiting Africa two years
before – to open an office of the bank in Johannesburg – the Chase
led a loan to South Africa. Now, after Sharpeville, Rockefeller
realised that by supporting Pretoria in a time of trouble he could
be on the inside track; and the Chase lent $10 million to South Africa
and joined a new consortium to lend $150 million. Churchmen and
others protested against this stamp of approval, but the Chase
replied: 'We believe it would endanger the free world if every large
American bank deprived developing countries of the opportunity

for economic growth. If one hopes for changes in the Republic of South Africa or elsewhere, it would do little good to withdraw economic support.' Four years later the Chase involved itself much more deeply in the Republic by buying a 15 percent share of the Standard Bank, its second-biggest bank which was also now spreading round the world – discreetly omitting the words 'of South Africa' from its name.

By 1964, with the black leaders in jail or in exile and the government clearly in control, the way was open for the great boom, a wonder-decade in which South Africa's economic growth was outstripping nearly all Western countries, averaging 6 percent a year during the 'sixties. The first recovery after Sharpeville had been achieved without much help from foreign investors who were wary of the political risk; but by 1965 they were piling in faster than before Sharpeville, contributing heavily to the high growth-rate and bringing in new technology which added to future growth. By 1970 foreign investment totalled $7.9 billion compared to $3.6 billion in 1960, and the annual net inflow of capital was $343 million – six times what it was before Sharpeville.*

Multinational corporations could not resist the prospects of rapid expansion and a return on investment averaging 15 percent by 1967 – far higher than in Europe.† The Pretoria government wanted to become less dependent on Britain – particularly since leaving the Commonwealth – and successfully encouraged corporations from the rest of Europe and the United States: by 1970 the big three American car-makers (Chrysler, Ford and General Motors) had invested over $75 million in ten years, and six out of ten of the cars and trucks made in South Africa were now made by American companies.‡ France acquired a special importance as the provider of arms, particularly Mirage fighters. But the most dynamic and confident new partner was West Germany, which increased its investment from R70 million in 1965 to over R1000 in 1970 and which by 1974 was providing more imports into South Africa than Britain. The names of Hoechst, Siemens or Mercedes sprung up on the hoardings and BMW established its only foreign plant in South Africa, from which they began exporting cars to the Middle East. And the 'Bonn–Pretoria Axis' was soon to have a special importance in providing military technology.§

* Johnson, *op. cit.*, pp 28, 30. *Also* Jim Hoagland, *South Africa, Civilizations in Conflict*, London, Allen & Unwin, 1973, p. 338
† UKSATA, London, Purpose and Progress 1965–7
‡ Hoagland, *op. cit.*, p. 338
§ R W Johnson, *How Long will South Africa Survive?* London, Macmillan, 1977, p. 35

Britain remained by far the biggest investor. By 1968 South Africa had moved from fourth to third place among Britain's investment territories (excluding oil, banking and insurance), overtaking the United States. 'Considering the relative size and growth prospects of these two countries,' wrote John Stopford and Louis Turner, 'one must conclude that the lure of easy profits remained, for many firms, more important than building for the future.'* And while South Africa accounted for only about 1 percent of America's total investment overseas in 1970, it made up 10 percent of Britain's.† Most British multinationals were still increasing their stake, often in close partnership with South African state corporations; while the Afrikaner government was strengthening its hold on the economy, and trying to ensure that expanding industry would support the system of apartheid.‡ Industry was usually happy to oblige. Courtaulds not only made fabrics, stockings and paper in South Africa, but invested heavily in a wood-pulp company, Saiccor, which exported to its rayon factories elsewhere (the state industrial development corporation had a one-third stake in Saiccor, and appointed the chairman). Rio Tinto-Zinc bought 39 percent of the huge Palabora copper mine (the American Newmont mining company owned another 30 percent). The mine employed 2,000 blacks close to a homeland in the Northern Transvaal, and brought RTZ – as they explained – into a 'very, very close understanding with the government'.§

Some multinationals with big interests in black Africa were worried about investing more in apartheid. 'It would be undesirable to appear to be expanding our interests in South Africa,' said the Special Committee which ruled Unilever in 1964, 'in view of the attitude to South Africa of other African States.' But when this policy was questioned the chairman Lord Cole explained revealingly that:

> in principle there was no objection to risking more money in South Africa provided this was not done in such a way as to provoke repercussions in other African states and that any new projects were sufficiently remunerative short term for us to see the possibility of getting our money back in five to six years.

* John M Stopford and Louis Turner, *Britain and the Multinationals*, Chichester, UK, 1985, p. 81
† Ruth First, Jonathan Steele and Christabel Gurney, *The South African Connection*, London, Temple Smith, 1972, p. 31
‡ Lipton, *op. cit.*, p. 303
§ House of Commons Expenditure Committee, 1973: Wages & Conditions of African Workers, Evidence, Vol. 1, pp. 88, 251

In fact many profits were high enough to offer such returns; and only a few months later Unilever bought the Robin Cheese company in South Africa. Unilever saw itself as firmly at odds with Pretoria: 'Unilever's commercial interests put it in the anti-apartheid camp in South Africa,' wrote a historian of the company, 'as surely as his desire to sell more soap to the English working-class had buttressed William Lever's enthusiasm for social reform in Britain half a century earlier.' But it continued to pay its black workers a quarter the wages of the whites, and like most British companies it was reluctant to interfere with the apartheid patterns. The Special Committee stressed that they had to 'proceed slowly in the replacement of Europeans by Africans . . . we had to take care not to upset the white community.'*

The flow of investment and trade was hardly affected by political changes in Britain, and after 1964 the Labour government actively encouraged it. In 1967 John Davies, the director-general of the Confederation of British Industry, went out to South Africa armed with a supporting letter from Anthony Crosland, the President of the Board of Trade, which stressed that a third of South Africa's exports still went to Britain and said: 'Our concern to see this valuable trade develop and to avoid any economic confrontation with South Africa has been repeatedly made clear in parliament and the UN.' And the British trade department issued *Hints to Businessmen* which pointed out that the two main political parties in South Africa 'do not disagree about the principle of separate treatment for those of European and non-European descent'. In a craven sentence it recommended: 'When engaged in business dealings visitors would be well advised not to become involved in controversy on political and social matters that arouse deep feeling in South Africa.' †

Many industrialists suggested that they were discreetly persuading Pretoria to modify its policies; but there was no real evidence of it, and the trade lobbies almost imperceptibly turned into lobbies to defend apartheid. In 1966 British businessmen set up the UK-South African Trade Association, or UKSATA, as an offshoot of the CBI, which soon became a zealous apologist for Pretoria, working closely with its sister-body in South Africa, SABRITA. UKSATA's vocal chairman William Luke – who was also chairman of Lindustries which had much business in South Africa – went frequently to Pretoria, where he always saw cabinet ministers. 'Since I know them, lunch with them and sometimes joke with them,' he said in

* Fieldhouse, *op. cit.*, pp. 133, 139, 140–2
† First *et al.*, *op. cit.*, pp. 214–16

1973, he believed he could 'quietly influence them . . .' UKSATA's president Sir Nicholas Cayzer, the very wealthy chairman of British and Commonwealth Shipping, who was a major contributor to the Tory party, usually saw the prime minister when he went to Pretoria.* What right had Britain or any other nation, he asked, 'to create moralistic barriers to the natural process of evolution in South Africa?'†

British and American businessmen also worked closely with a well-funded new lobby, the South African Foundation, which had been formed just before Sharpeville to improve the country's image abroad: 'It was the desperate need of the times that shaped its aims.'‡ It was supported by leading South African industrialists including Harry Oppenheimer and Anton Rupert; and its first president was Sir Francis de Guiringaud, formerly Chief of Staff to Lord Montgomery, who had emigrated to Johannesburg. Charles Engelhard (*see* below) was one of the original committee; most major American companies, including General Motors, Mobil, Chrysler, Union Carbide and Caterpillar, subscribed to it; and in Britain both Luke and Cayzer were among its trustees. Throughout the 'sixties the Foundation was very effective in inviting British and other grandees, including Field Marshal Montgomery, to visit and praise white South Africa. By its tenth anniversary it could claim that it had helped to 'stem the tide of ignorance, criticism and misrepresentation against the Republic'.

Businessmen were still more buoyant after 1966, when Verwoerd was assassinated and Balthazar John Vorster took over as prime minister. He was hardly a liberal: he had been imprisoned as a supporter of Hitler during the Second World War – together with Van den Bergh who became head of his secret service, Boss – and as Verwoerd's Minister of Justice he had been relentless in stamping out black opposition. But he had visibly mellowed, enjoyed golf and drinking, and was welcomed to the Rand Club, the traditional stronghold of English finance. He was not a theological fanatic like Verwoerd, and he faced up to the need to do business with South Africa's black neighbours, by launching a policy of *detente* with alternate bullying and friendship. The old fears of physical contact with blacks – which had precipitated the ejection from the Commonwealth – now dissolved in the face of diplomatic necessities, as black leaders were received in style. Many businessmen looked to Vorster to open up wider markets to the north, while maintaining order

---

* House of Commons Expenditure Committee, November 1983 Vol. 1, p. 9
† First *et al.*, *op. cit.*, p. 220
‡ Johannesburg *Sunday Times*, May 14, 1967

in the south; yet he was never really interested in the views of industrialists. He took the view, as Gavin Relly of Anglo-American later complained, 'that the politics of our country was none of our business. I think he was scared of businessmen, but in any event he found it offensive if they ever voiced a view about the political situation in the country.'*

South Africa was certainly acquiring a special dynamism and an exciting sense of the future – at least the short term – encouraged by entrepreneurs who were well able to compete internationally. Much of the pace was set by a remarkable group of descendants of Jewish immigrants who had nearly all been refugees from the same region of Lithuania on the edge of Russia in the late nineteenth century: many first arrived as pedlars, but quickly built up fast-growing businesses. Joffe Marks who arrived in 1884 began importing flour and bought up the small Premier milling company which was inherited by his nephew Harry Jaffe and by *his* nephew Joe Bloom, whose son Tony Bloom is now chairman of the present wide-ranging Premier Group. Heris Hersowitz who also arrived in 1884 had a son, Bob, who became a mining engineer and went into partnership with Simeon 'Slip' Menell, the son of a London furrier, to form a new gold-mining company Anglo-Vaal – which is still run by the founders' sons, Basil Hersov and Clive Menell. Meyer Ackerman arrived in 1883 and began dealing in ostrich feathers: his son Gus, financed by another Lithuanian, Morris Mauerberger, built up a chain of Ackerman's stores, which were then bought by another ex-Lithuanian group; while Gus Ackerman's son set up his own successful group of Pick 'n Pay supermarkets. One of the last Lithuanian immigrants was Nathan Gordon who arrived in 1918 and became credit manager for Advance Laundries: his son Donald, an accountant, raised money to set up his own Liberty Life assurance company, now the third biggest in the country, interlocked by the Standard Bank and South African Breweries.† These and other immigrant families were able to mobilise South African savings and capital to transform local industries, services and life-styles, with a speed of innovation and enterprise which surprised American as well as European business rivals.

The economic euphoria of South Africa in the 'sixties was promoted in *The Economist* in 1968 by their star writer Norman Macrae, in a survey called 'The Green Bay Tree' which encouraged both businessmen and diplomats in the west (*see* page 118). Macrae

* Interview with Hugh Murray, *Leadership* magazine, 1985
† For a full account of Jewish immigrant families see Mendel Kaplan, *Jewish Roots in the South African Economy*, Cape Town, C Struik, 1986

insisted that it was 'almost certainly to everybody's advantage' that
the Republic should continue to get richer. The business community
was visibly to the left of government, and in South Africa 'richer
and securer generally means lefter'. It was true that apartheid was
wickedly unequal and full of unnecessary cruelties; but the notion
of a 'revenging black tide' sweeping down from the north was
'good-hearted balderdash' in the light of the disasters in black
Africa, while the urban blacks in the Republic were benefitting from
the industrial advance. Moreover South Africa had the benefit of a
new generation of bubbling entrepreneurs including Afrikaners such
as Jan Marais of Trust Bank and Anton Rupert of Rembrandt
tobacco, together with civil servants with a 'wickedly admirable
detachment'; while the Reserve Bank, within the limits of its appalling social system, was 'the very best sort of central bank' run by
crisp and efficient Dutch bankers; and since black trade unions
were prohibited 'the country has the real economic good fortune
of not generally suffering from a trade-union-generated cost-push
inflation.' The military seemed to have a complete grip on any
black revolt, which was visibly incompetent and fifth-class. 'This
white nationalist government of South Africa,' Macrae concluded,
'is meeting a tryst with the twentieth century in its continent,
even though so many of its social attitudes belong deplorably to
pre-nineteenth century days'.*

At the heart of this business optimism was Harry Oppenheimer,
the chairman of the Anglo-American Corporation which was now
riding high on the boom. He still seemed diffident and self-effacing,
talked softly, listened carefully. He still liked to hire and promote
Oxford graduates (to the annoyance of some Afrikaners including
Wim de Villiers who thought they 'never got to grips with problems
on the shop-floor'). But in action he was now far more confident, like
his father but more proudly South African. He was also extending
Anglo's interests to the north: his group was by far the biggest
investor in the continent, with its income dwarfing most emerging
black states. His personal sensitivity made him a patient diplomat,
as he became the object of anti-imperialist rhetoric in Tanzania or
Zambia: he became friendly with President Kaunda, even though
he took control of Anglo's copper mines. But South Africa remained
all-important, and Anglo was soon dominating the gold-mines still
further.

Oppenheimer acquired an important new partner when in 1958
Anglo bought control of Central Mining (the old Wernher-Beit
'Corner House'), with the help of the bulky and grunting American

* *The Economist*, 'The Green Bay Tree', June 29, 1968

tycoon Charlie Engelhard, who was suspected of being the original of Ian Fleming's character Goldfinger. He was the son of a German emigrant to America who had set up the Engelhard Metals and Minerals Corporation in 1890; but Charlie made his own bigger fortune, and became the 'Platinum King'. He joined the board of Anglo – thus making it more genuinely Anglo-American – and bought a mansion in Johannesburg. Unlike Oppenheimer he loved flaunting his wealth, gambling, over-eating and flying in his private plane, the Platinum Plover, complete with two butlers. After Sharpeville he did much, together with Oppenheimer, to attract new investment and loans from America. As a friend of Presidents Kennedy and Johnson, he could make South Africa more acceptable to Americans. When Vorster took over he explained that his policy was 'as much in the interest of South Africa as anything I can think of . . .'* But he never challenged colour bar customs: after the black singer Miriam Makeba had sung to his white guests in his Johannesburg home she was taken to the kitchen for supper.

Anglo-American soon extended its intricate web. The Oppenheimer–Engelhard interests merged Central Mining to form the conglomerate Charter Consolidated based in London; and in 1960 Anglo was able to buy Johannesburg Consolidated Investments (Johnnies), Barney Barnato's old company, forestalling Afrikaner interests. Four years later and more far-sightedly Oppenheimer deliberately allowed the Afrikaner group Federale Mynbou to gain control of another group of gold-mines, General Mining, with Anglo as a minority shareholder. For the first time in eighty years an Afrikaner group owned a major stake (9 percent) in the country's gold industry. By the end of the 'sixties, Anglo also had minority interests in two other gold-mining groups, Gold Fields of South Africa and Union Corporation, all of them interlocked with directorships. Only the smallest of the six groups, Anglo-Vaal, now remained separate from the Oppenheimer network: the group which was still controlled by its two founding families, the Menells and the Hersovs.†

As his gold-mines needed less capital during the 'sixties Oppenheimer seized every chance to expand into manufacture, finance and property, frequently in partnership with foreign companies who brought in advanced technology; though he found that the companies which ran themselves performed better.‡ With ICI Anglo built up the chemical-and-explosives company AE&CI to become

* First *et al.*, *op. cit.*, p. 132
† See above, p. 91
‡ Innes, p. 193

South Africa's biggest industrial company, making plastics, ammonia and textiles as well as ammunition and explosives; and also SA Nylon Spinners, the country's biggest producer of synthetic fibres. The twin giants faced little competition: Courtaulds complained that AE&CI had told them: 'your chemicals go up by 10 percent from this evening. If you do not accept, you get no chemicals': though ICI angrily denied it.* In steel, Anglo used Newmont from America and Davy from Britain to establish its biggest single project Highveld Steel and Vanadium, to produce high-grade steel, which became the country's fourth biggest manufacturer; and with the help of General Steel Industries and the Abex Corporation in America it built up Scaw metals to make steel parts and grinding balls. With Bowater from Britain it formed the Mondi Valley Paper Company. Anglo's newspaper empire, however, came to it by accident, when it bought JCI in 1960, bringing with it effective control (40 percent) over the Argus Group which included the influential Johannesburg *Star*: eventually in 1971 the Argus gained control of South African Associated Newspapers (SAAN) which included the liberal Rand *Daily Mail*, thus giving Anglo indirect control over seventeen out of twenty English-speaking papers – but no Afrikaans.†

Behind all these companies lay a growing financial network. Already in 1955 Sir Ernest had formed Anglo's own merchant bank called Union Acceptances, with the help of Lazards and Barclays in London, which soon produced its own offspring the Discount House of SA. By 1968 UAL was the seventh biggest bank in South Africa, and the biggest merchant bank. Anglo also built up its own property subsidiary called Amaprop, run by Oppenheimer's ex-son-in-law, a hearty rugby footballer and son of a Glasgow stockbroker, Gordon Waddell. Its chief monument is the Carlton Centre in Johannesburg, the biggest hotel complex in Africa and one of the first multiracial hotels.

Oppenheimer dominated the country's economy in many ways more pervasively than Rhodes sixty years earlier; but like Rhodes he remained in awkward tandem with the Afrikaner political monopoly. Anglo was as consistently English-speaking as Pretoria was Afrikaans-speaking; and the government had plenty of leverage over Anglo, through contracts, taxes and military links: in some ways a semi-monopoly was much easier to control. Oppenheimer financed a spectrum of political groups, like Gianni Agnelli in Italy whose Fiat empire had similar ramifications, including both the

* Expenditure Committee Vol 1, pp. 87, 298
† Innes, p. 205

Progressive Party formed in 1959 with its courageous and solitary
MP Helen Suzman, and the South African Foundation which helped
to whitewash the country abroad. Later Anglo helped Chief Buthelezi in KwaZulu, and even offered some support to the Black
Consciousness Movement. Within South Africa Oppenheimer appeared emphatically liberal, always advocating reforms in his
speeches; but abroad he felt compelled to defend his government,
and discourage foreign pressure.

Inside Anglo's spacious womb the white executives could easily
believe that their benign expansion was resolving the racial problems, like booming companies in the American Deep South – a
confidence which radiated from the lush house magazine *Optima*.
Anglo estates and Anglo factories spread out across the virgin veld,
built on Anglo land financed by the Anglo bank. It seemed almost
a state within a state – like De Beers in Kimberley half a century
earlier – with its own diplomats, intelligence and mine police. From
inside its rational, self-enclosed world, with smiling black chauffeurs
and clerks, the compounds and slum houses of Soweto seemed a
world away. Oppenheimer was a masterly financial and industrial
manager, and he knew how to pick British and other executives and
give them motivation and drive. The 'Anglo boys' in Johannesburg
became a distinctive and confident breed, riding at the Inanda
Club, swimming at the Country Club, flying in private Anglo
planes. Developing Africa was rewarding psychologically as well as
financially: it was their wives who were often left to try to mitigate
the insoluble social problems of black families in the wake of their
industrial progress.

White businessmen and overseas visitors could be reassured by
what was known as the 'Oppenheimer Thesis': that economic
growth would make apartheid wither away, as blacks were drawn
into skilled jobs and middle class life. It was supported by a
much-quoted historical analysis, written in 1964 by an Anglo executive Michael O'Dowd, which insisted that South Africa's political
and social development was not abnormal for a country just emerging from the first stage of industrialisation – like contemporary
Mexico or like Britain in the 1850s – where a minority government
ruled harshly. Social injustice, he argued, was not merely normal
in a developing economy but 'it is absolutely universal and if not
inevitable it has certainly never yet been avoided'. He explained
that 'a watershed is reached when the supply of unskilled labour
ceases to appear inexhaustible and the ruling minority starts to find
that it actually needs the rest of the population.' He predicted (with
some accuracy) a period of major reform in about 1980 but his
analysis did not accept that South Africa's development posed any

special racial problem; and like most businessmen he showed little interest in the black political attitudes that might be forged in the meantime.*

Black nationalists as well as communists began to see Anglo as the living model of monopoly capitalism. This is how the ANC secretary-general Alfred Nzo depicted it in the Congress magazine *Sechaba* in 1970:

> South African companies like the Anglo-American Corporation under Harry Oppenheimer and many others have all got interlocking interests and directorships with British and US companies. Economically therefore, the South African racists who cling to apartheid are an integral and key part of the sinister plot of exploitation by the imperialists on an international scale. The merger of White S.A. capital with international finance has been a specific feature of S.A. penetration in the economies in many countries in Africa and elsewhere. There is no other country in the world in which the imperialists have been prepared to relegate their differences to the background and unite their efforts economically, technically and militarily as they have done in South Africa.†

The debate about capitalism and apartheid would continue over the next two decades. Certainly many foreign investors welcomed features of the apartheid regime, after the black political leaders were out of sight: and Pretoria made the most of its appeal to the union-ridden industrialists abroad. And viewed from the black side of the curtain there was little evidence that economic growth was in itself liberalising apartheid. 'South Africa's most dramatic period of economic advance between 1967 and 1976,' said Joe Slovo, the later Chairman of the South African Communist Party, 'was also a period during which more was done that at any time during our history to implement the worst features of apartheid.'‡ A new school of young Marxist South African writers emerged during the 'sixties who maintained that apartheid was really an extension of capitalism; and neo-Marxist historians and sociologists were to acquire a dominating position in many South African universities.

But many Marxists had an oversimplified view of the capitalists, who themselves had increasingly divergent interests, particularly as manufacturing and retailing rivalled mining. The old colour bar

* From Adrian Leftwich (editor), South Africa: Economic Growth and Political Change, London, (Allison and Busby) 1974, pp. 34–42
† *Sechaba*, February 1970
‡ Speech to SACP, July 1986: *see* Chapter 17

in jobs which had been entrenched in the gold-mines long before the apartheid government was getting in the way of more sophisticated industries. Mechanised factories called for more skilled black workers, living in stable conditions: there were not enough white workers to fill the jobs, and their rapid turnover became absurdly rapid and inefficient; while it was becoming obvious that black workers could do the same jobs for much lower wages. The sheer cost of Verwoerdian apartheid, including decentralising industry to the borders of the homelands, was increasingly evident. And both manufacturers and shopkeepers were looking enviously towards the black middle class to provide a market for their goods. By 1970, according to the Bureau of Market Research at the University of South Africa, the blacks accounted for 22.5 percent of total personal income; by 1975 25.4 percent.*

The gold-mine owners were also having doubts as to whether the colour bar and the use of cheap migrant labour were in their interests, or even in the interests of the white workers. It was true that they had kept down black wages with extraordinary success. Between 1889 and 1969 (according to Francis Wilson in his pioneering study) the real wages of black miners seemed actually to have fallen. But Wilson also showed that the colour bar added to the cost of producing gold, restricting both output and total employment, including the employment of skilled whites. 'Is it possible,' he asked, 'that the existence of the colour bar is actually against the interests of white workers?'† The mine-owners were reluctant to challenge the government on which much of their profits depended. But by the late 'sixties most major industrialists were beginning to press for a relaxation of job bars: though this did not mean (as Merle Lipton points out), that they necessarily rejected all aspects of apartheid.‡

The Afrikaner government in the meantime was gradually becoming more influenced by economic arguments. In the first years of apartheid under Malan and Verwoerd, the Afrikaners' tribal pride and fierce racial doctrine seemed almost immune: while they were able both to get richer and to extend the apartheid system. But by the late 'sixties the tribal unity was beginning to crack, while apartheid was not so obviously acting in all their interests. The Afrikaners were also more keen to extend their own share of the free-enterprise system, encouraged by their own emerging business leaders. The most remarkable of them was Anton Rupert, the

* See Financial Mail, Johannesburg, September 14, 1979
† Francis Wilson, *Labour in the South African Gold Mines 1911–1969*, Cambridge University Press, pp. 141, 118–19
‡ Lipton, p. 146

scientist who had built up the Rembrandt tobacco company with
the help of German capital from the small Voorbrand tobacco
company. He had always had Afrikaner backing and links with the
Broederbond: 'we were asked to smoke and cough for Volk and
Vaderland' as one Broeder complained.* But he was intellectually
adventurous, sounding often more like a don than a businessman,
and sometimes in trouble with the Broeders. When I met him in
his house in Stellenbosch in February 1960, just after Macmillan's
wind-of-change speech, he said it was just what he would have
written himself, and insisted that 'the coloureds must be admitted
into the white world – even with the vote'. He built up his global
tobacco empire, including Rothmans in Britain, into what he
claimed was 'the world's first truly multinational group'. He depicted Afrikaners as the much-needed catalysts for developing a
continent full of incompetents: 'The more disillusioned men there
are in the chancelleries of the West, the more we shall be needed.'†
He became more critical of the harsher aspects of apartheid, yet in
the end he was always loyal to his Volk, and never wanted to be
accused of damaging their interests. He continued to see his own
people, like the Jews, as having a special destiny and leadership
after surviving the ordeals of Africa. 'As fourteenth-generation
Africans – and indeed the first freedom fighters in Africa – we are
in a position to take the lead . . . Since the early 'thirties, when one
of every three Afrikaners was indigent, we have fought for and won
a place in the economy of the country through study, diligence,
daring, audacity and perseverance.' He preferred to discuss blacks
– like his fellow-Afrikaner Laurens van der Post, in terms of flora
and fauna, or catalysts and chemicals, rather than as ordinary
people or a practical political problem.‡

But most of the new Afrikaner businessmen were not so much
entrepreneurs as managers of the state-owned industries and
nationalised services – including the state steel company Iscor, the
state electricity Escom, the airline SAA, the railways SAR, the radio
(and later TV) SABC, and the state oil and gas company Sasol; while
the new development corporations for the homelands, like the Bantu
Investment Corporation or the Xhosa Development Corporation,
gave new jobs to Afrikaners as well as blacks. The Industrial
Development Corporation, which Hertzog had set up in 1927,
had now become an industrial conglomerate which (as Andries

* Ivor Wilkins and Hans Strydom, *The Broederbond*, New York, Paddington
Press, p. 428
† Anton Rupert, *Progress through Partnership*, Cape Town, Nasionale Boek-
handel, 1967, p. 157
‡ Anton Rupert, *Priorities for Co-existence*, Cape Town, Tafelberg, 1981, p. 26

Wassenaar of the insurance group Sanlam described it) 'tended to enter into direct competition with the private sector instead of assisting it'. Many English-speaking businessmen would complain that South Africa had become (as Gavin Relly of Anglo-American put it later) 'one of the most socialist countries in the world, because the Afrikaners, like any strong tribal group, have built it up to distribute the wealth among themselves'.* Even Afrikaners were worrying about the incompetence of this bureaucratic state network and Wassenaar later wrote an explosive book which infuriated politicians by complaining about 'the natural inclination of Afrikaners towards socialism' and the Jekyll-and-Hyde attitude of South Africa: 'It is obsessed with anti-communist legislation, but it follows economic policies which appear to move in the opposite direction.' He blamed gold for many of his country's problems and asked: 'Would this psychosis have come about had it not been the need, so it was thought, for Afrikanerdom to fight the power of money? It is difficult not to see behind all this the shadow of Gold.'†

At the iron heart of this Afrikaner state sector was the fast-growing arms industry; and it was here that the multinational corporations were most vulnerable to attack for supporting apartheid. For much of the new business in the long South African boom was interlocked directly or indirectly with the military and police machinery, with its cogs and levers for the control of the black population. It had become far more dominant after Sharpeville: between 1960 and 1969 the defence budget had risen from £22 million to £136 million a year, amounting to 17 percent of the total budget and 2.4 percent of the country's GNP. But the formal statistics understated much of the increasing penetration of defence and police contracts into apparently civilian activities. The defence forces took a huge leap under the new minister of defence P W Botha in 1967, who in one year doubled the numbers in military training in the Citizen Force and Command Units, to 32,500.‡

Most of the new spending went into the home-grown arms industry. During the 'fifties, South Africa had imported most of its arms, including tanks, submarines and destroyers, from Britain: when the new Buccaneer strike aircraft was produced in 1955 for the Royal Navy its only other customer was South Africa which ordered sixteen. But after Sharpeville, where British Saracen tanks rolled in to control the crowds, it became harder to distinguish

* Interview with author, May 1986
† Andries Wassenaar, pp. 123–51
‡ Foltz & Bienen, *Arms & The African*, Yale University Press, 1985, p. 127

between external defence and internal repression, and arms sales
to Pretoria were fiercely attacked. By 1964 the United Nations,
pressed by its new black members, had called for a total embargo
on the sale of arms, ammunition and arms-making equipment to
South Africa. The British Conservative government had abstained,
but the Labour government joined a full embargo of arms. It was
never as full as it looked: it let through existing orders, including
the Buccaneers, while Marconi (a subsidiary of the British General
Electric) still equipped the underground radar base at Devon in the
Transvaal. Both the British and the Americans did restrict their
arms exports, but their purpose was soon frustrated by the French
who became the chief arms suppliers to Pretoria: over the next
decade they provided sixty-four Mirage fighters and seventy-five
helicopters to South Africa which became their third biggest arms
customer; while they were also supplying weapons, with their
customary impartiality, to black clients further north. The Germans
also became important suppliers of technology, particularly to the
Simonstown military communications centre.

Pretoria still importuned the British and Americans for weapons,
and in 1967 the Labour government nearly relented, pressed by the
Minister of Defence Denis Healey who was desperate to increase
exports, before the prime minister Harold Wilson turned the tables.
(After losing office in 1970 Healey quickly went out to South Africa
to rebuild his bridges with blacks, delivering an attack on apartheid
in Durban and visiting Mandela on Robben Island. When an ANC
journalist asked him about selling arms he admitted 'I now think
I was wrong even to support the matter being considered.'*) Pretoria
still pressed, warning foreign companies that they would suffer
unless the embargo was lifted. British businessmen responded
obediently, and tried to lobby their government. The trade association Uksata protested against the 'adolescent action' of the arms
embargo, and the President of the CBI Sir Stephen Brown complained about the 'irresponsible obstacles' to trade.† One of
the most powerful lobbyists was the managing director of Shell,
Sir Frank (later Lord) McFadzean, who was friendly with the
prime minister Vorster, and warned his government that the
arms embargo would 'have repercussions in other commercial
fields'.‡

Pretoria tried again when the conservatives returned to power in
1970 under Ted Heath, pledged to resume arms sales. There was

* *Sechaba*, January 19, 1971, p. 15
† *Cape Times*, December 21, 1967
‡ Bingham Report, p. 258

an open split in the cabinet, led by Jim Prior; but eventually Pretoria only asked for a few Navy helicopters – which were never supplied. As Harold Wilson pointed out, what Pretoria now wanted was not so much the weapons as a 'certificate of respectability', or 'to get pregnant' (as the Pentagon elegantly put it) by the Western powers, to commit them to their support. For South Africa was now becoming more self-sufficient in arms. Already in 1962 ICI had helped Pretoria (through AECI) to build three armaments factories to produce ammunition, tear gas and rockets; by the next year Pretoria claimed to be producing all the ammunition they needed. After the UN embargo Pretoria embarked on extravagant new arms-making programmes, discreetly helped by American and European companies. By 1967 Vorster had opened the first aircraft factory to make Impala planes based on British and Italian technology;* and the next year the defence minister P W Botha established the new state-owned Armaments Development and Production Corporation (Armscor) which became the centrepiece of the military-industrial complex. Armscor was protected by strict secrecy – no newspaper could publish details of any defence deal – and the full collaboration with Western industrialists may never emerge. But it commanded great patronage and leverage and Pretoria's grand design was to commit companies deeply to the military expansion and 'strategic investment'. It was becoming harder to distinguish, not just between external and internal security, but between civil and military purposes. The issuing of pass books, the surveillance of townships, the tapping of telephones and the monitoring of car rentals all used computerised technology which appeared peaceful but could easily be adapted to a sophisticated police state.

By the time the UN voted for mandatory sanctions in 1977, thus cutting off most of the French arms connection, South Africa was already very well equipped. Many opponents of sanctions would argue that the arms embargo had been counter-productive, by helping Pretoria to become self-sufficient in weapons, and thus to pursue military policies unrestrained by the West. In fact Pretoria was never as self-sufficient, or as successful in exporting weapons, as the government propaganda made out: the more sophisticated weapons required hundreds of components, many of which still had to come from abroad, with the help of intricate evasions; and the ageing French Mirages, and still older British Buccaneer strike aircraft – which were frequently used for deadly cross-border raids – had to be replaced with a South African version of the Mirage

* UN Special Committee on Apartheid: Note on Military and Police Build-up, February 21, 1968

which still needed components smuggled in from France and Israel. The black opposition claimed that Pretoria's arms programme was itself dependent on general Western investment. 'This enormous expenditure on arms and other weapons of war,' said Tambo at the time of the ANC's sixtieth anniversary in 1972, 'is only possible because of the thousands of millions of imperialist investment in the South African economy. Without this support, without the backing of the imperialist countries, South Africa would long have gone bankrupt even while we were fighting, literally, with our bare hands.'*

By the early 'seventies the long South African boom was petering out, and in 1971 the growth-rate was down to 3.3 percent compared to 7.1 percent three years earlier. The economy was partially saved by the sudden revival of its old staple, gold – which still accounted for 60 percent of the world's supply. For forty years the gold-price had been fixed at $35 an ounce, which had become increasingly unprofitable: by the late 'sixties Consolidated Goldfields was considering moving out altogether. But the crisis of the dollar in 1971 produced a new demand; the market price was unfixed; and Pretoria discreetly restricted production to force the price up. By June 1972 the gold price in the free market was above $60; by the beginning of 1974 it was $130; by the end of 1974 it was $198. The gold-mines once again became the key source of profits, and Anglo-American made more mergers and deals with weaker industrial rivals. In finance Anglo merged their own bank UAL with Syfret's Trust and the Dutch bank Nedbank to form a powerful financial group called Nedsual, and increased their stake in Barclays National. In cars they emerged with a three-quarter stake in a new Sigma motor corporation, with the other quarter owned by American Chrysler. The biggest merger was in reverse: the engineering group Thomas Barlow took over Rand Mines to form Barlow Rand, which could use gold to underpin its industrial business. But Anglo, through its subsidiaries, could control nearly 25 percent of the shares of Barlow Rand. By 1976, according to Duncan Innes, 'Anglo group companies held top positions in every one of South Africa's economic sectors except agriculture.'†

But the gold boom could not solve the fundamental problems of manufacturers, who found too small a market: much of Africa was closed to them, while their products could not compete outside the continent. The cheapness of black labour was often illusory, as

* *Sechaba*, April, 1972
† Innes, pp. 212–18

factories needed to mechanise with skilled and stable workers. And as markets turned down and inflation turned up the black workers who had been brought in by the boom were beginning to show the first signs of giving serious trouble.

7

The Roots of Revolt

No other workforce in the history of industrialisation has been so
excluded for so long from the system it made possible.

Heribert Adam and Kogila Moodley, *South Africa without Apartheid*,
Berkeley, University of California Press, 1986, p. 22

Whatever the failures of apartheid, for a long time it succeeded
brilliantly in sweeping the black opposition under the carpet. During
the election campaign of 1970, when I was back in South Africa,
the white voters saw scarcely a sign of black unrest or protest. The
Vorster government was preoccupied by the threat from the right,
from the breakaway Herstigte (reconstituted) National Party led
by Jaap Marais, a passionate advocate of ethnic purity. 'No other
will ever love us,' he said. 'That is a law of international politics.'
But Vorster was returned in triumph, with much business support,
and there was little serious concern about a black revolt. 'The
government can't lose so long as they've achieved the basic fact of
apartheid,' said the editor of the *Johannesburg Sunday Times*, Joel
Mervis: 'putting the African danger out of sight.' Western diplomats
in Pretoria seemed to accept that apartheid had come to stay, and
could only hope that it would become more liberal. 'Diplomats are
always looking for glimmers of hope: they have to find a reason for
doing nothing,' said the Afrikaner commentator Stanley Uys, 'so
Pretoria has a special department to supply glimmers.'

Yet some Afrikaner intellectuals, having built up their great wall
of apartheid, were already beginning to see its shortcomings and
contradictions. Pretoria went ahead with establishing the 'independent' homelands, beginning with the Transkei in 1963, which they
hoped would divert black ambitions away from urban revolts, back
towards their own tribal roots. But the Transkei under its prime
minister Kaiser Matanzima – a nephew of Nelson Mandela – was
already under a permanent state of emergency and its parliament
had no real autonomy, while no Western nation would recognise
the homelands as independent nations. And the blacks were still
surging into the white cities, where industry depended on them
more than ever. When I talked in 1970 to the Afrikaner editor Schalk
Pienaar, who had confidently argued the case for Verwoerdian

apartheid with me ten years earlier, he began by saying: 'I no longer think that the blacks can be denied a permanent place in the white cities.'

Behind the great wall there were rumblings of trouble to come. The churchmen were more perceptive than the businessmen. 'Nowadays when visitors want to talk to African priests it's hard to get anyone to meet them,' said the dissenting Afrikaner pastor Beyers Naude in 1970: 'Of course the Africans are becoming more interested in Black Power . . . some of the government are realising that they unleashed a social-political force which they can't control.' The membership of black separatist churches had doubled in five years, and blacks were abandoning the conventional Christian churches. 'When I ask them why they're leaving the Anglican Church they talk about Black Power,' said Father Leo Rakale, a more conservative black theologian. 'But when I ask them about it they don't come again.' Western culture, led by the Bible and Shakespeare, still held its attractions, but partly because of its revolutionary implications. (When the former headmaster of Eton Sir Robert Birley went to teach in Soweto he was surprised to find that his black pupils took the side of Bolingbroke against King Richard II, and that they understood the conspirators' scenes in Julius Caesar better than he did.)

I found it much harder now to talk politics with the blacks in Soweto. 'You know I don't dare tell my own brother what I'm thinking,' said one young black politician. 'So you've come to pick up the old threads?' said a veteran campaigner. 'Well, they're broken.' Informers were everywhere, and the young tsotsis or gangsters were paid to give any news of saboteurs or guerillas. Some blacks were even complaining that it was guerillas who got people tortured and killed in detention; but cases of sabotage were now rare. What would happen if a guerilla did appear in Soweto? I asked blacks in a shebeen: 'Someone would give him away just for a quiet life.' A few were beginning to talk about total terrorism: only real massacres, they said, would interest the outside world, and only when blacks feared their own people more than the police would the informer network be broken (a forewarning of necklaces to come). The government's policy of harrassing urban blacks, separating them from families and herding back to reserves, was taking its toll. But blacks were still refusing to behave like American Indians (as one of their banned leaders put it) – losing their sense of identity, or being decimated by drink and despair.

The ANC and the PAC remained banned. No word by Mandela or Sobukwe could be published; to be seen with a Congress document was to go to jail. 'By the end of the 1960s,' wrote Thomas Karis, the American historian of black politics, 'the ANC seemed to be little more than a shadowy presence in South Africa.'* Mandela's wife Winnie was soon being pressed into politics herself: in 1969 she and twenty-one others were arrested and charged with supporting the banned ANC; the evidence showed how frail their own communications were and how deeply informers had penetrated. But after two trials, acquittals and re-arrests, and after 491 days in solitary confinement, Winnie Mandela emerged a far more determined political figure who was (she said) not afraid of anyone.

Sobukwe of the PAC was under house arrest in Kimberley, writing a novel about his childhood, and under constant surveillance. (When I visited him in 1970, we drove in a hired car as we talked, but a police car was following us after a few minutes.) He still carried authority, with his strong eyes and huge laugh, though he suffered from paranoia after his long isolation and he was convinced the police had inserted a listening device into his body. He sounded much more moderate than the young blacks of Soweto: he deplored the growing signs of black vengeance, but was not surprised. He despised John Vorster and thought the split among Afrikaners would widen. Not a word of his moderation could be published.

Oliver Tambo, the president of the ANC in exile in Zambia, faced an unpromising prospect. Western governments and the UN were condemning apartheid, but with no visible influence on Pretoria. Only the sports boycott, preventing South African teams from competing at international games, had visibly dented apartheid thinking. The armed struggle was having its own problems: in 1965 some of the ANC's guerillas in their army Umkhonto were in Rhodesia on their way back to South Africa, but they suffered humiliating setbacks, causing discontent in the training camps. Tambo himself remained a devout Christian, close to radical priests including the Anglicans Father Huddleston and John Collins, the Canon of St Paul's. But he had to reconcile very different strands, including Christians, communists and straightforward black nationalists; and since Congress had little help from the West the communist influence inevitably increased. ANC members were invited to Moscow or East Germany and weapons were supplied from the Soviet Union. The communist influence among exiles worried some former Western supporters of the ANC; but in the meantime within South Africa a new black generation was taking a different direction.

The first serious signs of renewed resistance came from the factories, where the rising inflation and recession of the early 'seven-

* Thomas Karis, 'Black Politics in South Africa', *Foreign Affairs*, Winter 1983–4

ties quickly had their impact on black workers, who were demanding not so much political rights, as higher wages. By the beginning of 1973 black workers were striking illegally in Durban, and later in East London and on the Rand, revealing an unexpected new militancy and organisation, with no formal leaders who could be picked off or victimised. Afrikaners noted with relish that English-speaking Natal was the focus; it was 'the irony of the year', said the pro-government paper *Rapport*, that 'it should be Durban that shows the country how scandalously some industrialists treat their non-white workers.' Several strikes originated in the factories of a single large company, the Frame textile group whose wages were notoriously low. The chairman Philip Frame, a nationalist member of Vorster's economic advisory council, complained he was a scapegoat 'for the total system of wage differentiation for which every white citizen in this country shares responsibility.'* The employers could not easily replace these semi-skilled workers who thus gained wage-increases, which encouraged trades unionism; but the workers were politically cautious, linking themselves to the white-led unions of TUCSA which the ANC condemned for being preoccupied with white living standards. But the ANC nevertheless looked forward with some prescience to 'the most turbulent period of industrial and political unrest in South Africa's history. Coupled with the power the workers have shown they can exert, is the growth of a new and dynamic concept among the youth in particular and the people at large: the concept of black consciousness, of black unity against white racism.'†

Black consciousness provided the ideological impetus to black revolt, personified by the articulate young leader Steve Biko who in his short life helped to 'conscientise' a new generation of blacks. Tall and quick-witted, he made his first impact as a black student in the Eastern Cape, when in 1969 he rejected the white leadership of the partly-multiracial students' union NUSAS to form the new all-black South African Students' Organisation (SASO) – which in turn became the 'nursery' for the Black People's Convention (BPC). But both movements were deliberately not competing with the existing political bodies, the ANC and the PAC, and not trying to be an alternative force.‡ Biko always denied that SASO was anti-white, but his break from white liberal leadership undoubtedly helped to give blacks a new confidence. His movement was part of a new insistence, influenced by African writers including the Algerian Frantz Fanon, that blacks had their own values and traditions; and

* *Sechaba*, March 1973
† *Sechaba*, May 1973
‡ Sam Nolutshungu, *Changing South Africa*, Manchester University Press, 1982, p. 149

the word 'black' was now being proudly adopted as part of a new
pride and spirit, in Africa as in America. Many ANC supporters
inside South Africa were worried that the new movement might get
in the way of their own plans; but Winnie Mandela, banned from
active politics, welcomed the young vigour and Steve Biko first
visited her in Soweto in 1979, with his lieutenant Barney Pityana
(now a vicar in Birmingham, England). As Pityana later recollected:

> We knew that the younger generation wanted to get on with
> things, with a broader base. Winnie had no ifs and buts, and
> opened her heart to us. Steve always went to see her when he
> was in Johannesburg.*

Like most African leaders Biko resented the influence of both
superpowers: 'We have no illusions about the African policies of
either the US or the USSR,' he told a Canadian interviewer in 1977.
But he warned the West that 'many persons within the liberation
struggles look upon the Marxist analysis of repression as the proper
diagnosis of their situation. And on top of all this there is the
overwhelming evidence of America's involvement in the Third
World for the sake of its own economic self-interest. Russia has
no investments to protect in Johannesburg. America does.' Biko
opposed all foreign investment in South Africa as 'nothing but an
exploitation of the blacks' (as he said at a trial in 1976). 'Harold
Wilson stands up to criticise the system here,' he complained, 'and
several of his firms come to invest in this country, among other
reasons, precisely because there exists in the country cheap labour
from the blacks.' But he remained pragmatic and tactical, and he
saw 'this whole foreign investment question as a vehicle for generating pressure to sympathise with our point of view.' He also attacked
foreign investors for not using their strength: 'when these people
have got a point of leverage, because they are not South Africans,
because they are subject back home, probably, to more liberal
attitudes, they don't make use of this.'†
    By 1973 Biko was sufficiently effective to attract the interest of
the police: he was banned from leaving his home district in the
Eastern Cape, and he remained restricted, at a time when the black
political temper was rising again all over South Africa. The growing
pride in blackness and the clamour for freedom were fired by the
sudden collapse of white rule in the Portuguese colonies of Angola
and Mozambique which had long provided a buffer between South

---

* Interview with author and others, November 1986.
† Donald Woods, *Biko*, New York, Paddington Press, 1978, pp. 95–103, 134–6

Africa and independent black Africa. When Mozambique became independent under the black government of Frelimo in June 1975, followed by Angola under the MPLA five months later, they appeared to black South Africans to mark at last a break in the white wall. The South African army, under its minister of defence P W Botha, had been humiliated in Angola by the counter-offensive helped by Cuban and Russian support; while Mozambique now provided a base for black troops to invade Rhodesia, the last remaining white bastion apart from South Africa. The crumbling of the white buffers brought premature hopes to the South African blacks: and young blacks shouted 'Viva Frelimo!'

But it was the growth of Soweto with over a million intensely urbanised blacks which showed up all the contradictions between apartheid theories and the facts of industrial integration. In the industrial heart of South Africa, Soweto was a greater threat to Pretoria than any border state. Many young Sowetans were inspired by the new pride in black consciousness and became more militant with the recession on top of the repression. It was appropriate that the language teaching should be the cause of their explosion; but it was not because the blacks – like most nationalist movements – wanted to be taught in their traditional language. They wanted to learn in English which they saw as the language of Western culture and opportunity, while Afrikaans was the oppressor's language. English-speaking industrialists, who now desperately needed articulate black employees, should have shared their crusade but they did not. The issue of language went to the heart of the disunity behind the union of 1910 which had promised equality to Afrikaans. 'It is ironical,' wrote two students of Afrikaner politics in 1978, 'that the Broederbond, born out of the frustration caused by Lord Milner's policy of anglicising Afrikaners, should blunder a few decades later by trying to force its own language on blacks.'* The Broederbond was pressing for blacks to speak Afrikaans as their second language, while preserving their own Bantu language at home, and in 1974 the director of education in the Johannesburg region instructed black schools, against strong protests, to teach mathematics, history and geography in Afrikaans.

In January 1976 the new minister in charge of black education, Andreas Treurnicht, insisted on further teaching in Afrikaans. The Soweto schoolboys, and many teachers, were enraged; and in May students began striking in protest. The Institute of Race Relations in Johannesburg warned the minister of a serious crisis; students stoned buildings and a black Afrikaans teacher was stabbed. A

* Wilkins and Strydom, *op. cit.*, p. 217

Soweto councillor, Leonard Mosela, warned the police that enforc-
ing Afrikaans teaching could lead to another Sharpeville. Few
revolts had been so accurately predicted; and two days later on
June 16 Soweto exploded. Ten thousand black students marched
peacefully to the school where the strike had begun, where they
were confronted with police with tear gas. The children threw
stones, the police fired back and killed a child: the children ran riot
and killed two whites, including Dr Edelstein who had devoted his
life to black welfare. The first day's deaths were estimated at
twenty-five; but rioting, arson and strikes spread through Soweto,
which became a battlefield complete with armoured cars and helicopters.

The schoolchildren soon achieved their immediate object, the
relaxing of rules about Afrikaans; but the rioting and striking
continued, spreading to Cape Town and Port Elizabeth and revealing all the pent-up fury behind the previous surface of calm. The
students turned to organising major strikes, with unexpected success, while white vigilantes and Zulu tribesmen fought back at the
students and the police began mass arrests.* By the end of the year
the death-roll was estimated at between 500 and 1,000.

The Soweto fury was more deeply-rooted and long-lasting than
the anger in Sharpeville sixteen years earlier, for it was led by the
children who were in fundamental revolt against their schooling
and indoctrination. The leader of the first protest march, the
nineteen-year-old Tsietsi Mashinini, explained afterwards how 'the
black student in South Africa is being fed the type of education that
will domesticate him to become a better tool for the white man . . .'
And many parents, in spite of the cost in lives, admired their show
of strength. 'The buildings in Soweto and all over still went down
despite the guns, you know,' said Mrs Phakathi, the national
president of the YWCA.†

The government had denied that language was the main cause
of the riots, and had tried desperately to defuse the anger by
belatedly meeting black leaders. But they were determined to re-
impose order in the townships, particularly Soweto; and the Broederbond promised its members, that 'the routines and methods
which their own police will use among their own people will sometimes be different from those of a white community'.‡ The promise
was hardly necessary: twenty-six blacks had been tortured to death
in two years. When a year after Soweto three former black students

---

* For a thorough analysis of the revolt *see* John Kane-Berman, *Soweto*, Johannes-
burg, Ravan Press, 1978. *See also* R W Johnson, *op. cit.*, pp. 189–201
† *This Week*, 'South Africa – there is no crisis' London, September 2, 1976
‡ Wilkins and Strydom, *op. cit.*, p. 236

who had trained abroad killed two whites in Johannesburg the government had a further pretext for a new purge of potential terrorists.

The most famous victim was Steve Biko. Not directly involved in the Soweto uprising, he saw it as vindicating his principles. When asked in July 1977 for evidence that younger blacks were supporting his Black People's Convention he answered: 'In one word, Soweto! The boldness, dedication, sense of purpose, and clarity of analysis of the situation – all of these things are a direct result of black consciousness ideas among the young in Soweto and elsewhere.'*
'The real contribution of black consciousness to the revolt,' wrote Sam Nolutshungu, 'was in the demon it had roused: the defiant attitude among the youth in the face of police violence, and the solidarity which emerged among blacks in the year and a half of the revolt.'† After Soweto Biko was inevitably a marked man. A year after it, in August 1977, he was stopped in his car near Grahamstown by the police, imprisoned for the fourth time without trial and interrogated. A month later the police announced that he had died in jail. The Minister of Justice, James Kruger, later told the delegates to the Afrikaner Nationalist Party, in a much-repeated phrase, 'Dit laat my koud' – 'it leaves me cold'. In the inquest the police interrogators, cross-examined by the family's lawyer Sydney Kentridge, described how Biko had been kept naked in his cell for two days, in handcuffs and leg-irons; and how when he collapsed he was driven 1,200 kilometres, naked in the back of a land-rover, to Pretoria prison hospital where he died on a mat on a stone floor. The torture to death of this intellectual who had never advocated violence probably did more than any single act to discredit apartheid among Americans and Europeans – and also among many South Africans. But it did not deter Vorster's government. A month after Biko's murder it cracked down on any further potential black leaders, many of them known for their moderation. It banned the black consciousness movements and the Christian Institute, detained forty-seven black leaders including Dr Nthato Motlana in Soweto, and closed down the influential black newspaper the World, edited by Percy Qoboza.

The official report on the Soweto riots by Judge Cillie blamed the ANC, the PAC and the communists for encouraging the riots; but in truth the revolt came largely from schoolboys who were little influenced by Congress. 'We didn't deserve so much credit for Soweto,' Winnie Mandela told me afterwards, 'but we don't mind

* Interview with Bernard Zylstra; Woods, *op. cit.*, p. 98
† Nolutshungu, *op. cit.*, p. 185

at all.' The ANC's prospects were fundamentally changed by the
Soweto revolt, or 'the South African Uprising' as they preferred to
call it. When police reprisals drove thousands of young Soweto
rebels over the frontiers, many eventually joined the ANC or its
military wing Umkhonto. By mid 1978 Pretoria claimed that 4,000
refugees were being trained in Angola, Libya and Tanzania. The
ANC's national executive in Lusaka had carefully not opposed the
theories of black consciousness even though they cut across their
own multiracialism, and claimed to have helped to establish the
new militancy;* while Tambo explained in 1977 that it was a stage
of development:

> In a way we started from the point of black consciousness too.
> We formed the ANC from just Africans – because the British had
> delivered themselves of a constitution which cut us out of power.
> They transferred power to the white settlers and we had to
> organise ourselves to defend our rights. But we have not stayed
> there. We have developed to the position where we expect all the
> people in South Africa to form part of the movement for the
> transformation of the social, political and economic situation.
> Black consciousness, looked at from this point of view, is thus a
> phase in the struggle . . .†

The ANC still faced problems with dissenters who objected to collaborating with other races and with the communist party. In 1975
a breakaway group of 'ANC African nationalists', led by Tennyson
Makiwane and including Luthuli's son-in-law Pascal Ngakane, had
publicly attacked the communists' influence. The secretary-general
of the ANC Alfred Nzo denounced the 'treacherous faction and
conspiracy', and expelled them; Makiwane later worked for the
Transkei government and was killed in 1980 – some suspected by
ANC agents. The ANC also had a more serious new rival in the
Azanian People's Organisation (AZAPO) which was formed in 1978
with its roots in black consciousness. It was a more dogmatically
socialist movement which saw capitalism as the enemy, more than
apartheid; and its documents advocated much more specific policies
than the ANC's, including the nationalisation of heavy industry and
land, confiscation of emigrants' property, and disallowing most
inherited property.

As for the PAC, whose thinking had helped to inspire black

* *See* interview with Tebello Motapanyane, the secretary-general of SASM,
Sechaba, second quarter, 1977
† Interview with *Sechaba*, fourth quarter, 1977

consciousness, it had been facing growing disputes in exile. It turned to communist China for funds, and made a splash at the UN with the help of its exuberant ambassador plenipotentiary David Sibeko, who had once plotted to assassinate Dr Verwoerd. But after the death of its founder Sobukwe in 1978 the PAC was more confused, and its acting leader Potlako Leballo had betrayed or alienated many of its supporters. In May 1979 he was succeeded by a three-man council led by Sibeko; but the following month Sibeko was assassinated by three men from a rival faction; and the movement never recovered its original unity and purpose.

Inside South Africa the ANC was beginning to face its most formidable challenge in the shape of the Zulu leader Gatsha Buthelezi. He had a traditional background: he came from the Zulu royal family and briefly worked as a clerk in the government's native administration. But he had also been through the same stable as many other black nationalists; he was at Fort Hare college with Sobukwe, before being expelled, and then joined the Congress Youth League. At twenty-nine he was installed as chief, while the ANC leaders were on trial for treason; but for years he appeared to resist Pretoria's pressure for a Zulu homeland. When Pretoria established KwaZulu in 1970 he was elected its chief executive; but he denounced apartheid from his new political base, explaining privately how he could buck the system, and still kept in touch with ANC friends in exile. It was the ANC who encouraged him in 1975 to set up his own movement, Inkatha, a revival of an earlier Zulu cultural organisation. The ANC (they later explained) wanted Buthelezi to 'use the legal opportunities provided by the Bantustan programme to participate in the mass mobilisation of our people . . .'* And Buthelezi always stressed his early friendship with ANC leaders: 'I cajoled Western governments for not supporting the mission-in-exile' (as he always studiously called the ANC leadership). But the ANC had seriously miscalculated, as they later candidly admitted:

> Unfortunately, we failed to mobilise our own people to take on the task of resurrecting Inkatha as the kind of organisation we wanted, owing to the understandable antipathy of many of our comrades towards what they considered as working within the Bantustan system. The task of reconstituting Inkatha therefore fell on Gatsha Buthelezi himself, who then built Inkatha as a personal power base far removed from the kind of organisation we had visualised, as an instrument for the mobilisation of our people in the countryside into an active and conscious force

* ANC NEC Political Report, *Sechaba*, December 1985

for revolutionary change. In the first instance, Gatsha dressed Inkatha in the clothes of the ANC, exactly because he knew that the masses to whom he was appealing were loyal to the ANC and had for six decades adhered to our movement as their representative and their leader. Later, when he thought he had sufficient of a base, he also used coercive methods against the people to force them to support Inkatha.

Buthelezi was undoubtedly a force among Zulus. His tactics were necessarily devious, since he was both benefiting from the apartheid system and denouncing it. Vorster saw him as a tool of the English-speaking press; but he sometimes liked to compare Zulus to Afrikaners. 'The Afrikaner himself did not ascend to power only through bloodshed,' he told a rally in Soweto in 1975. 'My daily prayer for him is that God should give him the grace he gave the English to bow to the inevitable while there is still time.'* To Steve Biko and other black consciousness leaders Buthelezi appeared as the stooge of Pretoria, and when he appeared at Sobukwe's funeral in 1978 he was shouted down and attacked. The ANC was soon painting him in the colours of Tshombe in the Congo or Muzorewa in Rhodesia: a puppet of the capitalists. But to white businessmen he appeared to be a welcome alternative to the revolutionaries of the ANC as he talked the language of negotiation and power-broking without violence while supporting free enterprise and safeguards for the whites.

Yet the ANC remained the chief beneficiary of Soweto, in spite of its sixteen years underground and in exile. The schoolchildren chanted the names of Mandela and Tambo at funerals and the slogans and flags began coming into the open again. The ANC retained its historic position as the oldest and broadest liberation movement; and its martyrs and prisoners had all the greater glory in their absence. The Soweto children had also rediscovered the fearful truth which the ANC had painfully reached in 1961: that when all political expression is suppressed, their only effective communication is violence. And the violence was now beginning to make some impact on the business community.

The schoolchildren of Soweto, on top of a depression and troubles in Angola, had provoked a crisis in many ways more serious than Sharpeville. On the morning of June 16, 1976 the gold-mines index in the *Financial Times* fell by 8 percent, and by another 3 percent the next day. There was less outflow of capital than after Sharpeville since exchange control was in force; but the London stockbrokers

---

* Ben Temkin, *Buthelezi*, Durnall, 1977, p. 152

Williams de Broe reported that the situation was 'sufficiently serious to advise against new investment in South Africa until calm is clearly shown to be re-established in the area'; and Graham Hatton in the *Financial Times* warned that 'South Africa will need upwards of R1 billion of new capital every year if it is to achieve a rate of economic growth that is high enough to prevent black unemployment from rising.'* Land values fell rapidly, bankrupting some property companies and threatening the banks, and several European and American companies began selling off their South African subsidiaries. Pretoria had to impose import controls and strict measures to save fuel.

And the Soweto riots shocked most South African businessmen into realising how much the young blacks hated their system. A week of violence had achieved more than decades of petitions. At Anglo-American, Oppenheimer was now much more worried: he felt the responsibility to improve black conditions, but recession made it harder to reassure white trades unionists. He conceded that Western pressure could be helpful, but the West must not expect Afrikaners to commit political suicide.† Basil Hersov of Anglo-Vaal told his shareholders in 1976 that 'private enterprise must re-examine its role in society' and that 'businesses will be weighing short-term expenditures against the longer-term rewards of helping to ensure greater possibilities of stability and growth in our society.' The Transvaal Chamber of Industries sent a memorandum to the prime minister explaining that 'the rising generation is no longer prepared to accept the limitations which its parents accepted as a penalty of having been born without a white skin'. But the average businessman's reaction, said the well-informed *Financial Mail* in Johannesburg, was to be comforted by the muted reaction overseas and to be convinced that Vorster still held a tight rein: 'whether he believes the next fifteen years will be as profitable as the last fifteen is another matter. His time horizon simply does not stretch that far.'‡

Soon after Soweto Harry Oppenheimer persuaded Anton Rupert and other business leaders to set up the 'Urban Foundation', which aimed to improve conditions for Soweto and other townships with the help of new housing, electrification, sewage or building societies. It was described as a non-political fund, which could thus raise foreign loans, but it tacitly accepted that businessmen now accepted a wider social responsibility. 'There were still many people in

---

* *Financial Times* June 19 and 23, 1976
† Interview with author, May 3, 1978
‡ Kane-Berman, *op. cit.*, p. 160

government who clung to Verwoerdian ideas,' said Anton Rupert
later, 'in the belief that you could think away the problems of
Soweto if you tried hard enough. But of course we in business know
that is not possible.'* The Urban Foundation and other business
groups were now anxious to build up a black middle class as a
bulwark against revolutionary elements, and to provide a stable
community with solid materialist values – a strategy which also
suited Pretoria. But they were tactless in spelling out their motives,
which soon aroused resistance from radicals; and when they tried
to meet black leaders many businessmen became rapidly aware of
how few they could talk to – even fewer after the arrests of October
1977. When they did talk to them their message was not reassuring:
Dr Motlana, the elder statesman of Soweto who kept in contact
with the young rebels, told Oppenheimer that change was now more
likely to come through chaos than through prosperity. Motlana was
much criticised by the young – including his son – for even talking
to whites; and he was now pessimistic of any help from the West.
'Why do the West hide their stick behind their back when they talk
to South Africa?' he asked me in Soweto in 1978. 'The Africans like
to see that stick out front. I wish the Russians would show more
interest in South Africa – to compel the West to intervene.'

The business leaders were coming up against a deeper alienation
than most of them realised. As the Johannesburg market-researcher
Eric Mafuna put it: 'In the early 'seventies most blacks were aspiring
to be part of the first world. But after 1976 many of them felt they
did not want to be part of an artificially enriched world: they
preferred to be in the third world.'† And the anger of the Soweto
children continued to seethe below the surface, passing down the
school generations.

* HFO: some personal perspectives *Ibid*.
† Interview with author, June 19, 1986

8

Western Revulsion

What the hell would you do if you found out that God was black?

Bobby Kennedy, to a meeting of Afrikaner students at
Stellenbosch, 1966[*]

Through the boom years the Western protest against apartheid and repression had been frequently passionate, but largely ineffective. It had been the British with their long involvement with South Africa who were most vocal, spurred on by South African exiles; and it was one of them, Peter Hain, who achieved the most damaging blow against apartheid, the sports boycott. The Americans were slower to become interested, with less historical involvement and investment and far more interest in Latin America than Africa. Yet it was the Americans who were eventually to mount the more effective pressure, not so much through diplomatic leverage as by mobilising the machinery of capitalism itself.

In the years after Sharpeville American policy towards Africa was given low priority compared to Vietnam, Latin America and Europe. President Kennedy was genuinely revolted by apartheid and supported the UN arms embargo, while the State Department reduced its support for Pretoria. In July 1963 the American embassy in Pretoria – far ahead of the British – invited blacks to a reception for the first time. Bobby Kennedy made a much-publicised visit to South Africa in 1966: as his plane took off back to Washington he said: 'If I lived in this country I would gather up everything I have and get out now.'[†] Lyndon Johnson as President maintained the Kennedys' hostility to apartheid, but he knew little about Africa and (as Anthony Lake wrote) 'as the rhetoric of American policy toward Africa took on a more elevated tone, the gap between word and deed became more noticeable'.[‡] American blacks were largely preoccupied with their own civil rights campaign. The chief lobby for black South Africans was the American Committee on Africa

---

[*] Arthur Schlesinger Jr, *Robert Kennedy and his Times*, London, André Deutsch, 1978, p. 746

[†] Schlesinger, *op. cit.*, p. 748

[‡] Anthony Lake, *The 'Tar Baby' Option*, New York, Columbia University Press, 1976, p. 74

(ACOA), set up by a dedicated Methodist minister George Hauser after the defiance campaign in 1952: but it gained only limited support from black Americans.

Washington was still much influenced by British policies and it was not until the arrival in 1969 of Nixon and Kissinger that American policies became more distinctive. Kissinger was bored by South Africa and Rhodesia – he did not refer to either in the first two volumes of his memoirs – but he was instinctively in favour of the *status quo* of the existing white regimes. Both the Pentagon and the National Security Council argued that economic growth supported by American businessmen could play a liberalising role, and officials were impressed by *The Economist*'s arguments that 'richer means lefter'.* Kissinger, exasperated by the State Department's influence, ordered a secret policy review by the NSC which was thoroughly sceptical about external pressure on Pretoria, and maintained that:

> For the foreseeable future South Africa will be able to maintain internal stability and effectively counter insurgent activity . . . The Whites are here to stay and the only way that constructive change can come about is through them. There is no hope for the Blacks to gain the political rights they seek through violence, which will only lead to chaos and increased opportunities for the communists.

It was an analysis which took little interest in black attitudes, and the ANC called it an 'infamous document'. Kissinger was presented with five options and chose number two, which proposed relaxation of American measures against South Africa – including easing the arms embargo – while giving more aid to black Africa, particularly Botswana. The National Security Council discussed it with some ignorance (Vice-President Spiro Agnew praised the South Africans for having achieved independence with a declaration modelled on America's, until Nixon suggested 'Ted, you mean Rhodesia don't you?'). The State Department, dismayed by the choice of option two, quoted the story of Brer Fox who made a Tar Baby to catch Brer Rabbit: each time Brer Rabbit hit the Tar Baby, he got more stuck to it. They called it the Tar Baby Option: the name stuck and so did the policy.†

The theory behind the policy, as David Newsom at the State Department described it, was that 'isolation can breed resistance

* Lake, p. 127
† Lake, *op. cit.*, p. 129

to change. Open doors can accelerate it.' But who or what would come in through those open doors? Soon after the policy-shift the American ambassador to South Africa, John Hurd, went pheasant-shooting with government leaders on Robben Island, while the head of the defence forces in Pretoria, Admiral Biermann, was welcomed at the Pentagon. In the event, the Nixon–Kissinger policy effectively condoned Pretoria's apartheid system, and left it to corporations and banks to try to liberalise it.

But by early 1969 Americans outside Washington were showing one of those mysterious surges of concern with a distant part of the world. Students and church leaders became suddenly aware of the evils of apartheid, and their interest merged with the eagerness of the disciples of Ralph Nader to challenge the social responsibilities of American corporations. European protesters were determined to use capitalism as an instrument of change rather than to attack it wholesale; and their patient application of pressure from share-holders was to prove the most effective leverage of all.

The first stirrings had already begun in the mid 'sixties. After his visit to the Republic, Bobby Kennedy had begun writing to American businessmen, asking them to define their responsibilities to their workers in South Africa. And black organisations, civil rights campaigners and churches launched a campaign against ten US banks which were lending to South Africa, picketed annual stockholders' meetings, asked awkward questions of chairmen, wrote letters to shareholders, leafletted depositors and sent del-egations to the banks' headquarters. A chief target was the Chase Manhattan, which already featured large in student demonology. At its annual meeting in 1967 they held signs which adapted the bank's current slogan to say: APARTHEID HAS A FRIEND AT CHASE MANHATTAN. The chairman, David Rockefeller, declared: 'None of us holds any brief for apartheid. In fact we regard it as a dangerous and shocking policy'; but he went on to explain that 'the black people of South Africa are far better off economically than the black people anywhere else in the African continent'; and he insisted that the bank could 'exert a constructive influence on racial conditions in South Africa'. The Chase view of South Africa during the 'sixties was later described in suitably cold-blooded prose by Joel Stern, the President of the Chase Financial Policy in 1976. 'It was a period of exceptional growth in a highly industrialised and exceptionally productive and efficient society in the utilisation of physical and human resources.'*

* Senate Foreign Relations Committee: Subcommittee on African Affairs. Hearings on South Africa, September 6, 1976

But in 1969, when Kissinger was leaving it to corporations to liberalise apartheid, the limitations of that policy were revealed, when the Council for Economic Priorities in New York commissioned a study of how American companies actually behaved in South Africa. One young researcher, Tim Smith of the Council for Christian Social Action, went out to interview executives in twenty businesses in South Africa, armed with letters of introduction from parent companies. He elicited some candid replies. When R J Scott, the chief executive of Ford in South Africa, was asked if he had any non-white friends he replied: 'No, I don't mix with them here, and if I went back to the States, I wouldn't mix with them there either.' What did International Harvester think about the Bantustan policy? 'I agree with it 100 percent,' said their South African managing director James Hatos: 'It is economically and politically sound. I am sympathetic with what the South African government is trying to do. I don't want hundreds of Africans running around in front of my house.' Esso South Africa had provided a memorandum for their visiting executives, prepared by a young South African economist, David Knowles, which faithfully echoed Pretoria propaganda and explained that there would soon be total literacy among Bantu children. The chief executive of Goodyear, John Purcell, explained that American companies must inevitably be 'counter-revolutionary' in their concern to avoid radical political change. Many of the white managers who were interviewed talked confidently about black culture and problems, but none had any black friends. All of them were opposed to Washington's condemnations of apartheid. 'Individually, American businessmen generally support the racial policies of the South African government or a slightly modified form,' said Smith, and he concluded that 'it seems clear that one of the costs of doing business in South Africa is the establishment of a friendly working relationship with the government.'

Few executives were actively trying to mitigate the effects of apartheid. A survey in 1969 of American and Canadian businessmen had shown that 31 percent of them would vote for the government policy if they had the vote. The multinational corporations stressed the importance of following local law: the first of the eight 'Principles of Caltex' was 'to comply in letter and spirit with laws and regulations, and to co-operate with government officials.'* But many executives seemed unaware of how much of the segregation – as in elevators or canteens – was dictated by custom, not law; and few

* Timothy H Smith, *The American Corporation in South Africa: An Analysis*, New York, United Church of Christ, 815 Second Avenue, 1970

exercised any 'sovereignty behind the factory gates'. And these impressions were corroborated by the *Washington Post* correspondent Jim Hoagland who concluded in 1972 that 'American investment has not had a liberalising effect on race relations in South Africa and in fact has probably strengthened the apartheid government's logistical and financial position.'*

Already some American shareholders were beginning to call for their companies to disinvest; and some South African industrialists became worried that the sports boycott could overspill into a business boycott.† The protesters' chief target was the biggest company General Motors, which now had 5,000 employees (40 percent white) in its plant near Port Elizabeth, and which announced in 1970 that it would soon launch the first South-African-built car, the Ranger. General Motors was already under fire for its attitudes to black Americans, and had elected a black director, the Reverend Leon Sullivan, to join the board, who soon became closely involved in South Africa. He was a tall and resonant preacher from a popular Baptist church in Philadelphia, who was influenced by the Moral Rearmament movement: and he knew how to mobilise black and liberal opinion. When the Episcopal Church which owned shares in GM asked it to withdraw from South Africa, it was supported by Sullivan, causing an unprecedented and much-publicised split on the board. Only 1 percent of the stockholders backed up the protesters, but they now had a beachhead.‡ After visiting South Africa Sullivan modified his demands (see page 128) but he still retained his weapon of demanding their withdrawal.

A highly publicised American protest came from inside the booming camera company Polaroid, whose inventive president Edwin Land was also a trustee of the Ford Foundation. In late 1970 two black employees began picketing Polaroid to stop selling cameras or film to South Africa where they were used for the hated passbooks. South Africa provided only 1 percent of Polaroid's revenues; but the company eventually sent four employees out to investigate, who came back proclaiming that 'South Africa alone articulates a policy contrary to everything we stand for'. Polaroid then gave a third of its South African profits for black education, and their agent's black wages went up by 22 percent, but the campaigners were not satisfied and asked for total disengagement. Polaroid claimed they had shown others what could be done. But the South African Institute of Race Relations concluded that the Polaroid

* Hoagland, *op. cit.*, pp. 348, 350
† *Financial Mail*, September 11, 1970
‡ Hoagland, *op. cit.*, p. 352. *Also* Corporate Information Centre, National Council of Churches, New York

experiment had failed to improve the wages and working condition
of blacks in general and reckoned that thirteen out of seventeen
companies which had revealed their wage-rates were paying wages
below the poverty line – including Unilever, AE & CI, African Oxygen
and NASA.*

The American protesters had produced some results. They had
begun to learn how to use the engines of capitalism to challenge
the apartheid system, with shrewd deployment of shareholders'
resolutions. American companies put money into educational funds
and wage increases: by April 1973 the State Department had issued
its own guidelines, recommending wages of at least R100 a month.
But the first hopes that American companies could challenge the
whole apartheid system soon fizzled out. 'American executives
running South African companies began to realise that they must
make more sympathetic public statements to improve their public
relations in the US,' said Tim Smith afterwards, 'but their co-
operation with the South African government remained the same.'†
The movement lacked staying power without major support from
black Americans. 'If the anti-apartheid movement really is to get
anywhere in the US,' Hoagland had concluded in 1972, 'it must
rapidly develop truly concerned, articulate and informed black
leadership.'‡

South Africa continued to lure new American investment with
its dazzling opportunities. As John Blashill, *Time*'s bureau chief in
Africa, wrote in *Fortune* magazine in July 1972:

> The Republic of South Africa has always been regarded by foreign
> investors as a gold mine, one of those rare and refreshing places
> where profits are great and problems small. Capital is not
> threatened by political instability or nationalization. Labor is
> cheap, the market booming, the currency hard and convertible.
> Such are the market's attractions that 292 American corporations
> and subsidiaries have established subsidiaries or affiliates there.
> Their combined direct investment is close to $900 million, and
> their returns on that investment have been romping home at
> something like 19 percent a year, after taxes.§

The American agitation moved to Britain which had four times as
much investment in South Africa. A young reporter on the *Guardian*,

* First *et al.*, *op. cit.*, p. 200
† Interview with author, June 1986
‡ Hoagland, *op. cit.*, p. 359
§ John Blashill, 'The Proper Role of US Corporations in South Africa', *Fortune*,
July 1972, p. 49

Adam Raphael, who was in Washington during the Polaroid furore, toured South Africa (where he had family connections) looking into the wages paid by British companies. He found that most of them were paying less than the Poverty Datum Line (PDL) as reckoned by South African bodies including the Institute of Race Relations.* In March 1973 Raphael produced articles in the *Guardian* revealing that out of a hundred British companies investigated only three – Shell, ICI and Unilever – were paying all their employees above the poverty line. Among the worst offenders were the Illovo sugar estates owned by Tate & Lyle, Wilson Rowntree owned by the Quaker group Rowntree Mackintosh and the cement works at Lichtenberg controlled by Associated Portland Cement. 'The whole apparatus of apartheid,' said Raphael, 'has created a labour market where the only discipline is the employer's conscience.'† The articles soon led to hearings by members of parliament on the Trade and Industry sub-committee of the Expenditure Committee chaired by William Rodgers, who invited chairmen to give evidence. They provided a unique insight into the workings of British companies, many of which had been evidently paying blacks as little as they could get away with. 'We were horrified by what we read,' said Jim Slater after he had seen the *Guardian*'s revelations about the subsidiaries of his own group Slater Walker: 'We had tended to look at our investments in South Africa as an investment and we had not really looked into the problem in great detail.'‡

Rio Tinto-Zinc which controlled the huge Palabora copper mine were paying more than half their workers below the poverty line until they put up wages by 50 percent after Raphael's revelations: yet their chairman Sir Val Duncan (when asked about reinvestment) explained that 'Palabora is in the position of being so profitable that the question of African wages is, in that context, irrelevant.'§ ICI had to admit that 57 percent of the labour force in AECI (joint-owned with Anglo-American), was paid just below or just above the minimum.¶ British Leyland and others still paid many of their workers below the line. Courtaulds quickly doubled wages for some workers and their chairman Lord Kearton explained that 'The tide of publicity has helped us to accelerate along the path on which we were already going . . . we try to push things along, not because we are saints, but because we think we owe it to ourselves.'‖

* *Guardian*, March 12–14, 1973
† Expenditure Committee, Vol. 1, p. 354
‡ *Ibid.*, p. 395
§ *Ibid.*, p. 244
¶ *Ibid.*, p. 308
‖ *Ibid.*, p. 88

The trade association, UKSATA, through its chairman William Luke, explained that 'it would be unwise to have a black African union', that blacks lacked the 'mental capacity' to do many industrial jobs, and that 'there is a tendency for the black African, if you pay him more money, to put in less time.'* (which Unilever firmly contradicted).† 'The tribal Africans have really only been in contract with the Europeans perhaps during this century,' said Donald McCall of Consolidated Goldfields: 'Let us not try and jump too far in seventy or eighty years what has taken us, say, a thousand years to achieve.'‡

'British companies may wish to behave well and many believe they are doing so,' said Adam Raphael in his own evidence, 'but in many cases the wish has yet to be put into practice.' And he ended by quoting Byron's *Don Juan*:

> Alas! How deeply painful is all payment,
> They hate the murderer much less than a claimant.
> Kill a man's family and he may brook it,
> But keep your hand out of his breeches pocket.§

To which the committee's chairman William Rodgers replied by quoting from T S Eliot's *Murder in the Cathedral*:

> The last temptation is the greatest treason
> To do the right deed for the wrong reason.

The industrialists played down any relationship between their high earnings in South Africa and the low wages, which were made possible by the lack of unions and the constraints of apartheid; but as the conservative *Economist* wrote when discussing the high British profits: 'It is impossible to pretend that this above-average rate does not come to a large extent from the very low wages paid in South Africa.'¶ The connection was reassuring to Marxists: 'Apartheid, far from being a doctrine peculiar to Afrikaner needs,' wrote the authors of *The South African Connection* in 1972, who included the communist ex-editor Ruth First, 'is an economic instrument, organically connected with the various sources of capital control in South Africa, and with the operation of international capital in the country.' But it was significant that Courtaulds admitted that they

* *Ibid.*, pp. 1–10
† *Ibid.*, p. 167
‡ *Ibid.*, p. 222
§ *Ibid.*, pp. 359–60
¶ *The Economist*, June 5, 1971

needed prodding by publicity into doing what might well be in their long-term interests anyway. They *were* doing 'the right thing for the wrong reason'; and Lord Kearton of Courtaulds said he had many letters from shareholders 'who would prefer to see lower profits if that would mean better conditions in South Africa.' Unilever emphasised that higher overall black wages would increase the market for their goods; but none seemed anxious to start the process themselves. What was striking about much of the evidence was the short-term view of the companies involved, which was sometimes explained by their expectation that they might not be able to stay there much longer anyway.

The anti-apartheid campaigners, on their side, had taken a surprisingly long time to focus on the wretched wages which were a larger component of black misery. Many of them had been preoccupied with condemning the fundamental system, or demanding total disinvestment, while some did not want to suggest that capitalism could ever be made tolerable. In fact the threat of disinvestment proved the most effective pressure to get companies to improve wages and conditions, by pressing them to justify their presence; while these material improvements did not appear to diminish the black anger against apartheid.

In the United States, the combination of Soweto and Jimmy Carter, who became President six months later, heralded a major change in Washington's policy. Carter himself was committed to fighting apartheid, though he had been slow to support black Americans in the South. At the State Department Cyrus Vance was determined to stiffen the line, supported by a wiry Southerner Richard Moose as assistant secretary for African affairs. Even Walter Mondale, the cautious vice-president, warned Pretoria that they should not 'rely on any illusions that the United States will, in the end, intervene to save South Africa'.

Carter's boldest step was to appoint the thirty-nine-year-old black Congressman and preacher Andrew Young as ambassador to the United Nations, with a special brief on Southern Africa. Young soon identified with black South Africans: he visited Soweto, where he advocated an economic boycott as in the South, and agreed that the Pretoria government was 'illegitimate'. He was convinced that neither politicians nor businessmen in South Africa would change their policies unless they were constantly pushed from outside: 'you always have to keep up the pressure to achieve anything,' he told me. 'I learnt that with civil rights in the South.' But his policies were never as extreme as they sounded – particularly towards business involvement. Like other black Americans he could compare South Africa too readily to the South, and put too much faith in the 'Oppenheimer thesis' – that prosperity would in itself undermine apartheid. He looked to enlightened capitalists as allies, impressed that they were to the left of the government; and he stayed with Harry Oppenheimer in Johannesburg. 'You are meeting one of the most dedicated and brilliant minds', he told the Foreign Policy Association in New York when he introduced Oppenheimer in October 1977, 'one of the most sensitive and humane businessmen anywhere in the world.' Oppenheimer himself thought Young was too impressed by the influence of American companies and Atlanta banks on the Southern whites, and not sufficiently aware of the total difference of South African law and history.* Many blacks were more critical. 'Carter uses Andrew Young's colour as a special passport to the Third World,' said Steve Biko in July 1977. 'But Young has no programme except the furtherance of the American system. That's why he plays tennis in Soweto. Carter is doing more skilfully what Nixon and Ford did: to make the American system work more efficiently.'†

The Carter administration took some important steps away from Pretoria: after the murder of Biko, through the insistence of Andrew Young they voted for the mandatory arms embargo at the UN in 1977; they stopped sales of military equipment in the 'gray areas' and withdrew their naval attaché. Pretoria soon reckoned that their relations with the US were at an all-time low – reaching a new nadir when Donald McHenry, Andrew Young's black deputy, interrupted his negotiations over Namibia in Pretoria to attend Biko's funeral. But Carter also (as the Ford Foundation's Study Commission put it) 'emphasised the positive side of economic relations and enlightened capitalism as a positive force for change within South African society'. But the administration often seemed unaware of how easily capitalists identified themselves with apartheid. Just after Pretoria's ruthless mass arrests in October 1977 the US Chamber of Commerce cheerfully opened a branch in Johannesburg, and the head of its international division boasted that 'commerce could disagree with the wishes of politicians and trade with whomsoever it chose'.‡

But Soweto also provoked a new wave of American indignation against corporations conniving with apartheid, and in September 1976 the Senate sub-committee on African affairs held hearings to investigate them, chaired by Senator Dick Clark of Iowa who was becoming passionately concerned with South Africa, and who soon

* Interview with author, May 3, 1978
† Woods, *op cit.*, p. 100
‡ *South Africa: Time Running Out*; report of the Study Commission on US policy towards Southern Africa, University of California Press, 1981, pp. 360, 362

afterwards flew to South Africa to see Biko to give him American support. General Motors were the Senators' chief target, and their manager of overseas operations, Alex Cunningham, explained how they had constantly tried, within South African law, to modify apartheid provisions at their plant in Port Elizabeth; while the chairman Thomas Murphy had personally asked John Vorster to legislate for equal opportunities. The company believed they would 'continue to be a positive influence for improvement of economic conditions and social well-being of all races there'. But, Clark replied: 'I never met anyone who studied German society, economic politics in the 1930s and 1940s from the time Hitler came into power, who didn't say that the German people were a good deal better off under that system . . . but there is the political aspect, the human aspect . . .' 'We feel we can influence change from within with progressive policies,' said Cunningham, 'whereas, if we are not there, we could do nothing.' But Clark replied that none of the investments had 'brought us closer to what we would all agree is a more just society. Indeed, it seems that during the time of investment it has really gotten worse . . .'*

Clark was still more sceptical about IBM. It did not make computers in South Africa, and had only 1,460 employees there (out of 289,000 world-wide); but contracts with the Pretoria government provided a third of its business in South Africa. IBM's vice-chairman Gilbert Jones had toured Africa earlier that year with his chairman Frank Cary, and Jones told the senators that his company opposed apartheid as 'a concept completely incompatible with the most fundamental principle of IBM – respect for the individual.' But IBM also 'recognised many years ago that our products could be used in ways possibly inimical to individuals and society . . . I must point out that once our equipment has been provided, we do not always know when a customer may change his applications to perform entirely different tasks.' Jones agreed that IBM had once bid to provide computers for the hated black pass-books, and did provide computers for the 'book of life' carried by non-Africans. How is that compatible,' asked Clark, 'with the principle that you have laid down for IBM – respect for the individual?' Jones explained that IBM had to deal with the government if it wanted to stay and 'there is no way that we can apply moral judgment to the South African government or to any other government.'†

Eighteen months later Senator Clark published a critical report

* Hearings before the Subcommittee on African Affairs, September 22, 1976 p. 445
† Hearings, pp. 656–701

on American corporations in South Africa, written by William Raiford, which condemned their 'abysmal performance' in the past and explained that the American economic interest 'has been pivotal in directly assisting the South African government during its worst economic difficulties in the past, and, if permitted, could do so in the future.' He recommended the US government actively to discourage American investment; to stop promoting the flow of capital and credit; and 'to deny tax credits to American corporations that invest or lend to South African government projects, or to companies which did not enforce fair labour practices.'*

American shareholders were also on the warpath again after Soweto: 'There is hardly a shareholders' meeting' said *Fortune* in June 1978, 'at which the chairman doesn't have to face cross-examination and criticism, mainly from church and university groups, pressing them to explain why they are still in South Africa.' Americans still accounted for only 16 percent of total foreign investment compared to 57 percent from the European Community, but they were much more vocal. Leon Sullivan, the black director of General Motors, had by 1977 persuaded a group of twelve American companies – later much enlarged – to sign the six 'Sullivan Principles' which included a commitment to improving black living conditions, training and promotion, and more specifically promised non-segregation in cafeterias, washrooms and workplace; equal and fair employment practices; and equal pay for comparable work. They were not revolutionary, and were soon approved by Pretoria. Many companies were worried that their white employees would resent them; and General Motors themselves did not follow them closely: they removed the signs in their lavatories saying 'EURO-PEANS' and 'NON-EUROPEANS' but replaced them with blue doors for whites and orange for non-whites.† But the principles did something to counterbalance the local pressures towards social apartheid; and the monitoring of the Sullivan rules was much more effective than the similar rules agreed by the European Community, which were widely disregarded.

Soweto also reactivated the campaigns against American banks, forcing many of them to declare themselves more openly against apartheid and to admit some connection between banking and morality. The Chase under Rockefeller were criticised not only by shareholders and depositors, but by some senior executives and directors including Father Theodore Hesburgh, the President of

---

* US Corporate Interests in South Africa. Report to the Committee on Foreign Relations, US Senate, Washington, 1978
† *Fortune*, June 1968

Notre Dame University. In 1977 Rockefeller felt obliged to proclaim a new 'Code of Ethics' which specifically excluded any loans that 'tend to support the apartheid policies of the South African government or reinforce discriminatory business practices'. The Bank of America under Tom Clausen resisted any moral commitment, but eventually in 1979 announced in bankers' neutral prose that 'the consequences of apartheid policy create social unrest that adversely affects the country-risk rating of that nation. Hence the Corporation's lending activities in South Africa are restrained and will continue to be so.' Morgan's were under fire from august bodies including Harvard and Yale which both sold off their Morgan bonds. But the bank was non-committal, insisting that credit did not imply political approval, and that withholding loans could lead to hardship for blacks. The Chemical Bank in New York were vulnerable as bankers to the UN down the street: eventually their chairman, Donald Platten, pronounced that his bank was 'strongly opposed to apartheid, and consequently has a policy of prohibiting any loan transactions with the government of South Africa'.

Citibank was responsible for nearly a quarter of the American bank loans to South Africa and its combative chairman Walter Wriston became the target for protesters who wore buttons saying CITIBANK FINANCES APARTHEID. But Wriston was unrepentant and George Vojta, a Citibank vice-president, told the Senate that 'the rule for all multinational corporations round the world must be "hands off!"' Vojta also claimed that Citibank's presence in South Africa benefitted all its people, and contributed to 'a more pluralistic social system'.* He was quickly contradicted by Tim Smith, now Director of the Interfaith Center, who argued that American firms were promoting the pro-white position, while the gap widened between black and white wages. 'US bank loans subsidise South Africa's military capability,' said Smith, 'and thus are a direct resourcing of machinery of oppression for the black majority.'† Eventually shareholders forced even Citibank to announce that they were no longer lending to the South African government or to state corporations: 'We regard apartheid as having a negative effect on South Africa's economic viability.' But it refused to promise that it would not resume lending to the government if its 'economic viability' improved.

In London Barclays Bank also came under greater fire, and tried to distance themselves with some embarrassment from their South African subsidiary. Soon after Soweto their chief executive in

* Hearings, pp. 530–42
† *Ibid.*, pp. 542–6

Johannesburg, Bob Aldworth, remarked on the difficulties of raising loans and was sharply rebuked by Pretoria: he made amends by buying fifteen million pounds' worth of Defence Bonds which the government had recently launched without much success, and explained that the bank was showing its social responsibility and supporting their staff: 'We do have a large number of our boys called up continually. We stand behind them.' The commitment to the army – from an old Quaker bank – outraged some British shareholders and an uproar broke out at the next annual meeting. The chairman, Sir Anthony Tuke, insisted that the British tax inspectors would not allow him to give instructions to the subsidiary (which was only part-owned), but when pressed he explained: 'I have suggested to the South African board that these bonds will be . . . er . . . should be sold as soon as it is permitted to do so.' Barclays were now increasingly caught between their banking in South Africa and in other black African states, which were protesting that Barclays cease lending to South Africa altogether. Nigeria, thanks to its oil, had become a more important trading partner to Britain than South Africa; and had a network of Barclays branches, 40 percent owned by the London parent. The Nigerian government, under President Obasanjo, warned 'double dealers' that they would have to choose, and by March 1978 they were insisting that Barclays should withdraw from South Africa: when Tuke refused they withdrew their deposits.

The coldest-blooded lenders were the International Monetary Fund in Washington. Just before Soweto, Pretoria had asked them in January 1976 for a loan of ninety-three million dollars and a stand-by agreement to tide over its economic crisis which (as an IMF study reported) had been precipitated by military spending. The representative of black states, Antoine Yameogo, insisted that Pretoria's falling exports were due to their treatment of black workers. But the British representative, Peter Bull, explained that the stand-by arrangement would give Pretoria 'some feeling of international support, which they deserve'; and the loan was agreed. Five months after Soweto, when the gold price was falling further, South Africa asked the IMF for a new loan of $186 million which was granted by the IMF executive board without discussing arms spending or Soweto. During 1976 and 1977 the IMF had lent South Africa a total of $571 million, more than to all the rest of Africa and more than to any single country except Britain and Mexico. And the IMF loans almost exactly corresponded to the increase in South Africa's arms spending.*

* James Morrell and David Gisselquist, *How the IMF slipped $464 millions to South Africa*, Washington, Center for International Policy, January 1978.

But in commercial banking, if not in the IMF, moral objections were already having some effect in restricting loans to South Africa. Bankers would continue to insist that they were concerned only with profitability and credit-worthiness; and they took a short-term view that the Pretoria government could suppress political revolt for some years to come. But they were also concerned – at least in America – not to lose important customers, who were offended by their complacency towards apartheid. It was ironic that the bankers needed these 'moralising critics' as they like to call them, to tell them where in fact their own long-term commercial interests lay – in disengaging themselves from a dangerous commitment.

9

Botha's Businessmen

If ever a historical tide of change was determined by necessity, it is
the move towards full political participation by blacks here in South
Africa ... The notion that the West's economic interests in South
Africa give us a stake in the status quo is therefore old fashioned and
dangerously misleading.

Edward Heath, Johannesburg, 1981

The arrival of P W Botha as prime minister in September 1978
came as an immediate relief to businessmen both in South Africa
and abroad. It had been preceded by the spectacular 'Muldergate'
scandal, in which the cabinet minister Connie Mulder had conspired
with the head of the secret service, General van den Bergh, and the
information director, Eschel Rhoodie, secretly to buy media and
influence and spread propaganda round the world, leaving a web
of corruption and blunders. The prime minister John Vorster was
disgraced, and Botha emerged as the clean candidate in contrast to
his tainted rival Mulder.

But as a reformer Botha seemed in many ways less promising
than his predecessor. Like Vorster he had been steeped in Afrikaner
nationalism from his childhood. He had been brought up on his
father's farm in the Orange Free State, still in the shadow of the
Boer War. After studying law he became an organiser for the
National party, an accomplished heckler and the leader of gangs to
break up the pro-British United Party. For part of the Second
World War, like Vorster, he joined the pro-Nazi Ossewa Brandwag.
When the nationalists won in 1948 he became an MP, and loyally
supported every step in the steady build-up of apartheid laws and
repression. He was never much involved in the business world, and
his roots were rural. Dr Verwoerd made him a cabinet minister,
and by 1966 he had reached the key post of minister of defence,
where he stayed for twelve years, building up the military machine
and founding the state armaments company Armscor which made
South Africa more self-sufficient. Defence gave him a secure power-
base and the friendship of the generals including Magnus Malan
who later became his defence minister. As minister of defence he
was fortified against most international criticism, and he developed

his populist rhetoric – with constant finger-wagging, swaying and leering – which was unappealing to non-Afrikaners. 'If he were a woman,' said Helen Suzman, 'he would ride into parliament on a broomstick.'

But defence helped to broaden some of his attitudes: he promoted English-speaking generals and admirals, and even promoted some blacks to positions above whites. In his quieter moments he did have some worries about the clash of nationalisms and the humiliation of the blacks – and particularly the coloureds. 'The people I belong to,' he told Samora Machel the President of Mozambique in March 1984, 'know the feeling of powerlessness in the face of an external force greater than ours.' He was certainly more thoughtful than his predecessor. 'He remains a political enigma; a mixture of sentimentality and intolerance . . .' wrote his liberal parliamentary opponent Van Zyl Slabbert. 'His political instinct told him that to pursue the old road would deepen the crisis of government, even if he did not know where the new road was or where it led. He initiated the search we are involved in and he is going to receive very little gratitude from the hard right or left for it.'*

Other Afrikaner leaders, facing the black danger and the 'total onslaught', were also modifying their old hostility to the English-speakers; and the mythology of the Boer War was beginning to fade. 'Afrikaner interests now required the co-operation of English-speaking white South Africans,' wrote the historian Leonard Thompson, 'and the sympathy and governments of America and Europe, including the United Kingdom.'† Botha wanted to produce a new image, particularly to businessmen, whom he met in November 1979 at a much publicised conference at the Carlton Centre in Johannesburg. Most of the tycoons were relieved, after Vorster's resentment of any business advice, to find Botha listening apparently intently. The prime minister outlined his proposals for a 'constellation of states', a plan which Oppenheimer said had 'imagination and charm'; but the businessmen were too flattered to utter much criticism. It would be an exaggeration to compare Botha's meeting with Hitler's first meeting with German businessmen as Chancellor in February 1933, when he rallied them behind him with promises to fight the Red Terror and to build up the army. But the South African businessmen proved almost as easy to manipulate. 'If the Carlton meeting is an indication of how organised business will deal with government in future when hard bargains need to be struck,' warned the *Financial Mail*, 'it is clear the

---

* Frederik Van Zyl Slabbert, *op. cit.*, p. 147
† Thompson, *op. cit.*, p. 212

prime minister has managed to stack the odds in his favour.'* Many
businessmen later looked back at the meeting with recriminations.
'What we rather naïve businessmen failed to realise was that we
were, in fact, being "set up",' said John Wilson of Shell seven years
later: 'that those conferences were nothing more than a forum for
the propagation of government policies.' By the time of the next
meeting in Cape Town two years later many tycoons were already
disillusioned: 'Perhaps the best lesson the business leaders learnt
was that government has no plans to modernise apartheid,' said
the *Financial Mail*. '. . . it would be naïve to believe that, in the
South African context, economic power determines political power.
The history of Afrikaner nationalism and the modern history of
black nationalism refute this theory.'†

Botha and his government did give way to businessmen on one
critical area: on recognising black labour unions. The outbreaks of
illegal strikes from the early 'seventies had strengthened the case
made by many industrialists that it was safer to deal with black
grievances inside a union than outside. Tony Bloom of the Premier
Group had called for recognising black unions in 1974, and Anglo-
American followed. 'After 1979 I was sure the right thing for the
mining houses was to help the blacks to build up a powerful trades
union leadership,' recalled Gavin Relly, soon to become chairman
of Anglo. 'It was an illusion for the mines to think that the old
paternalistic process could continue to work. And the self-interest
of the unions may not make them the natural bed-fellows of the
black political leaders.'‡ 'I was not so foolish to suppose that this
would make the life of industrialists like me easier,' Oppenheimer
recollected later, 'but I still thought that it was much better to have
this than to sit on the safety valve.'§

In 1979 a commission on industrial relations, which had been
appointed by Vorster two years before, chaired by Professor Nic
Wiehahn, reported that to recognise black unions would provide 'a
more structured and orderly situation' and would allow official
surveillance and 'responsible behaviour'. Wiehahn recommended
that job reservation in industry should be abolished and that (as in
the army) industry might work under blacks. He also paid a
significant tribute to foreign business pressure: 'The presence of
subsidiaries of multinational enterprises within a country's borders
creates a conduit through which strong influences and pressure can
be exerted on that country's policies and practices.' The Botha

* *Financial Mail*, Johannesburg, November 30, 1979
† *Ibid.*, November 20, 1981
‡ Interview with author, May 6, 1986
§ Interview with ABC TV, March 20, 1985

government faced a storm of protests over the Wiehahn report, particularly from the white unions. 'It was the greatest treachery against the white employees of South Africa since 1922,' said the secretary of the (white) Mineworkers Union. But it was supported by most industrialists, including the Afrikaanese Handelsinstituut which now saw black unions as 'a new safety valve so that we do not land in the minefield without warning.' After much wrangling and many exemptions, Botha was persuaded that legal unions could be effectively controlled, and could defuse political agitation; and the government accepted most of the recommendations. It was a much more radical reform than most of its authors realised. 'Not only did the unions gain unprecedented power in the workplace,' wrote the Labour correspondent Steven Friedman looking back on it afterwards, 'but they soon began to use it to press for political rights . . . The reform achieved the opposite to the one its architects intended – and if they were surprised, so too were the commentators, including this one, who believed the reforms were the product of a sophisticated plan which would bolster white control within the factories and outside them.'*

The new leaders of black unions still faced many obstacles. The union movement was split, between the white-based group TUCSA which worked closely with management and now formed its parallel black unions, and the federation of independent black unions FOSATU which saw the TUCSA unions as stooges of the managers; while the old ANC unions of SACTU still had a shadowy existence. The black unions still had to be registered, and were strictly forbidden from engaging in politics. In November 1979 black Ford workers went on strike after one of their colleagues, Thozamile Botha, was dismissed for belonging to a militant community group in Port Elizabeth, PEBCO. The dispute was settled after three months, but the government detained Botha and three of his colleagues without trial. When black municipal workers in Johannesburg struck because their union was not recognised, the government deported some workers back to the Bantustans and detained others, to encourage the rest back to work. But many black unions, by providing organisation and communication, were soon helping to politicise the workers; and the political steam among workers was far too strong to be released by this kind of industrial safety valve. As Sam Nolutshungu wrote: 'Even "reform" under such conditions merely highlights to the deprived the enormity of their political disabilities.'†

* *Weekly Mail*, May 30, 1986
† Nolutshungu, *op. cit.*, p. 128

The most spectacular manifestation was in the gold-mines which had so long rejected black unions. The most right-wing mining groups – Gold Fields of South Africa, the only British-owned group, and Gencor controlled by Afrikaners – still refused to recognise black trades unionists. But the others, including Anglo-American and Anglo-Vaal, preferred to deal with organised workers who were now represented by the black National Union of Mineworkers. Its young secretary Cyril Ramaphosa was already thoroughly politicised: as a student at Turfloop university he had been chairman of the local black consciousness organisation SASO: he was detained for a year, rejected from the university, and detained again. He now found himself organising half-a-million black mineworkers and building up 100,000 fee-paying union members in the next four years. He soon realised the political potential: 'You only need to attend our meetings to tell how radical they are. It began as soon as they realised that the union organisation gave them a chance to show their real feelings.'* He knew he was creating a much more disciplined organisation than the political parties, and he never concealed his political interests. 'We have to make a link between economic and political issues,' he said later. 'We all agree that the struggle on the shop floor cannot be separated from the wider political issues.'†

Botha's government could also reassure businessmen by pointing to some progress in providing for a black middle class. By 1980 the blacks had 30 percent of the GNP, compared with 15 percent fifteen years earlier.‡ Already by the 1970 census there were 44,000 black teachers, 28,000 nurses, and 9,700 'working proprietors'; and in 1979 there were 6,800 Africans at university (and another 9,000 doing correspondence courses). It was certainly a long way from 1924, when Z K Matthews had become the first black graduate of a South African university. But the figures were still tiny compared to 118,000 whites at universities of both kinds, and in 1970 there were no black architects or senior engineers in the population of 15 million. And the apartheid system continued to ensure that black professional people could still not be absorbed into any kind of white world: those that did go abroad often returned in a more rebellious mood, while many teachers had been radicalised by the events following Soweto in 1976. Black graduates were still forming the spearhead of radical movements. The hope that the growing

* Telephone interview with author, August 1985
† Interview with Barry Streek, Africa Report, March 1986
‡ Symposium on Current Issues Facing American Corporations in South Africa, New York, Interfaith Center on Corporate Responsibility, September 28, 1981, p. 53

middle class would provide a bourgeois buffer was negated by the segregation which pushed graduates back among their own people.

But many white South African businessmen believed that Botha was bringing in the new era of industrial liberalism which Oppenheimer had so long asked for. Apartheid was no longer a complete obstacle to economic expansion. Blacks could now perform skilled jobs; a few earned wages comparable to whites. Soweto had a few two-storey houses and a handful of black millionaires (in rand), and Botha was much more willing than Vorster to seek out the views of more moderate blacks. He was the first prime minister ever to visit Soweto, arriving by helicopter and talking to some residents. 'We are all South Africans,' he told the Sowetans, 'and we must act in that spirit towards each other.' And his sophisticated economic adviser Simon Brand warned that 'blacks must be allowed to take part fully in the free enterprise system if we want them to accept it, defend it, and make it their own.'

Not only businessmen, but also some persistent overseas critics of apartheid were persuaded. 'South Africa had changed almost beyond recognition,' wrote the influential South African exile Colin Legum having returned to his home country after twenty years. 'The army, I discovered, has become the outstanding institutional model for the kind of multiracial society South Africa could one day become . . . in South Africa's first line of defence, apartheid (as preached) no longer exists.' Legum found that, even though the political system had not altered, the Afrikaner establishment had fundamentally changed its attitudes to apartheid.*

Pretoria was making renewed efforts to reassure businessmen overseas after the embarrassing images of Soweto, Biko and the Muldergate scandals. In November 1979 a delegation of South African businessmen, led by Gerry Muller, the chief executive of the Afrikaner group Nedbank, came to Britain to encourage trade: at a conference at Ditchley Park they explained how rapidly government attitudes were changing, and Simon Brand quietly and convincingly described how the prime minister had a new blueprint, a total strategy for modernising the country, and how the government was becoming much more business-like, less military. The Afrikaners admitted that their reforms had been the result of international pressure, though they still seemed to lack interest in black opinion. 'We will know there's progress,' said the American scholar Sanford Ungar, 'when the blacks tell us.'

British businessmen were glad to forget about Soweto and Biko, and to share the renewed South African optimism, helped on by

* Colin Legum, 'An Enemy Goes Home', *Observer*, April 26, 1981

the revived growth rate and the mounting gold-price. Their trade association UKSATA, with its 300 corporate members, boasted in a new pamphlet in 1979 that South Africa still made up 10 percent of all British direct investment overseas, which together with portfolio investment amounted to about £7 billion; while trade brought in about £2 billion a year. It warned that 'the managerial class must extend far into the black and brown sectors of the population,' and that 'an enormous investment in the human infrastructure of the country is necessary if the South African economy is to grow, and if black advancement is to develop.'

British governments still encouraged investment and trade: even the Labour government before it lost office in 1979. Their ambassador to the UN, Ivor Richard, had insisted that while Britain should disapprove of South Africa's policies 'it should be treated in precisely the same way as any other country with which we have economic relations . . . Gesture politics don't work. It is transparent, intellectually dishonest, and morally specious . . .' But when Mrs Thatcher became prime minister in 1979 she showed a more positive sympathy for white South Africa – one of the few topics on which she was influenced by her husband Denis, with his business friendships. It was true that she was soon very pragmatic in agreeing to negotiations with terrorist leaders from Rhodesia–Zimbabwe, which led to independence under Robert Mugabe; but she never expected Mugabe to win the elections, and she still saw the African National Congress in terms of the terrorists of the IRA or the PLO. It was left to Thatcher's predecessor and rival Edward Heath to try to dissociate British business interests from apartheid, more extremely than Macmillan in his 'wind of change' twenty years earlier. 'Neither in peacetime nor in war', Heath said in Johannesburg in August 1981, 'would the West stand in strategic alliance with South Africa as long as she pursues a system which she considers to be profoundly insulting to the rights of the overwhelming majority of her population . . .'*

The international bankers were also rediscovering South Africa's charms. For two years after Soweto even the Swiss bankers had been wary of lending. Robert Studer, senior vice-president of the Union Bank of Switzerland, had warned that apartheid could lead to revolution, civil war or even open war between West and East. 'The very existence of these incalculable risks,' he told a conference, 'would result in the decline of the flood of foreign capital in the future, or in it drying up completely.† In 1978 the South African

* Speech to conference on international political prospects, Carlton Centre, Johannesburg, August 31, 1981
† Africa Contemporary Record, 1977–8, p. b876

government was exasperated to discover that it was paying interest rates as high as Tanzania's, when it borrowed $12 million from the Bank of America. The next year the genial minister of finance Owen Horwood complained that 'there is not one foreign bank that talks to us that does not say that if they looked at this country from an economic point of view there is no reason why terms and conditions should not be better.'* Swiss and German banks continued to lend at high rates and in 1980 the Deutsche Bank caused a stir by appearing publicly at the top of a 'tombstone' advertisement announcing a loan to South Africa. But most British and American banks had stopped lending to the government or public corporations. In London Anthony Tuke, the chairman of Barclays, came under heavy fire for lending to a new SASOL oil-from-coal plant in 1980: 'I find it difficult to understand why it should be good for countries in the Western world to develop alternative energy sources,' he told an angry shareholder, 'but that it's bad for South Africa to do precisely the same thing.'

But South African businessmen were fostering a more humane image. Harry Oppenheimer made a forceful speech at a bankers' meeting in Mexico in 1978: 'Those who seek to bring about change in South Africa's racial attitudes by cutting us off from the capital markets of the world,' he said, 'should understand clearly that in practice, if not intent, they are aiming at change by violence.'† (It was the dead opposite of the argument of Oliver Tambo, the President of the ANC; that only through foreign pressure by disinvestment could much further violence be avoided.)

By 1980 gold was once again working its unpredictable magic, and had shot up to an all-time high of over $800 an ounce, while the growth rate was back to 8 percent. The South African government tried for the first time since Soweto to raise a major loan – which they presented as being 'socially productive' for the benefit of blacks. 'We did not really need the money,' the finance minister Horwood significantly explained, 'but it is important to fly our flag in the international capital markets.' The South Africans approached their friends in Citibank in New York, who were still feeling exposed. 'I feel that Citibank has borne the brunt really,' their voluble spokesman, Bill Koplowitz, explained, '. . . because we are so vulnerable to public pressure by selling our stock and taking accounts out of our bank.' Since Soweto, Citibank had lent nothing to the South African public sector, but they now (said

* *Euromoney*, June 1979. *See also* Anthony Sampson, *The Money Lenders*, Chapter 11, London, Hodder & Stoughton, 1981
† London *Times*, May 24, 1978

Koplowitz) agreed to lead a syndicated loan of $250 million, for
moral reasons:

> It caused us to re-examine the question of moral content of our
> earnings . . . We made that one loan because it was the right
> thing to do, as well as good business. The houses, the hospital,
> the 26 primary schools and 32 secondary schools, the facilities
> that are going up daily, are impressive.

The Citibank loan caused an uproar among the American churches
and other big shareholders. Harvard University sold $51 million of
Citibank's securities, and many churches stopped buying Citibank
notes. 'Citibank assisted in building South Africa's moral and
financial credibility as well as providing hard cash for apartheid,'
said William Howard, the President of the National Council of
Churches, with unconcealed menace. 'Those banks continuing loans
to the South African government will be met with massive withdrawal of deposits, accounts and divestiture of securities. There will
be a financial price to pay, in the United States, for supporting
apartheid.'* His words were truer than most bankers could have
imagined.

American industrial companies were also again being lured. In
June 1978 *Fortune* magazine had carried an influential report on
'The Case for doing Business in South Africa' by one of its editors
Herman Nickel – a veteran *Time* correspondent with an admiration
for Afrikaners – who was struck by the progress in what *Fortune*
had called 'the only real industrial complex south of Milan'. He
described how average incomes in black households had gone up
by 118 percent in the five years to 1975, whereas white households
had gone up by only 58 percent; how the ratio of black to white
incomes in industry had been narrowing steadily, from 1 to 5.85 in
1970 to 1 to 4.44 in 1976; while the white share in total incomes
had been going down by 1 percent each year, to 63 percent in 1977.
Nickel was confident that the 'Oppenheimer thesis' was being
vindicated, that economic growth – until the recession – had led to
many more good jobs for blacks, while 'the contradictions of the
system were bound to become ever more glaring, even to many of
its Afrikaner supporters.' As for public criticism: 'All the Carter
Administration has managed to achieve with its rhetoric so far has
been to stiffen the will of the forces of resistance, and complicate
the task of black leaders struggling for reform.'
Many American companies could now justify their presence by

* *Symposium*, p. 40

obeying the 'Sullivan Principles', and General Motors was still in the forefront. It was barely profitable in South Africa before 1979, when it injected $24 million into its plant – not (it stressed) to expand production but to improve efficiency and conditions. Roger Smith, who succeeded Murphy as chairman in January 1981, felt a personal commitment to oppose apartheid and back up Leon Sullivan on the board. 'We have the opportunity to be a positive force for change in that government's apartheid policies,' said a spokesman, Bob McCabe in 1981.* General Motors every year earned top marks under the Sullivan code – 'Making Good Progress' – and after its previous embarrassment over orange and blue lavatories it now provided integrated lavatories, dining rooms and lockers. By 1985 it even claimed to have twelve black car dealers.†
But Sullivan kept his options open, insisting: 'My aim is not to keep the American companies there. They can leave. But the companies must become part of the fiber of the liberation movement. If you can use the American companies, like a crowbar, to move a great big rock, you have to.'‡

It was a romantic idea, that companies should become 'part of the fiber of the liberation movement'; but it was far from being reciprocated inside South Africa – where many blacks accused them of encouraging apartheid and helping to build up the military machine. 'Multinational corporations are not yet involved in the business of helping to destroy apartheid,' said Desmond Tutu, later bishop of Johannesburg, in an open letter in September 1981. 'They are making apartheid more comfortable rather than dismantling it.'§ Donald McHenry, the former US ambassador to the UN, concurred: though there may have been some improvement in employees' lives, 'there has been little or no structural change in South Africa'. Ramaphosa of the mineworkers union in Johannesburg later insisted that the Sullivan principles '. . . have had absolutely no effect. None whatsoever'; and he claimed that the American mining company Union Carbide was far worse than the South African company Anglo-American.¶ Ramaphosa was being unfair to the Sullivan rules, which had not only improved black working conditions and wages, but had shown that apartheid could be broken down without industry collapsing. But several American

* *Symposium* p. 2
† Interview with President James McDonald, CTC Reporter, New York UN Centre on Transnational Corporations, Spring 1985
‡ Interview with Lindsey Gruson, *International Herald Tribune*, September 18, 1985
§ *Washington Post*, September 23, 1981
¶ Africa Report, March 1986

companies were still supplying equipment to the South African military or police – including computers for black pass-books – evading an embargo laid down in 1978. 'Most firms have been able to continue sales,' said a confidential cable from the American Embassy (quoted by the columnist Jack Anderson in May 1981), 'by shifting to non-US sources for components.' The American company Control Data had supplied disk-drives to the British ICL, which then supplied computer equipment used by the South African police. General Motors promised not to sell any 'vehicles with US content or technology' to the army or police; but they still sold them trucks and cars: stopping those, said their spokesman McCabe, would reduce GM's capability in the country, and thus prevent it from promoting change.*

This indeed was the nub of Pretoria's bargain: they wanted multinationals for their capital and technology, which they could also use for their military machine. This contradicted any notion of companies 'becoming part of the fiber of the liberation movement'. As the Botha government extended its military forces and its security net, foreign investors were inevitably locked more closely into the defence system. After the ANC had bombed SASOL oil plants the government passed the 'National Key Points Act' which put many industrial installations including oil refineries under special controls with great secrecy; and foreign industrialists found themselves working with government in planning and running their plants, in some cases keeping secrets from their own company headquarters.†

The renewed friendship between Botha and American business gained a new warmth from the arrival of Ronald Reagan in Washington after the cold years of Jimmy Carter. Reagan knew little about South Africa, which he seemed to envisage as a kind of very Deep South on its way to reform through prosperity. He explained in one interview in 1985 how it 'had eliminated the segregation that we once had in our own country – the type of thing when hotels and restaurants and places were segregated – that had all been eliminated. They recognise now interracial marriages and all'.‡ Reagan's ambassador to the United Nations, Jeane Kirkpatrick, was openly sympathetic to the Botha regime and had talks with its military and intelligence leaders; while both the American and British secret services began co-operating with South African intelligence, reversing Carter's policy and giving Pretoria information about the ANC in return for information about Soviet shipping and

---

* *Symposium*, pp. 33, 37
† *The Dilemma of Code Three*, SA Council of Churches, 1981, pp. 5–6
‡ Telephone interview with WSB Radio in Atlanta, August 24, 1985

other movements.* Reagan's first choice as ambassador to Pretoria was Patrick Buchanan, the right-wing polemicist who had written speeches for President Nixon. The eventual choice was Herman Nickel, the *Fortune* editor who had written glowingly about South Africa's prospects, who stuck to his view that its expanding industrial economy was constantly undermining the apartheid system.

A further signal of warmer relations was the appointment of Chester Crocker to be the chief formulator of American policy on South Africa, as assistant secretary of state – an urbane academic, passionately interested in South Africa and married to a white Rhodesian. Crocker was seen by Senator Helms and other conservatives as too liberal on Africa; but he was contemptuous of the 'verbal flagellation' of apartheid by the Carter administration: 'Indignation by itself is not foreign policy,' he explained. When I once asked him if he could really trust the Pretoria government he replied: 'Trust is a matter for lovers or families, not for diplomats. My job is to deal with the real forces in the region.' He called his own policy 'constructive engagement', which chimed well with Reagan's own faith in the free market as an instrument of diplomacy, and which proved not very different from Kissinger's 'tar baby option' ten years earlier. As Crocker described it just before his appointment: 'Our market economies will apply normal political risk criteria in the reading of the South African investment climate, thereby signalling a message of both hope and concern . . . engagement in its economy can be constructive for the majority . . . if there is a "tilt" in such a policy, it is in favour of sustained and orderly change.' But to many blacks inside South Africa it looked like a tilt from black to white; the black paper *City Press* reckoned that in three years from January 1982 Crocker only had formal meetings with fifteen black South Africans – all of them in the US.†

Crocker acclaimed Botha's economic reforms, achieved by 'tightfisted Friedmanites' who had freed the foreign exchange, labour and capital markets: 'The private sector will now be set free to become the engine of job creation and black socio-economic advancement.' He left it open as to whether economic expansion would strengthen the military machine, or create a more liberal climate, but he saw 'a window of opportunity to create such a climate in Southern Africa'; and he suggested that the defence chiefs were themselves 'a lobby of modernising patriots'.‡ And when the Sec-

* Seymour Hersh in the *New York Times*, July 23, 1986
† Johannesburg *City Press*, May 19, 1985. *See also* Sanford Ungar and Peter Vale, 'South Africa: Why Constructive Engagement Failed'. *Foreign Affairs*, Winter 1985–6
‡ Chester A Crocker, 'Strategy for Change', *Foreign Affairs*, Winter 1980–1

retary of State Al Haig was due to meet Botha's foreign minister
Pik Botha in 1981, Crocker wrote a secret briefing explaining the
'. . . possibility for a more positive and reciprocal relationship
between the two countries based upon shared strategic concerns in
South Africa'.*

Crocker, Nickel and Kirkpatrick all encouraged American
companies and bankers with the same hopeful message: that after
the shocks of Soweto, South Africa would be helped by American
capital and trade along the road to democracy; and over the next
years Washington showed few signs of criticising Pretoria. It was a
tragic misreading: for while capital in the long term might bring
reconciliation and peace, in the immediate future it could be easily
manipulated into building up a still more dangerous military system. And the Washington analysis showed little understanding of
the extent of black anger that was simmering behind the white wall.

With all the apparent reforms since Soweto, most blacks now saw
businessmen as closely arrayed on the same side as Afrikaner
politicians and policemen, maintaining white oppression against
them – all the more since their new public cosiness. 'More and
more blacks – especially young blacks – are beginning to identify
apartheid with the capitalist system,' Allister Sparks, the editor of
the *Rand Daily Mail*, warned in September 1979, 'and to see the
struggle to overthrow apartheid in terms of a struggle to overthrow
the capitalist system as a whole.' A survey of migrant labour
conducted by Schlemmer and Moller in 1982 showed that 82
percent thought that business leaders work with and support the
government, 72 percent thought they did not care about blacks,
and 94 percent thought that they ran to the police whenever there
was a dispute. 'Many big businesses in South Africa have, over the
last ten years, moved on to what one can call liberal capitalism,'
commented Hermann Giliomee, professor of political science at
Cape Town, 'which demands a well-paid and secure labour force
rather than badly-paid and repressed workers. But this does not get
these big businesses out of the dock. A vast underclass of migrant
labourers – men turned into atomised strangers in their own land
– will always be a living indictment of the exploitative nature of
capitalism.'†

Businessmen increasingly looked towards new moderate black
leaders; and particularly towards Chief Buthelezi in KwaZulu, who
was now becoming a more independent and unpredictable power
with a strong tribal base. By 1980 his Zulu party Inkatha was

* Washington, TransAfrica News Report, August 1981
† Leape *et al.*, *op. cit.*, p. 151

claiming 350,000 members. Its real democratic following was hard
to analyse, since its leadership virtually corresponded with the
government of KwaZulu which commanded much patronage, and
had its own private army of Zulu 'impis' who could intimidate any
opponents. Buthelezi had very variable relationships with other
black leaders, above all with the ANC: he praised Mandela while
criticising Tambo and his 'mission-in-exile', and publicly opposed
the armed struggle and the policy of disinvestment. The ANC executive agreed to meet Buthelezi secretly in London in 1979 'to explain
the position of our movement and ensure unity of approach to the
main strategic requirements of the struggle'.* But Buthelezi made
the meeting public, explaining that Inkatha and the ANC would
form a united front; after which the ANC faced a storm of criticism
for collaborating with him. By the following year, as the ANC stepped
up sabotage and encouraged schools boycotts, the deadlock between
Buthelezi and Tambo had hardened further.

Many business leaders inside and outside South Africa were
beginning to see Buthelezi as an attractive 'third force' who was
opposed to violence and encouraging to free enterprise. He supported the 'constructive engagement' of foreign companies, while
concerned that there should be more jobs in rural areas and that
'economic progress of blacks in South Africa should not be measured
by the performance of a few dozen large multinationals'.† He was
a favourite guest of the South African Foundation; he was supported
by the Institute of Race Relations; and he was befriended by British
and American corporations, including Barclays Bank and Mobil.
Above all, he was supported by Anglo-American and Harry Oppenheimer, who invited him to his seventieth birthday party. 'No
one, the ANC included, has done more to halt the ideological thrust
of apartheid than Buthelezi,' said Gavin Relly of Anglo-American
later. 'Because he has rejected violence as an instrument to bring
about national change, he naturally stands in a better light for
many than those who do not. It is easy today to forget that he was
the only black leader with an authentic power base to have faced
the heat, a long time ago, of a government still determined to enforce
apartheid . . . You can't expect us to run away from the single black
leader who says exactly what we think.'‡

While none of the ANC leaders could be quoted, Buthelezi was
the most publicised black leader in South Africa. He had his
own public relations team of white ex-journalists, including an

* *Sechaba*, December 1985. *See also* Time Running Out, p. 196
† Memo to Leon Sullivan, September 1980. *See* Kane-Berman in Leape *et al.*,
op cit., p. 36
‡ Interviews with author, May 1986

'Information Centre on South Africa' in Amsterdam, which was far more professional than the ANC's organisation: his long speeches were handed out to the press before being delivered. He could switch quickly from demagogic speeches to Zulu crowds in tribal costume to friendly and intimate discussions in a dark suit with Western businessmen. The more the ANC escalated their violence, the more attractive Buthelezi looked to businessmen – and even to Afrikaner politicians.

When Buthelezi first met Botha just after he became prime minister he was impressed that 'unlike his predecessor, at least this man was a human being'. Botha told Buthelezi that the whites must either adapt or die, and that as a Christian he would work for people of all races; and Buthelezi decided to give him a chance. Botha visited KwaZulu in August 1979 and invited Buthelezi to Cape Town six months later, together with the heads of the other homelands; but Botha, true to his ethnic theories, would only see them one by one; when Buthelezi's time came he wanted to make it public, lest his people would accuse him of negotiating secretly: Botha (according to Buthelezi) lost his temper, and for the next four-and-a-half years they did not meet.*

Buthelezi went his own way, developing his own links with businessmen and politicians in Natal. In 1980 he appointed a commission – whose members included Chris Saunders, chairman of the important Tongaat Group – to discuss how KwaZulu could work more closely with the whites in Natal. The 'Natal option' was beginning to take shape, which Saunders and other local industrialists began to see as a way of having harmonious relations with blacks without being dominated by a future black majority. Harry Oppenheimer persuaded Buthelezi to extend his commission to consider black rights in central government. The commission's report published in 1982 concluded that all the racial groups in Natal – including whites, Indians, coloureds and blacks – could accept multiracial governments in the province. 'Through the involvement of some of the leading corporations and business organisations in South Africa,' wrote John Kane-Berman of the Institute of Race Relations who was close to Buthelezi, 'it elevated "constructive engagement" to new heights. It took engagement beyond the conventional areas of industrial relations and wage levels into the realms of economic planning and development, social policy, urbanisation, and, of course, politics.'†

But the armed struggle was beginning to become more deadly on

* Interview with Hugh Murray, *Leadership*, December 1985
† Leape *et al.*, *op. cit.*, p. 37

both sides, with reprisals and counter-reprisals. Umkhonto, the military wing of the ANC, was by 1981 launching more effective raids, attacking the oil-from-coal plant at Sasolburg, the Koeberg nuclear power station and the defence headquarters at Voortrekker-hoogte. After the ANC representative in Zimbabwe was murdered in 1981, the ANC retaliated by exploding a bomb a few days later in the centre of Port Elizabeth. By 1982 the ANC's raids constituted, according to the historian Tom Lodge 'the most sustained violent rebellion in South African history and all the indications are that it will develop into a full-scale revolutionary war'.* (The ANC welcomed Lodge's assessment while complaining that 'he has not yet grasped and imbibed the spirit of the times'.)†

Pretoria's counter-attacks were fiercer. In August 1982, Ruth First, the veteran communist supporter of the ANC, was killed by a letter-bomb in Maputo where she worked in a study-centre. Her husband Joe Slovo, a key military organiser for the ANC, claimed that she was murdered because she was obstructing Pretoria's new plans to make bargains with surrounding states including Mozambique.‡ The South African defence forces wanted to eradicate the ANC bases in the border countries. In 1981 they raided the ANC offices in Maputo, Mozambique, killing thirteen people; the next year they raided Maseru in Lesotho, killing forty-two. In Lusaka, Oliver Tambo decided that 'something must be done about this succession of massacres' and in May 1983 a car-bomb exploded outside the air force headquarters in Pretoria, killing nineteen people and injuring two hundred, most of them civilians. In his jail in Cape Town, Nelson Mandela heard about it and regretted that people had been killed: 'We don't believe in assassinations,' he said. Tambo later explained: 'I can quite understand why he would regret it. It was a military target, but the press highlighted the civilian casualties . . . He was expressing the horror we ourselves used to have about hurting civilians.'§

Pretoria's forces remained far greater than anything the ANC could mount, including armies of informers. In 1982 the head of security, General Coetzee, told Joseph Lelyveld of the *New York Times* that the ANC was crippled by the risk of informers inside South Africa: 'I have them all the way to Moscow.' Tambo seemed to concur. 'He was right . . .' he told Lelyveld. 'They've been giving us a rough time, making us work very hard. At one time there was

* Lodge, *op. cit.*, pp. 339–40
† Francis Meli in *Sechaba*, February 1984
‡ *Sechaba*, February 1985
§ Interview with author, July 1985. *See also* Benson, *op. cit.*, pp. 222–3; Interview with Lord Bethel, *The Mail on Sunday*, London, January 27, 1985

a group of ten, and only one of them was genuine . . .'* The chief
of police Mike Geldenhuys seemed equally confident. 'I will only
begin to worry about the ANC', he told an American diplomat, 'when
we can't identify from our files every one of their guerillas when we
catch them: from their fingerprints we can trace exactly where
they've been.'

Oliver Tambo, in his base in Zambia, remained an improbable
terrorist leader. 'He seems far too gentle to head the revolutionary
African National Congress,' as Andrew Young described him. 'His
tone is too calm and reasoned; an almost casual objectivity pervades
his spirit. His eyes glow with warmth and affection . . .'† He still
seemed more like a monk manqué than a militant leader, with none
of the fiery style of Buthelezi. His wife Adelaide, a formidable
hospital sister, lived in London with his family, and their daughter
married an English banker in St Paul's Cathedral. The ANC had
offices in London, in a shabby house in Pentonville: the British
government gave it some protection, but no recognition. Most of
the London support for the ANC came from the Anti-Apartheid
Movement and the International Defence and Aid Fund (IDAF) set
up by Canon Collins, which both included a large intake of South
African exiles.

Yet the ANC was never as ineffectual as it looked. Tambo always
insisted that it must have its 'four pillars' – the underground
structure, the united mass action, the armed offensive and the
international pressure.‡ He still looked to world opinion as the
means of avoiding a bloodbath, and the ANC developed an increasingly sophisticated diplomatic approach, with the help of its chief
of publicity Thabo Mbeki (the son of the jailed leader Govan
Mbeki) who had been educated at Sussex University, and Johnny
Makatini, its representative in the US. Tambo and Mbeki travelled in
tandem, seeking support from the West, particularly from America.
Tambo put little faith in Washington's policy: 'Under the US policy
of "constructive engagement",' he said in 1983, 'there has been an
increase in US investments, loans and financing of apartheid; new
movements of military and nuclear co-operation with the racist
regime have been opened up.'§ But by 1981 he was beginning to
gain some support both from black American movements and from
some business interests who were beginning to look to a black future
(*see* Chapter 11).

And within South Africa the traditions of the ANC had survived

* Joseph Lelyveld, *op. cit.*, pp. 331–2
† African–American Institute, New York, Africa Report, March–April 1986
‡ *Sechaba*, March 1984
§ *Sechaba*, October 1983

the battering of twenty years of banning and suppression far more effectively than either the military or the business leaders had realised. Mandela had been in jail for fourteen years when Botha became prime minister in 1978, but his name was more famous than ever, proclaimed in chants and graffiti. Two years later the Soweto paper *The Post* launched a new 'Release Mandela' campaign. The ANC was still a baffling mixture of purpose and muddle, radicalism and conservatism, Christianity and communism; but it remained the chief forum for the aspirations of the blacks.

10

Slamming the Black Door

The most perilous moment for a bad government is when it seeks to mend its ways. Only consummate statecraft can enable a king to save his throne when after a long spell of oppressive rule he sets to improving the lot of his subjects.

De Tocqueville, *Democracy in America*, 1840, Part 3, Chapter 4, p. 196

It has become something of a cliche to say that whenever a country experiences a period of reform there is bound to be uncertainty.

P W Botha, *Wall Street Journal*, May 15, 1986

It was when Botha put forward his new constitution in 1983 that he provided businessmen with their most difficult and decisive choice. Determined to co-opt some other racial groups into the parliamentary system, he had tested his strength with a general election, which gave broader white support to his National Party. The liberal PFP had increased its seats and the right-wing HNP – still led by Jaap Marais – had gained votes, while the following year eighteen more right-wing MPs seceded from the National Party to form another right-wing group, the Conservative Party led by the Transvaal leader Andreas Treurnicht. But Botha gained support at the election from many English-speakers including businessmen, and retained a commanding majority.

Botha could thus put all his energies behind major constitutional changes; and in 1983 he proposed separate parliamentary assemblies for eighty-five coloured representatives and forty-five Asians on top of the existing 178 members of the white parliament. Each chamber would be responsible for its people's 'own affairs' – education, welfare, housing, local government – while all the three chambers would separately vote on finance, foreign policy and defence. An electoral college drawn from the three chambers – with whites in an overall majority – would choose an executive president. The Africans, the overwhelming majority of the population, were firmly shut out. To many Afrikaners it seemed rational to include the coloureds, predominantly Afrikaans-speaking and descended from Afrikaners, while keeping out Africans whom, they claimed, had different ethnic roots and their own homelands to vote in. But most Indians and coloureds opposed the new constitution, and for Africans it was the greatest provocation, to introduce reforms which gave concessions to others but took no notice of them.

Botha got his constitution through the white parliament and then submitted it to a referendum of whites, preceded by a passionate two months' debate. It was an awkward choice for the more far-sighted business leaders: they were worried about excluding the blacks, but more worried about undermining Botha's reforming leadership and reducing overseas confidence. 'It is all too likely that "no" would be an act of despair that would lead to the fall of P W Botha, if not of his government,' wrote the *Financial Mail*, 'the reduction of even our tentative reform process to stasis and a freezing of our international links from cool to frigid.' A few business leaders lobbied against the constitution, including Harry Oppenheimer and his ex-son-in-law Gordon Waddell, Clive Menell, the vice-chairman of Anglo-Vaal, and Tony Bloom, the chairman of the Premier Group. Oppenheimer himself gave a lunch for Van Zyl Slabbert, the leader of the PFP liberal party who was campaigning against the constitution because it excluded blacks, to try to persuade businessmen to vote No: 'Almost without exception they agreed with my reasons for rejecting the new constitution,' said Slabbert, 'but at the same time it was clear to me that most of them were going to support the Yes vote.'

For Oppenheimer, who had retired from the chairmanship of Anglo after twenty-five years in December 1983, it seemed a sad conclusion. He believed that the central issue was bound to be the black majority: Botha's constitution, he thought, might have been workable thirty years earlier – just when the government abolished the coloured vote – but not in the 'eighties. He was not entirely critical of the government and thought the homelands policy was now irreversible. But he was convinced that the blacks should have far greater mobility and freedom, and he was proud of his political role as an industrialist. 'We have produced the circumstances which have caused this great black population to accumulate in the towns', he told the London *Financial Times*, 'and where there simply aren't enough white people to do the jobs.'* But he had never fully faced up to the political consequences of that movement.

In the referendum the Yes lobby was much more powerful, assisted by a convincing advertising campaign mounted by Saatchi and Saatchi. A group of business leaders – including the local chairman of Rio Tinto Alastair Macmillan, the former chairman of

* Interview with J D F Jones, *Financial Times*, January 31, 1983

Goldfields Adriaan Louw and the chairman of Nedbank, Frans
Cronje – set up a Reform Fund to persuade others, on the grounds
that a No would discourage foreign investment. Influential businessmen – including Gavin Relly who succeeded Oppenheimer, Raymond Ackerman of Pick 'n Pay and Raymond Parsons, the head of
the Associated Chambers of Commerce (Assocom) – publicly said
Yes. And several multinationals welcomed Botha's proposal as far
as it went. 'It is a step in the right direction,' said Michael Peacock
of ICI. 'It could be a tentative step in the direction the country must
go,' said General Motors. 'It is a move to reform which will increase
confidence abroad,' said the Swiss Ciba-Geigy, 'provided it is
followed by real change.'*

   In the context of purely white politics the Constitution could
appear as the bold beginning of a new road. As Henry Kissinger
explained, playing devil's advocate over breakfast to Slabbert, it
showed 'how a dominant minority intent on maintaining control
could manipulate patronage by co-opting clients to assist it'.† Many
foreign diplomats were hopeful, and both the British ambassador,
Ewen Fergusson and the American Ambassador, Herman Nickel –
to Slabbert's chagrin – welcomed it as a positive step. Two major
English-language newspapers, the *Sunday Times* and the *Financial
Mail*, condemned the constitution but advised their readers to vote
Yes. But to the blacks that Yes was the last straw, the final
provocation to revolt; and a few white liberals gave clear warnings.
It was 'a step backward in terms of evolutionary change and
stability,' said John Kane-Berman of the Institute of Race Relations.
'It made absolutely no sense,' said Slabbert, 'if you accepted that
the legitimacy of reform also depended on the acceptance of the
constitution by a significant number of blacks, deliberately to exclude them from the constitution itself.'

   The referendum was hailed as a triumph for Botha: of the 76
percent of the white electorate who voted, 66.3 percent said Yes,
33.2 percent said No. Botha was soon installed with his new title of
State President, presiding over whites, Indians and coloureds – but
not blacks. For them, he set up a seven-member committee to
discuss their future in the cities. Most businessmen who had opposed
the constitution now thought they must defend it abroad. 'It is quite
wrong to think of the new constitution as a sham, or as a device to
entrench apartheid in a new form,' Oppenheimer said in New York
in October, 'even though the division of parliament into separate
racially constituted chambers is a clumsy device which reflects the

* *Financial Mail*, November 11, 1985
† Slabbert, *op. cit.*. pp. 113–14

prejudices of the past.'* But blacks saw it as much worse than a
sham: it denied them any hope of a political role, just when they
were being allowed an industrial role through trades unions. It
proved the decisive watershed in alienating a new black generation,
and in provoking a far more serious confrontation which threatened
to damage business interests irreparably.

Western governments continued to see Botha's constitution as
part of a new era of peaceful development and stability; and the
referendum had been followed in March 1984 by a striking diplomatic achievement. The president of Mozambique, Samora Machel,
who had taken over his country nine years earlier with such high
hopes from young black radicals, had seen his country devastated
by a combination of economic disasters and sabotage by guerillas
backed by Pretoria; and he had to plead to Washington for help.
Chester Crocker and his deputy Frank Wisner secretly pressed
Botha to reach a diplomatic detente: the South African generals
wanted to crush Machel, while the security service wanted to make
a deal with him, to eject the ANC guerillas from Mozambique. The
Americans could exploit the split, and in March 1984 Botha signed
an agreement at Nkomati on the Mozambique border with Machel,
in which both sides undertook to prevent guerilla incursions. The
small figure of Machel in military uniform looked up at Botha's big
smiling head in front of the television cameras, the symbol of
successful white paternalism. It seemed to many Western observers
and businessmen that the 'Nkomati Accord' was the beginning of
a new recognition of Pretoria's true power. 'For two decades,' said
The Economist on March 24, 'the politics of the region have been
distorted by fanciful predictions of continued black revolution.'

For Botha, the accord with Machel opened the way to a new
detente with the West, and two months later he made a tour of nine
Western European countries, beginning with Britain – the first visit
by a South African head of government since Verwoerd was forced
out of the Commonwealth twenty-three years before – where he met
Margaret Thatcher (while her husband Denis watched rugby on
television with Botha's security men).† The British press were told
that Thatcher gave Botha a dressing down and she explained later
that she told him that the forced removal of blacks was 'totally and
utterly and particularly repugnant to us';‡ while the South Africans
were told the talks were 'fruitful, extremely frank but not acrimonious': either way it was the beginning of a candid relationship

---

* Speech to Foreign Policy Association, New York, October 11, 1984
† Graham Leach, *South Africa*, London, Routledge, 1986, p. 59
‡ Interview with Hugo Young, *Guardian*, July 1986

through correspondence. Botha complained to Thatcher about the ANC office in London, which he insisted was master-minding terrorist attacks, and he pressed his argument through Europe that the ANC was a communist tool with no broad following inside South Africa.

Certainly the ANC saw the Nkomati Accord as an unexpected blow which had, as they admitted, 'surprised the progressive world'. They had been deprived of an important base for guerilla activity, which had been indispensable for Mugabe's Zanu army in attacking white Rhodesia. Yet the setback had its compensations, for the ANC was now compelled to think more seriously about its internal activity. 'Our principal task,' said the secretary-general Alfred Nzo just after the accord, 'is, and must be, to intensify our political and military offensive inside South Africa.'* Botha's own preoccupation with military power and the 'total onslaught' of communist forces distracted the attention of both government and businessmen from the more serious danger of a fundamental black revolt inside the country; while the provocation of the new constitution provided the ANC with many new supporters. 'Its diplomatic defeat at Nkomati,' as Adam and Moodley put it, 'turned into a psychological victory at home.'†

Botha returned to Pretoria with a new authority among whites as the architect of a new detente with Europe; and his political triumphs were beginning to reassure investors and bankers after some lean years. On top of the world recession South Africa had suffered two years of serious drought which had cut down the maize crop; exports had declined and the gold-price had sunk back again, to below $400 in early 1984. But the basic potential of the economy still impressed bankers, and it looked more attractive again in the light of Botha's promised political stability and apparently sound financial management which was in welcome contrast to the rest of Africa. The short term opportunities for capital soon won over the longer term dangers, as South Africa began to look like a golden boy of free enterprise in the continent.

The finance minister Owen Horwood, a chubby figure who enjoyed literary quotations, had been in office since 1975; and in 1981 the Reserve Bank in Pretoria acquired a new governor Gerhard de Kock, a donnish economist, the son of a previous governor, who had impressed Western bankers at the IMF – particularly Americans. He believed firmly in freeing markets and the benign consequences of economic expansion: 'Economic forces shape political history,'

---

* *Sechaba*, May 1984
† Adam & Moodley, *op. cit.*, p. 250

he said later. 'I think Indians, coloureds and blacks will come into the cabinet because the economy needs them. Like in the southern US, economic advance will lead to political advance.'* De Kock had already chaired a commission on monetary policy which had recommended liberalising the financial markets, and his free-market theories fitted well with Botha's own promises to businessmen, and with the prevailing mood in New York and London. Bernard Simon welcomed de Kock's arrival in *The Banker* magazine in May 1982:

> A new era is bursting on South Africa's banks, transforming them from an over-protected, over-controlled and downright stodgy sector of the economy to one more competitive and innovative than most others in a country not renowned for its free markets . . . South Africa is fortunate that its present appetite for foreign loans has coincided with a period of relative political stability at home and turmoil in some other countries far more heavily in debt to the banks. Pretoria is on good terms with foreign bankers. It has never defaulted on a foreign loan, nor has it asked for a renegotiation of debt repayments . . . Nonetheless, South Africa's uncertain political future and unrelenting pressure on many banks not to help maintain minority rule hamper Pretoria's credit rating.†

Faced with the declining exports de Kock and his deputy Chris Stahls actively encouraged South African corporations to borrow abroad, where dollar interest-rates were far lower than the local rates: 'We replaced lost real income with short-term finance,' said Stahls.‡ Most American and British banks were prepared to lend to public corporations, if not to the government, and as South Africa looked politically less risky again the extra interest-rate or 'spread' on its loans began to come down. The biggest borrower was the state-owned electricity company Escom – the symbol of South Africa's industrial expectations – which now planned to triple its generating capacity by the end of the century; and Escom's contracts for power-stations aroused frenzied competition from overseas bidders in spite of the political risks.§ The power-stations also required big loans which reached a new peak in 1984 when Escom raised a loan of $50 million for three years at a spread of only ⅝ percent above the standard interest-rate Libor. 'The political premium has disappeared,' said Escom's financial manager, Len te Groen, 'but

* *Euromoney*, December 1985, p. 67
† *The Banker*, London, May 1982
‡ *Euromoney*, June 1984. Supplement on 'South Africa – Land of Change', p. 68
§ Leape *et al.*, *Business in the Shadow of Apartheid*, Lexington Books, 1985, p. 5

there is still an economic risk in a country that is heavily dependent
on exports of one product – even if that does happen to be gold.'
Owen Horwood still complained that the spreads were too high.
'The banks tell us, without exception, that if they were to look at it
simply on an economic and financial basis, we would be right
among the top. But then they say: 'How do we assess the political
factor?' We can't.'*

By the summer of 1984 South Africa was once again a favourite
of international bankers, and their magazine *Euromoney* published a
glowing special report with no political clouds on the horizon. The
dual exchange rate designed to protect the currency had been
abolished the previous year. Of the two dominant banks, Barclays'
profits were up by 24 percent in 1983 over the previous year, while
Standard's went up by 47 percent; and they were both bringing
funds into the country. 'The fact that they are not seen on a
so-called tombstone does not mean that they are not responsible for
channelling a lot of money into the country, and I dare say out as
well,' said Owen Horwood. The third runner, Nedbank, was growing fastest of all: it liked to compare itself to Morgan's and in
1983 opened a branch in New York. 'I want Nedbank to be an
international bank,' said its chief executive Rob Abrahamsen,
'which happens to have its headquarters in Johannesburg.'† It was
a heady atmosphere for dynamic South African financiers who felt
they were opening up to the world; and there were few warnings
that money could flow out much faster than it flowed in.

Yet there were already signs that the new constitution had
triggered off a wave of fury among the blacks, with a new leadership.
The leaders could not come from the old political parties which
were banned or exiled; they could only emerge from less obviously
political organisations – from the new trades unions, from sports
or social bodies, and perhaps most important from the churches
which were now forced into politics as never before, and which
threw up two spokesmen whose voices could carry round the
world.

The most surprising of them, Allan Boesak, had emerged from the
Cape coloured people: an intellectual theologian with a high-pitched
voice who belonged to the Dutch Reformed Mission Church, the
coloureds' offshoot of the Calvinist Afrikaner church. Boesak had
been reluctantly involved in politics: after seeing his own suburb
bulldozed to conform to the Group Areas Act he had decided in the
early 'sixties that he could not reconcile apartheid with Christ's

* *Euromoney, ibid.*, p. 19
† *Euromoney*, June 1984

teaching; but on the advice of another dissident Afrikaner theologian, Beyers Naude, he stayed within his church, seeing it as a potential agent for liberation rather than oppression. He was so successful that by 1977, as President of the world's Reformed Churches meeting in Ottawa, he had apartheid denounced as a heresy. He became increasingly politically involved, grappling with the problem of violence and deciding that: 'it is irresponsible for me to tell people to protest non-violently if I know that the response will be violent'. The proposed new constitution outraged him, as an insult to the humanity of the blacks, and he joined cause with Indians who had revived the Transvaal Indian Congress, an old ally of the ANC which had never been banned. In January 1983 Boesak called for a united front of all kinds of bodies, to 'inform people of the fraud that is about to be perpetrated in our name'.

Eight months later in August a meeting of 10,000 people near Cape Town launched the United Democratic Front (UDF), which was pledged to oppose the new constitution. It was a federation of 570 different bodies ranging from bicycle clubs to trades unions with members of all races: its structure was deliberately planned to make its leadership less vulnerable to picking-off, and to spread across the whole country. 'We thought Cape Town would be our weakest region,' one of its anonymous founders told me, 'so we sent most of our organisers down there . . . We knew the leaders would be cut off, but others could always take over.' The UDF took care not to challenge the existing exiled organisations, and its own declaration was even vaguer than the ANC's Freedom Charter: it stood for 'a single non-racial, unfragmented South Africa, free of Bantustans and group areas' and it was against 'economic and all other forms of exploitation'. In the words of its young general-secretary Popo Molefe – who was later arrested and tried for treason – 'it was the voice to say that there was still a chance to bring about change without loss of life'. The ANC in Lusaka which was also calling for everyone to reject 'dummy institutions' soon warmly welcomed the UDF which included many former ANC figures among its patrons. 'The UDF mobilises all people into one mass movement and co-ordinates community resistance,' wrote *Sechaba* in October, 'but it does not purport to be a substitute movement to accredited people's movements.' The ANC did not claim credit for creating the UDF, and explained that its members did not necessarily support the Freedom Charter; but it saw the UDF as a 'historic development in our people's march to freedom'.* In fact the UDF was much less

* Interview with Mac Maharaj, *Sechaba*, March 1984

radical in its economic attitudes than its rival AZAPO which criticised both the UDF and the ANC for not being sufficiently revolutionary against the existing racist-capitalist system. AZAPO had also formed its own coalition called the National Forum just before the UDF and in the following months the rival groups had bitter and sometimes violent conflicts – with some apparent connivance from the police who were noticeably more permissive towards AZAPO.

By the end of 1984 another black priest was achieving international political importance. Desmond Tutu had become the general-secretary of the South African Council for Churches in 1978, and eight years later became the first black bishop of Johannesburg – a position which gave him high exposure and unusual mobility as he moved between his small house in black Soweto and his big house in a white suburb – where the front lawn could (he said) accommodate ten Soweto houses. As a child Tutu had been much influenced, like Tambo, by Father Trevor Huddleston (after whom he named his son). Tutu's mother, an uneducated woman, worked in a menial job at the school for the blind run by Arthur Blaxall. 'I'll never forget seeing this tall white priest walking by, and *raising his hat* to my mother. I realised that here was a white man who treated everyone as human beings.' Later when he was seriously ill he had regular visits from Huddleston, and from him and others he gained a picture of the church as both compassionate and militant. Tutu liked to re-tell the old joke about how the blacks first had the land, when the whites came with the Bible: then the whites had the land, and the blacks had the Bible. 'But perhaps it was not such a bad exchange,' Tutu reflects. 'The Bible was very revolutionary. It was a tremendous idea, to be the partner of God in the dusty streets of the townships.'

Tutu was quite prepared to mix politics with religion, speaking with both passion and wit – rather like Cardinal Sin in the Philippines – grinning and rubbing his hands as he went into the attack. He made increasingly political statements, and when in 1980 he predicted that Mandela would be prime minister in five to ten years the government did not intervene. He did not overtly support the UDF or the ANC; but he did not criticise them and he kept his distance from Buthelezi. Many blacks talked of him as 'Mandela's caretaker': but he also took risks by mediating with the police. He warned American and European businessmen that they could not duck out of political involvement: 'By coming out here you make a political statement.' When in December 1984 Tutu was awarded the Nobel Peace Prize – twenty-three years after Albert Luthuli's in 1961 – he reached a new level, on which even President Reagan felt obliged to receive him. He soon became a persistent public commentator on successive crises: the first black South African to gain regular and effective access to the American media.

By September 1984 the UDF and other opposition groups showed the first signs of their strength when coloureds and Indians were elected to parliament under the new constitution. The UDF had called for a total boycott and out of the potential voters who had registered only 30.9 per cent of the coloureds and 20.3 percent of the Indians voted. And at the same time there were already signs of a new wave of black discontent, focussing once again on the inferior education. The new radical students union COSAS, set up in 1979, was an important ingredient of the UDF and was agitating both for better schooling and also mobilising pupils behind the broader policies of the UDF. During the elections black and coloured schoolchildren were protesting violently against their schools and the constitution. The black anger was increased by sharp rent increases, particularly in the townships in the 'Vaal Triangle' south of Johannesburg, which the black local councillors had to enforce on behalf of the government. On the same day that new members of parliament arrived in Cape Town a demonstration in Sharpeville – where the massacre had occurred twenty-four years before – led to riots, burnings and reprisals against black councillors. The new parliament coincided with the beginning of an almost continuous upsurge of protests and violence in black townships all over the country.

The links between the new resistance and either the UDF or the ANC remained very uncertain. But at the beginning of the new year Oliver Tambo delivered a dramatic new year message called RENDER SOUTH AFRICA UNGOVERNABLE. He claimed that the ANC had already 'taken impressive strides towards rendering the country ungovernable' – by such measures as boycotting community councils and the new constitution – and he warned that: 'In the coming period we shall need to pursue, with even greater vigour, the task of reducing the capacity of the colonial apartheid regime to continue its illegal rule of our country. The destruction of the organs of government weakens the regime and is a necessary part of our continuing mass offensive.'* The new slogan was still part of a broader strategy. As Tambo explained it later: 'There are many ways of making it unworkable of course, not just by violence. We think that economic sanctions, disinvestment and so on have the effect of creating problems for the apartheid system – therefore making it less efficient, less desirable as a system to the people of

* Message of the NEC of the ANC, January 8, 1985

South Africa overall.'* But it was not clear how far the ANC had really expected, or was ready to control, the escalation of violence that was to follow.

Many black townships were certainly becoming virtually ungovernable by the official authorities. The police now dared not suppress many demonstrations which openly advertised the ANC and the name of Mandela. Nor did they try to silence Winnie Mandela, who was now a major politician in her own right and who had herself almost become a no-go area, talking of the government with undisguised contempt. 'Just about every aspect of our lives is deteriorating,' she said in January 1985. 'When the army has to be called in to surround a township because people are demonstrating against the increase in rents – because people are protesting as they do in every democratic country – then that political situation must have deteriorated to zero. Things are cracking up. They are losing control.'† By March 1985 the twenty-fifth anniversary of Sharpeville precipitated a new wave of protests beginning in Uitenhage, an industrial town near the Volkswagen factory in the Eastern Cape. A procession of blacks walking to a funeral was met by the police who, unaware of the anniversary, panicked and killed nineteen.

No one could be sure how far the riots and protests were inspired by the ANC and its 'underground structures', how far they came spontaneously from a grass-roots fury, or from groups of children. Tambo had no formal organisation inside South Africa to compare with that of his rival Buthelezi, whose organisation was always free to hold meetings and who insisted that 'the myth that the ANC is the dominating black political force in South Africa is being falsely propagated'.‡ But the ANC still invoked its past record of defiance and martyrdom, and it could look back on its own warnings. As Winnie Mandela recalled: 'The leadership prophesied when they went to prison in 1964 that if violence is not controlled – which is what they were trying to do, to contain it, to direct acts of sabotage – violent revolution would be inevitable. Well, from that day we have picked up children's bodies from the streets because they dared to protest.'§

In June while the riots and protests were escalating Tambo presided over the second 'consultative conference' of the ANC in exile, at Kabwe in Zambia, attended by about 250 delegates including some who had just escaped from South Africa. They elected

* Telephone interview with author, July 1985
† Telephone interview with author, January 1985
‡ Letter to the author, January 1985
§ Telephone interview with author, March 1985

an enlarged national executive, with thirty members instead of twenty-two, embracing for the first time some non-Africans including the veteran white communist Joe Slovo. 'Some white participants opposed this admission,' Tambo said later. 'They thought it was wrong, ill-timed. But the conference ultimately came round to accepting that the time had come to practise complete non-racialism.' The chief leaders were re-elected uncontested, including Tambo. Some Congress-watchers suggested that Tambo was not the real boss of the movement, and that the real power lay with the 'Revolutionary Council' which included more guerilla leaders. Certainly Tambo's measured statements in private often contrasted with the fierce rhetoric of the ANC's 'Freedom Radio'. But Tambo had a very visible command over his colleagues; and he was able to unify them with all the authority of his friend Mandela behind him. Tambo told the conference that the violence in South Africa would inevitably escalate, and that it would be much harder to make the distinction between hard and soft targets. The ANC had so far been careful to avoid acts of pure terrorism against civilians, like those of the PLO; and in the previous August Tambo had reprimanded the people who had exploded a car-bomb in Durban, killing five.* But he now saw the country coming much closer to civil war. As he explained later: 'I didn't call for a general uprising. I can't say that because I wouldn't get it. But we did say that the black policemen must begin to prepare to turn their guns against their masters. We called on them to join our ranks rather than fight to defend the apartheid system.'†

Botha and many business leaders were now stepping up their warnings that the ANC was the tool of foreign communists 'marching to the beat of a distant drum'. Certainly the enlarged executive included many members of the South African Communist Party, which worked closely with the ANC – which was hardly surprising since the ANC in its quarter-century of exile had depended on financial and military support from the East, while most doors to the West had been closed. The fact of exile had inevitably shifted the balance, and many ANC politicians looked to the release of their leaders and the unbanning of their party to redress it. What was threatening to the West was not so much foreign communist influence as the hatred of capitalism by the young blacks inside the townships, who had never even heard of Marx but who naturally identified white business with apartheid. As Tom Lodge analysed the situation after the Kabwe conference:

* Lodge, *op. cit.*, p. 85
† Telephone interview with author, July 1985

With the renaissance of popular political culture during the post-Soweto era there has developed a profound and widespread antipathy to capitalism ... It is evident in the anti-capitalist polemic of virtually every black trade union spokesman regardless of his organisational affiliation ... If in the future the ANC shifts to the left in its social and economic prescriptions this will not be the result of any kind of manipulation of the movement by communists; it will rather be a reflection of the wider political culture of which it is part.'*

Tambo still insisted that the ANC remained ideologically uncommitted. 'Our broad movement for national liberation,' he said in the political report to the conference, 'contains both a nationalist and a socialist tendency.'† And to avoid a catastrophic civil war he still looked for intervention from the West – and particularly from the United States.

* Tom Lodge: The Second Consultative Conference of the African National Congress, South African International, 1985
† *Sechaba*, October 1985

11

The American Crusade

For America, 1985 has become the year of South Africa. A great nation has been stirred by the presence of a monumental evil in a small country. The moral sensibilities of our citizenry have been roused to a pitch that has no parallel elsewhere in the world and few precedents in our own history.

> Franklin Thomas, President of the Ford Foundation, in his speech
> to Commonwealth Club of California, May 31, 1985

I'm going to keep order in this country. And nobody in the world is going to stop me keeping order . . . South Africa is a tough country. We nearly brought the British Empire to its knees. And I would advise some superpowers not to try and destroy us.

> President Botha, to ABC Television, March 22, 1985

It was the United States, much more than Europe, which quite suddenly provided new hope for black South Africans despite Reagan's policies. But the outcome remained very uncertain: how far would Americans really intervene?

Black Americans were now the prime movers, as they found a common cause and exploited their leverage in Washington. For years black South Africans had been advised to follow the example of the Israelis whose survival had depended on mobilising American Jews. Why not likewise use the political pressure of the 27 million black Americans – more than the 20 million black South Africans themselves? But they had faced a much harder task than the Israelis. Most black Americans had been bored with Africa, preoccupied with their own campaigns, impatient of the passivity of black South Africans: others were full of romantic cross-purposes about tribal life. Black South Africans had their own superiority, conscious that they were in a majority in their own continent, and worried that American blacks were in the end too American, too caught up in materialism and capitalism.

Andrew Young, now mayor of the prosperous city of Atlanta – 'the city too busy to hate' – personified the new reconciliation of middle-class blacks with capitalism. He had seen the snags of socialism in Africa, when aid programmes took two years to get through to socialist Sudan, three months to capitalist Nigeria. 'I've

made peace with capitalism,' he said later. 'There's nothing better
for coping with sin. It rewards people for working hard.'* Young
was convinced that the experience of the civil rights movement,
including its financial pressures and boycotts, was relevant to black
South Africans, as they became more urbanised and industrialised.
'Atlanta's future twenty-five years ago was no more certain than
South Africa's is today,' he explained. 'The saving grace was that
Atlanta's white business leadership recognised that conflict was
self-defeating; they sat down with the black leadership and began
working out ways to accomplish their goals together.' Many civil
rights veterans shared the same faith in peaceful pressures. As
Franklin Thomas, the black president of the Ford Foundation later
put it: 'The civil rights cause was best served not by the violent
gestures and anarchic agendas of the Black Power movement –
though it helped draw attention to the issue – but by the persistent
and purposeful efforts of established leaders who were familiar with
the levers of change.'† And the coalition of interests, including
blacks, churches and liberal businessmen, who had come together
for the civil rights campaign but who had been frustrated in other
fields, found a more hopeful common interest in South Africa.

Civil rights could be a misleading precedent. 'There was one fundamental difference,' as Bishop Tutu put it. 'The law in the United
States was on the side of those campaigning in the civil rights movement, claiming their rights under the constitution. Here, the constitution and the law are against us.'‡ Black Americans who were proud
of the discipline of their passive resistance and boycotts were often
worried by the ANC's commitment to violence in South Africa. Yet it
was the violence, demonstrating that blacks were at last beginning to
fight back, which was a major cause in attracting American attention.
'Without the blacks rising up,' said the black American columnist
William Raspberry, 'the story was not complete.'§

The example of Israel had first been taken up by a small lobbying
group called TransAfrica which had first been set up after a conference of the African-American Institute in Lesotho in December
1976, just after the horrors of Soweto. The black American participants, including Andrew Young, inspired by their 'physical com-
munion with the land of our forefathers', resolved 'to take vigorous
action for positive policy changes'.¶ TransAfrica planned to lobby

* *International Herald Tribune*, June 7, 1986
† Thomas, *ibid.*
‡ *Witness to Apartheid*, Channel 4, April 4, 1986
§ Media Conference on South Africa in the News, Harvard, March 12, 1986
¶ Statement by the Afro-American participants. The African American Confer-
ence, December 2, 1976

for black Africa as the American-Israel Public Affairs Committee lobbied for Israel. It was run by Randall Robinson, a conservative-looking young aide to Congressman Charles Diggs of Michigan, whose brother Max was an anchorman for ABC. He had been brought up in segregated Virginia, graduated at the Harvard Law School and worked for a year in Tanzania. He was more radical in his approach to South Africa than Leon Sullivan: he had even written a novel in 1973 about a black soldier who refused to fight for a white regime in Southern Africa. When the political scientist Robert Rotberg argued in 1980 that 'the ultimate interests of Americans and white South Africans are probably not very different,' Robinson insisted that was 'fundamentally misguided. The long-range interests of the United States lie in accommodation and identification with the black majority, that will inevitably inherit South African Society.'*

TransAfrica was a small outfit which for years hardly dented the American apathy about Africa: but by the early 'eighties it was becoming more effective. In June 1981 it sponsored a conference in Washington attended by Oliver Tambo which concluded with a 'national declaration' advocating a massive educational drive about Southern Africa and stating that: 'We, as a people, have an immediate, direct hands-on impact capability.' Randall Robinson continued to maintain close links with the ANC, and with other radical groups in Africa and the Caribbean. Right-wing groups liked to depict TransAfrica as a leftist menace: 'TransAfrica is a spokesman, not for black Americans,' said the right-wing Lincoln Institute in Washington, 'but for the Soviet and Cuban supported terrorist groups.'† But many Republicans as well as Democrats came to be impressed by Robinson's campaign. 'It was not a Congressman, a Senator, or a President who brought the matter of South Africa to the attention of the American people,' said Senator Lowell Weicker in 1986: 'It was a citizen – Randall Robinson.'‡

But the ANC was also beginning to gain some friends in business circles in the United States, through the African-American Institute in New York under its senior vice-president Frank Ferrari. In June 1981, Oliver Tambo had his first meeting in New York with representatives of American companies including General Motors and Ford, and had a very friendly talk with the President of Gulf Oil International, Melvin Hill. In spring 1985 he visited New York and Washington, where he addressed Congressional staffers, spoke

---

* Randall Robinson, 'Investments in Tokenism', *Foreign Policy*, Spring 1980
† TransAfrica, A Lobby of the Left, Washington, The Lincoln Institute, 1985
‡ US Senate debate, August 14, 1986

to the Council of Foreign Relations, and met more businessmen
and bankers including David Rockefeller. 'I found it interesting to
talk to business people in the United States,' Tambo said in July
1985. 'I suppose they look at things slightly differently, but they
are businessmen all the same . . . I was really impressed by what
was going on (in America): the situation has been changed by
people at all levels: Congressmen, Senators and the population
generally.'*

The campaign of Jesse Jackson in the 1984 presidential elections
gave some encouragement to black South Africans, but without
much obvious response, and Reagan's re-election gave little indication of an impending crusade. 'I'm not naïve politically,' commented Buthelezi. 'Both Mondale and Jackson made apartheid an
election issue, but people still elected Reagan.' Then in November
1984 – just after Reagan's re-election, and after Tutu had won the
Nobel Peace Prize – Robinson planned a new kind of protest: he
and two other black leaders, Congressmen Walter Fauntroy and
Mary Frances Berry, a member of the Civil Rights Commission,
protested outside the South African embassy until they were
arrested and taken to jail. It was on the eve of Thanksgiving Day
(chosen, said Fauntroy, because 'there's nothing to report but
turkeys'). At first it only made a news story for black Washington,
but the national media quickly took it up. Robinson hastily called
his campaign the 'Free South Africa Movement', and persuaded
others to follow. Many people saw it as a distraction from the
humiliation of the Democrats and the black lobbies in the election,
and Robinson did not conceal his resentment that the Reagan
administration had 'almost entirely shut out blacks'. But the campaign very soon became bi-partisan and went far beyond black
politicians: by March, 2,000 people, many of them newsworthy,
including Republican Senators, had been arrested outside the embassy in Washington. Robinson was now stepping up his campaign.
'We have a commitment to be relentless,' he said. 'The South
African regime won't negotiate in good faith until they're certain
that the us is prepared to impose the stiffest of sanctions.'†

Many black politicians now saw American business as sharing
the blame for apartheid, and insisted on sanctions as the only
effective response. Already by 1982 the black Congressman for
Pennsylvania William Gray – who became chairman of the budget
committee – had introduced the first proposal in Congress for
sanctions against South Africa. 'Apartheid may have been nurtured

* Interview with author, July 1985
† *Wall Street Journal*, October 10, 1985

by a degenerate theocracy born in the seventeenth century,' he said later, 'but profits sustain it in the twentieth century . . . I decided that America cannot be loyal to its own democratic creed and at the same time provide the economic fuel for apartheid.'*

By early 1985 there was much more pressure for sanctions – ranging from banning the gold Krugerrand coins to banning all trade and investment or withdrawing landing rights for airlines from South Africa (which Andrew Young had long advocated). The pressure was now much more intense in America than in Europe. The motives were mixed and often muddled: some were crudely punitive; some self-righteous; many were ignorant of conditions inside South Africa, or the problems of opposing sanctions. But the consistent theme in the American campaign was the determination to pressurise companies and banks operating in South Africa, as part of the growing concern for the social responsibility of capitalism. The activists were determined that capitalism should not be allowed to give support to apartheid and oppression, and to pull the levers of investment away from the all-white world.

Television, as it began to show nightly scenes of riots, whippings and police raids, was bringing South Africa much closer to American homes. In January 1985 Senator Edward Kennedy visited South Africa, invited by Tutu and Boesak, emulating his brother Bobby's visit nineteen years before – to show support for the blacks and to take up the cause of disinvestment. He was received in a blaze of TV publicity, with little overt support from the ANC or the UDF, and with angry demonstrations from the black consciousness party AZAPO, which the police were glad to allow. When he addressed a lunch of businessmen, Ambassador Nickel introduced him with a long critical speech. The white press reported Kennedy's travels with mockery and vitriol, and depicted the visit as a fiasco. In fact it did much to pressurise local businessmen into committing themselves further against the apartheid system: and Kennedy stopped in Zambia on the way back for a friendly meeting with Tambo and the ANC. 'It took a Kennedy to emphasise the conditions we have had to live with to the rest of the world,' said Winnie Mandela later. 'It was one of the most significant political visits. But the Reagan administration is a lost cause. That clown is committed to constructive engagement to protect his investments.'†

Bishop Tutu also impinged on American TV with the suddenness of a jack-in-the-box: he had been granted a passport after pressure from Washington, and he proved to be one of the few black benefici-

* Africa Report, March 1986
† Interview with author, August 1985

aries of constructive engagement, projecting a quite new perception
of South Africa. Before him the main spokespeople for the blacks
had been distinguished white liberals, like Helen Suzman or Alan
Paton, who had emphasised the horrors and inhumanity of apartheid without necessarily supporting any black agenda. But Tutu
invited a much clearer identification with the black side by-passing
the white Liberals – to the chagrin of many. He always insisted
that Western politicians and businessmen had a responsibility to
intervene, to avoid further bloodshed; and in May 1985 he spoke
to huge student crowds – including 30,000 on three California
campuses – stressing repeatedly the blacks' desperate need for
Western help. 'Every time we have called for a change,' Tutu
explained back in South Africa, 'the effect has been not even a
minimal change but a tightening of the rules . . . If international
pressure doesn't work, we are for the birds . . . We need the world.
Most business people know we can't make it on our own. I would
not like to see this country destroyed.'* Tutu never at this stage
specifically called for economic sanctions or disinvestment – which
were illegal to advocate inside South Africa. But he gave an impetus
to the sanctions movement in the United States.

Washington now saw a far wider coalition against apartheid than
the familiar band of campaigners, as Senators and Congressmen
began proposing laws to enforce differing degrees of sanctions; and
the assumption that investment was in itself benign was fast fading.
Senator Proxmire, the senior Democrat on the banking committee,
said that 'at long last, people like myself feel we ought to begin
doing something about it,'† and proposed legislation to ban any
new investment. Stephen Solarz, the liberal Democrat who had
been four times to South Africa, argued that 'the apartheid system is
more entrenched today than ever before.' He doubted that American
corporations could be a major vehicle for change, and insisted on
external pressure: 'I know of no examples in history where ruling
establishments have voluntarily divested themselves of their power,
and their position.'‡

Inside South Africa nearly all whites, from right or left, were
appalled by the idea of sanctions, and the liberals were among the
most vociferous. 'The best hope for reform in South Africa lies in
economic advancement of the blacks,' said Helen Suzman. 'Anything that retards the economic advancement of blacks is counter-
productive.' Alan Paton insisted that 'punishment is no proper

* *Leadership* magazine, Johannesburg, special issue on Disinvestment, July 1985,
pp. 15–16
† *Leadership, ibid.*, p. 37
‡ *Ibid.*, p. 50

treatment for erring countries . . . The Afrikaner nationalist is ready to behave better . . . He is in fact attempting to return to the West.' Harry Oppenheimer continued to insist that new investment and business initiatives had helped to liberalise South Africa.* The black political leaders were divided. Chief Buthelezi warned that 'only those working for a future communist state see disinvestment as being in the best interests of South Africa.' But the UDF leaders and most activist groups insisted that sanctions offered the only alternative to mounting violence and chaos. 'Disinvestment is a practicable, possible and necessary tool for pressing against apartheid,' said Allan Boesak, one of the UDF founders. 'I do believe that without economic pressure on the South African government, there will be no movement towards change.'† The opposing views about sanctions helped to widen the gap between blacks and white liberals, and to emphasise their different economic perspectives.

American viewers came still closer to South Africa when in March 1986 Ted Koppel of ABC television went out there to film every night for a week which coincided with the anniversary of Sharpeville and the police killings at Uitenhage. Koppel brought together South Africans on the same screen, many of whom had never exchanged views before – revealing all the tragic fragmentation. 'We have stirred up in South Africa what we tend to take so much for granted in the US,' Koppel said at the end of the series, 'debate and the public exchange of views.' The head of the black mineworkers' union Cyril Ramaphosa appeared on the same programme – though in a different studio – as the head of the white mineworkers union Arrie Paulus: it was the closest they had ever got to actually meeting.‡

Harry Oppenheimer told Koppel that disinvestment 'could only cause change by bringing about a state of despair amongst black people, which would lead, not to peaceful change, but to violent change.' Louis Wilking of General Motors said that his company was 'in the vanguard of enticing South Africa to make many of the political changes that you see today.' But Ramaphosa asked: 'Why would the white South Africans make noises in the US and all over the world about their disinvestment campaign if they were not worried about it? . . . In recent months it has finally resulted in making the government make a number of changes, which people would never thought could be made in this country.' 'We want US business to voluntarily get out,' said the more extreme Imrann

---

* *Leadership, ibid.*
† *Corporate Examiner,* Vol. 14, No. 6, 1985
‡ Interview with Ramaphosa: Africa Report, March 1986

Moosa of AZAPO, 'before we have to force them to move out.' Finally
President Botha himself appeared: 'I have the impression – and I
think my impression is right – that you Americans are fighting your
elections in America on South African grounds . . . You have too
many elections, that is my complaint against your country. You
can't lead the Western world with all the elections you have – you're
weakening yourself.'*

It was only part of the bombardment of South African news. TV
teams and special correspondents poured into the Republic to follow
the daily trail of violence. Foundations and commissions sent out
researchers and fact-finding groups to interview the small stage
army of famous blacks. Black and white South Africans were flown
over to America for seminars, conferences, fellowships, scholarships.
Television and direct dialling could by-pass Pretoria and bring
restricted black leaders like Winnie Mandela into the global community. The centre of real communications was no longer in Pretoria
or Johannesburg where TV screens and newspapers were muzzled,
but in the airwaves where the voices of Botha, Tambo, Buthelezi
or Oppenheimer could all come together as they could not at home.
The American interest and hospitality undoubtedly helped to boost
the morale of black leaders, particularly if they were granted passports: unlike the Afrikaners they could now see themselves as
citizens of the world, and could be more widely informed than most
whites. But the embrace of the black elite could easily cut them off
from the youth in the townships who were setting the pace, and
becoming increasingly anti-American and anti-capitalist; and the
world of the American media and liberal universities was very
different from the world of the American government.

How far was the United States becoming an actor, as well as a
spectator, in the South African melodrama? Were the media only
raising false expectations? 'Blacks are getting the idea that external
pressure and non-governability of the townships will give them
victory just round the corner,' said the progressive MP Helen Suzman
later in the year. 'The risk is that Western powers are inadvertently
encouraging blacks to launch violence against whites, and then the
government is really going to unleash its terrible power on these
kids.' The *Wall Street Journal* quoted a black student saying, 'America
is with us,' and commented: 'But America isn't with them. The US
Marines aren't going to land in Soweto or New Brighton or any
other black township if the South African defence forces, mightiest
in all Africa, are unleashed on blacks. All they can expect is a
rush to the television cameras by US congressmen, Reagan adminis-

* ABC News, March 18–22, 1985

tration officials and American businessmen to deplore the killings.'*

Certainly President Reagan still showed little desire to identify himself with black South Africans, or with sanctions. By September 1985, Reagan felt impelled to preempt a Senate bill for sanctions with his own half-hearted executive order which agreed on a modified package, including a ban on all computer exports to South African apartheid agencies, restricting nuclear technology and banning imports of Krugerrands. Reagan, like Thatcher in Britain, never concealed his reluctance to impose serious sanctions. And despite the growing friendship from Congress black South Africans became increasingly hostile to Washington – paradoxically more hostile than towards London, though the British investment was much bigger they were more hostile as Reagan began overtly supporting Savimbi, the anti-communist rebel leader in Angola, whom they saw as in league with Pretoria, threatening a legitimate black state. Yet many black leaders looked to individual Americans and organisations as allies in their struggle; and American companies were now under much more pressure than the British to confront apartheid visibly and boldly. The campaign for sanctions, though it fell short of its object, achieved an important by-product in improving black conditions in the meantime. The more vociferous the demands for disinvestment the more companies felt the need to justify their presence in South Africa. Leon Sullivan was aware that his original principles had been outdated by the rising militancy, while his supporters in the companies were developing their own missionary zeal to convert blacks to capitalism – and to award marks to companies like schoolboys. In 1985 Sullivan could point to 178 signatories, compared to 128 the year before. Of the 146 companies which reported, thirty-six were Making Good Progress, including most of the biggest such as General Motors, Citicorp and IBM; while only four Did Not Pass Basic Requirements – including Ashland Oil and McCann-Erickson.† The most zealous of Sullivan's apostles was Sal Marzullo, the exuberant government relations manager of Mobil who was a close ally of Chief Buthelezi, who was determined to restore Mobil's reputation among blacks after its elaborate sanctions-busting in Rhodesia in the 'sixties, and who shared Mobil's faith in publicity and advertising: 'The process of urbanisation and industrialisation has done more to doom traditional apartheid,' he promised in mid-1985, 'than any other single influence.'‡

* Karen Elliott House in the *Wall Street Journal*, November 1, 1985
† America Magazine, New York. August 2–10, 1985, p. 53
‡ Ninth Report on the Signatory Companies to the Sullivan Principles, Arthur D Little, Cambridge, October 1985

While Randall Robinson was launching his 'Free South Africa'
campaign in November 1984 Sullivan was announcing his 'Fourth
Amplification' which would press companies to recognise black
unions and to campaign publicly against specific apartheid laws;
and he now called for dismantling apartheid within two years. It
was a call for external political interference in bold contrast to all
the earlier philosophy of multinationals, and it soon provoked angry
responses from inside the Republic. 'The only effective role for
United States interests,' Arthur Hammond-Tooke, the director of
economic affairs for the Federated Chamber of Industries told
executives in New York in May, 'is to latch onto the internal
pressures and developments which are moving under their own
power in the right direction.'

The most far-reaching American pressures were from the church
and other groups who were now pressing shareholders and investors
to take stronger stands; and in New York the Interfaith Center on
Corporate Responsibility was stepping up its long crusade under its
persistent director Tim Smith. Christian shareholders were steadily
chipping away at the big corporations, submitting resolutions on all
kinds of social issues, but increasingly featuring South Africa. The
Grey Nuns of the Sacred Heart, with six shares in Eastman Kodak,
called on the company to withdraw from South Africa. There were
also universities, foundations and institutions with far bigger share-
holdings which were demanding disinvestment, while American
cities and states were threatening to refuse to order goods from
companies investing in South Africa. In May 1985, while Tutu was
touring America, fifty-four Protestant and Catholic groups announced a new campaign against twelve 'key investors in apartheid'
which all had, said the churches, 'long histories of providing products
and services which have built South Africa's racist economy and way
of life.' They included three computer companies (IBM, Control Data,
Burroughs) – 'user-friendly to apartheid' – three oil companies
(Mobil, Texaco, Chevron), two car companies (Ford, General
Motors), together with Fluor, General Electric and Newmont
Mining. The church groups called on the companies to tell Pretoria
that they would not stay in South Africa unless eight drastic conditions were met by the end of 1986 – including releasing all political
prisoners, unbanning all organisations, repealing the Group Areas
Act and abandoning the homelands policy. To press them, the
churches would organise further shareholders' resolutions and meetings with businessmen, and if necessary start divesting securities and
launch campaigns for selective buying.*

* New York: Interfaith Center on Corporate Responsibility: *The Corporate
Examiner*, Vol. 14, No. 4, 1985

The persistent protests at company meetings – together with nightly television coverage from South Africa, and, often, nagging from children and wives – were gradually wearing down the resistance of chairmen and directors, and changing their perspectives. Whatever the commercial benefits from their South African investment – which were now anyway dwindling – the 'hassle factor' was already looming much larger as boards were compelled to think more carefully about their involvements with apartheid. The typical American corporation, it was said, had 1 percent of its investments in South Africa, producing 2 percent of its profits – but occupying 10 percent or even 20 percent of its chairman's time. While black South African radicals continued to blame American capitalism for their oppression, American companies, many operating at a loss, were identifying themselves more closely with blacks than the administration.

They were much more active than the British, who still had four times the investment but were far less vulnerable to calls for disinvestment or sanctions. Leon Sullivan was very keen to involve British companies in his stepped-up campaign: 'No one can have more impact than the British,' he told me, 'but they need a crisis to move them.' In March 1985, with the help of Edward Heath, he summoned a secret conference of chief executives at Leeds Castle, the moated mansion in Kent much favoured for discreet palavers. It was a high-powered British team – including Sir Peter Baxendell the head of Shell, Sir Peter Walters of BP, Sir Tim Bevan of Barclays and Sir Alistair Frame, the very conservative chairman of Rio Tinto-Zinc – while the American tycoons included Roger Smith of General Motors, Rawleigh Warner of Mobil and John Reed of Citibank (who had asked to attend after Sullivan had pulled out a New York pension fund from Citibank, forcing it to stop new lending to South Africa). In the castle they discussed the role of the business community in a just society, education and job creation, and Sullivan talked vaguely about windows and goal-setting. 'I don't want the crisis, when it comes,' he said, 'to be so great that it's uncontrollable.' But the South Africans, who included Tony Bloom of the Premier Group and Judge Steyn of the Urban Foundation, turned out to be the most radical; while the British chairmen explained that they were not under much pressure from shareholders, and saw no need for bold commitments. To Sullivan's disappointment they would only agree on a weak communique about their 'common concern' which he wisely tore up.

The British were much less pressed by their shareholders. The great bulk of British church investments were held in a single portfolio by the Church Commissioners which in 1986 included

nearly £300 million of investments in South Africa, including £21
million in four British companies – British Petroleum, Thorn EMI,
BET and BPB – which paid some workers below the minimum rate
stipulated by the EEC 'code of conduct'.* But the Commission
insisted that profits were their main criteria and that they could not
use investment as protest. The all-party British demonstrations and
protests against apartheid in the 'fifties and 'sixties had dwindled
to a narrow base, and the Anti-Apartheid Movement was almost
exclusively the province of the Left. High unemployment, the long
fiasco of sanctions against Rhodesia and the economic disasters of
black Africa, had all contributed to the British protest fatigue; and
there was no black political lobby in Britain to compare with the
American campaigners.

While Americans liked to see South Africa in the image of their
own Deep South and the civil rights campaign, the British were
still inclined to see it in terms of African colonial wars, and particularly the Boer War eighty years earlier; and Mrs Thatcher among
many others invested the Afrikaners with a legendary resistance and
stubbornness. While Americans instinctively looked to economic
pressures which had prevailed in the South, the British constantly
warned that overt pressure on Pretoria would make the Afrikaners
'retreat back into the laager'. British businessmen had longer traditional links than Americans with their white South African
counterparts, often reinforced by relatives and friends, which made
them more reluctant to defy local customs and attitudes, even if they
disagreed with them. The headquarters of British multinationals
traditionally gave much more freedom of action to their subsidiaries
than their American equivalents, so that if the London boards
suggested that their South African companies might be bolder in
opposing apartheid or promoting black managers they were easily
shut up by warnings of the dangers of a white backlash – warnings
which usually turned out (*see* page 201) to be without real basis.

The British trade lobby UKSATA, run by the former diplomat John
McQuiggan, still stayed close to Pretoria and South African officials
– 'it's really the commercial arm of the South African Embassy,'
said one of its members – while the new South African ambassador
Denis Worrall, a sophisticated political scientist, was agile in de-
ploying the network of potential friendships. McQuiggan and his
chairman Neil Forster also kept closely in touch with the Foreign
Office, and in July 1985 they were reassured by the official in charge
of Africa, Ewen Fergusson (the former ambassador to Pretoria), that
UKSATA would be consulted before any changes affecting companies

* *Financial Times*, July 7, 1986

were made. The Foreign Office was equally cut off from black opinion and politics, having virtually no contact with the African National Congress, while its embassy in Pretoria was more nervous than ever of offending the Afrikaners, and the Secret Service still co-operated with Pretoria's intelligence services in return for information on Cubans and communists in the North. The job of keeping in touch with blacks was delegated to the deputy-consul in Johannesburg, whose reports were filtered through the embassy. British diplomats in London had their own traumas about implementing sanctions after their experiences with Rhodesia; and most of them accepted Pretoria's argument that sanctions would either be ineffective, or would hurt the blacks without persuading the whites. In fact the argument that sanctions would not work was not proven. Robin Renwick, the senior British diplomat who had run the Rhodesia department and was a key negotiator of Zimbabwe's independence, had written his own study of past sanctions which pointed out many snags but concluded: 'The idea that sanctions have no effect, impose no penalty, or that their avoidance (or termination) offers no incentive, is contrary to the evidence, as it is to common sense . . .'*

While British and American politicians debated sanctions in theoretical terms, the mounting violence and counter-violence inside South Africa was moving the ground beneath them. Pretoria's iron control was looking much less certain; the old religious faith in apartheid was fading; the might of the military machine looked less relevant. Businessmen and bankers were becoming less confident of the status quo that they were defending, and more reluctant to invest anything more. They thought that the blacks might well be winning; and while the transition would be bloody and unprofitable they might do business with them in the end. Without much likelihood of orderly white reforms the case for sanctions was already looking stronger. 'What is marginal in conditions of relatively internal calm,' wrote Ian Davidson in the *Financial Times* in July 1985, 'may become critical in conditions of unrest and uncertainty . . . Western governments need to consider whether, for the sake of the white South Africans as well as for the blacks, their intervention may improve the odds of a better outcome, however unlikely it may appear to be.'†

But the emotional clamour in America for disinvestment, and the eagerness of many chairmen to escape from the hassle, tended to

* Robin Renwick, 'Economic Sanctions', Cambridge, Harvard Studies in International Affairs, No. 45, 1981
† *Financial Times*, July 29, 1985

distract attention from the more critical question of what would happen afterwards. For any thoughtful view of South Africa's long-term survival, disinvestment and sanctions could only be part of the strategy: they would have to be accompanied by much more constructive measures by both companies and governments, including a more decisive alignment with the black opposition, more support for the neighbouring black states and the building up of an alternative infrastructure of rail and air routes, to limit the dangerous dependence on South Africa. It was an error of many campaigners for disinvestment that they too easily allowed both businessmen and politicians to opt out and evade their real long-term problem: how to safeguard the continuity of Western interests and influence in Southern Africa by gaining much broader black support.

12

Emergency

We've got a new breed of children. They believe that they're going to die – and the frightening thing is they don't care. Because it is their view the only language the government understands is violence.

Bishop Tutu, *Witness to Apartheid*, Channel 4 TV, April 4, 1986

By the middle of 1985 the Botha government was convinced that its authority was being seriously undermined by the growing black revolt. The ANC's policy to 'render South Africa ungovernable' was looking more credible inside the townships. The young blacks were beginning to build up their own 'alternative structures' with their own crude form of discipline and government. For months, many black families had refused to pay higher rents. The government-sponsored community councils were boycotted. Police terrorism and torture were opposed by counter-terrorism against black police and suspected informers. The 'necklace' – the tyre filled with petrol and set alight round the victim's neck – had already become black South Africa's grim contribution to the language of revenge.

The government blamed as the chief culprits a group of radicals within the students' body COSAS, which they accused of conspiring secretly with the ANC, and which they soon banned. The well-briefed BBC correspondent Graham Leach reported:

The government was disturbed by evidence that the radicals were trying to carry through a classic two-stage revolutionary programme in some of the townships. The first phase was to make the townships ungovernable as the ANC had urged. Local government in many areas had collapsed following attacks on black councillors and the resignation, out of fear, of others. Black policemen, also the victims of violence, had been evacuated from their homes and, along with their families, were living like refugees in tented camps behind barbed wire on the outskirts of townships. Law and order had broken down with even the simplest burglary unable to be investigated unless an officer entered the township accompanied by armoured personnel-carriers carrying police and troops. Indeed it appeared to the authorities that the second phase of the activists' programme was becoming evident.*

On July 20 President Botha announced a state of emergency in thirty-six magisterial districts. It was just over twenty-five years since the previous emergency after Sharpeville, whose anniversary had helped to precipitate the new crisis. Two days afterwards I asked two rival black leaders how they thought it would compare with Sharpeville. From KwaZulu, Chief Buthelezi of Inkatha said:

You'll remember how Sharpeville broke down people's morale to the extent that you could hardly hear a whisper. So now one does fear that everything might reach its lowest ebb. I doubt very much whether the emergency will increase the opposition, knowing how cruel the police can be. You know how tough the Afrikaners are: they cling together once they feel an onslaught on them. Apartheid has been here for thirty-seven years. It would be a mistake to think the Afrikaners have lost the will to rule. It's true that they are very confused about where they want to go. Dr Verwoerd was cock-a-hoop about apartheid, whereas this regime is ashamed now about apartheid, to the extent that Botha, I'm sure, wants to dismantle it. They do worry about what they are doing, and this does give some encouragement to the blacks. But that is very different from losing the will to rule.

From Zambia, Oliver Tambo of the ANC said:

Martial law will sanction the killing of hundreds of people without police or others being asked to account for it. There will be a lot of 'disappearances'. But a greater degree of repression produces a greater upsurge. My expectation is that the emergency is preparing conditions for a much more violent conflict – moving towards a real explosion . . . The townships are struggling against the apartheid structure. But the struggle will soon go far beyond the townships, questioning the whole right to rule.†

When I visited Johannesburg a month after the declaration of the emergency both sides seemed to think that anything might happen, with the same discrepancy between ideas and realities that was so striking after Sharpeville: the premature optimism of the young blacks, insisting 'This is it!', while the white businessmen pursued

* Graham Leach, *op. cit.*, p. 174
† Telephone interviews with author, July 1985

their business as usual, and their suburban life was untouched. But
this black revolt was now far more widespread; and the balance
of confidence, if not the balance of power, had clearly changed.
'Sharpeville was a revolt of the parents,' as the veteran photographer
Peter Mugabane put it. 'Soweto was the children. Now it's both.'
'In 1976 the kids began it, almost spontaneously,' said the editor
of *Drum*, Stanley Motjuwadi. 'But now the parents can't control the
children as they could in '76, and the kids don't care about the
consequences. The more kids they arrest, the worse it becomes.'
The revolt had spread from town to country – even to the down-
trodden farm labourers in the Eastern Transvaal – and from
middle-class to workers: the activists of the UDF were a much more
proletarian group than earlier middle-class leaders such as Mandela
or Tambo. The police were helping to unite black businessmen and
workers against them, and militant blacks sounded confident that
when the real terrorists emerged they would find it easier to hide.
'There are safe houses for freedom fighters,' one boasted, 'even in
small Afrikaner towns in the Orange Free State.'

Could it really be the prelude to a revolution? Could the state
really be losing control? President Botha repeatedly warned that it
had still only used a small part of its fire-power; and while the
50,000 police were clearly overstretched and prone to panic, the
government still had a potential army of 300,000. The violence was
largely limited to the townships, and no casual visitor to the white
suburbs would notice any cause for worry. Yet the army com-
manders knew that they could not impose a purely military solution
in the heart of an advanced industrial state; and General Magnus
Malan, the Minister of Defence, had said long ago that they must
win 'hearts and minds'. Each confrontation was now losing more
hearts and minds, and the young Afrikaner police were visibly
provoking more resistance with their brutality and arbitrary arrests.
The co-opting of the army into many townships had created its own
problems by providing the appearance of a civil war.

Most whites had clearly expected the emergency to restore order
quickly, but the first weeks revealed unsuspected resistance; and
the UDF's grass roots surprised everyone including the police. In
Cape Town where the UDF had thought they would be weakest
the organisation was the most effective; and it was there that its
co-founder Allan Boesak planned a march on Mandela's prison to
'turn South Africa upside down', until he was himself arrested and
jailed. Black militants were emerging everywhere, and it was hard
to find 'Uncle Toms', for most blacks were convinced that they
were winning. They gave different time-frames, but rarely less than
ten years, before they would share political power – or control it.

They disagreed widely about the cost of it, whether it would be
achieved after far more bloodshed or after the intervention of the
West. But the heightened expectations reverberated through the
townships: any middle-class black now thought carefully before he
identified himself too closely with whites, on the losing side.

The blacks had very few guns and faced massed forces and
weaponry. Their optimism seemed absurd: yet many whites including Afrikaners now seemed convinced that part of their system was
crumbling. A poll taken in August 1985 showed 63 percent of whites
as well as 59 percent of blacks saying that apartheid would not exist
in ten years' time. Businessmen and politicians were talking in
commonplace terms about the post-apartheid era and power-
sharing with blacks; and even conservative Afrikaners including
Anton Rupert were insisting that apartheid must be buried. The
conditions seemed to be ripe for at least two ingredients for revolution: the rulers had lost confidence in their theories, and the ruled
were convinced that they could win. But between words and action
there remained a huge gap. The white language of power-sharing
and post-apartheid remained coded, with far vaguer connotations
than among Westerners or blacks, while the means of transition to
any kind of black government were still quite undefined. And in
the meantime the political pressures were still pushing the two sides
further apart. When the same poll asked blacks what would happen,
69 percent thought there would be a civil war, and only 29 percent
that it would be resolved peacefully: compared to 30 percent of
whites who expected civil war, and 59 percent who expected a
peaceful resolution.* The lack of common perceptions, and the
suppression of news suggested that the civil war had already begun.
Riots and shootings were officially described as 'unrest'. The television films of baton-charges and whippings which were screened
round the world were never glimpsed inside South Africa. Blinkered
from the real news, the two sides were diverging still further.

Nine years after Soweto, the black children were still more in the
centre of the revolt; and again the most explosive issue was black
education which was deteriorating still further. The schoolboys were
now further alienated from existing structures, with a conviction in
their own cause which had changed the frontiers of politics. As the
sociologists Adam and Moodley described it:

The hysteria that sweeps the school and townships resembles the
Children's Crusades of medieval Europe. Immune to the strategic

* Robert M Worcester of Mori, in *Public Opinion* magazine, AEI Washington,
September 18, 1985

reasoning of parents, teachers or even Bishop Tutu, it cuts its deadly path outside conventional politics and traditional ideologies. Political socialisation now starts with tear-gas fumes.*

Pretoria was quick to compare the militant children with the teenage Shi-ite warriors in the Middle East, or the Khmer Rouge in Cambodia. But the teenagers who called themselves 'comrades' in the townships owed little to religious or ideological teaching, and much more to their street-schooling in the townships which had taught them to expect nothing from the white world, whether government or business. They continued to be enraged by their formal schooling, which they equated with enslavement. The traditional belief in education as the means to compete with the whites, which had permeated the earlier ANC political leaders, was being undermined by the schoolboys' slogans: 'liberation before education' or 'freedom now, education later'. But the schools and syllabi were still part of the battleground.

Behind many of the protests and boycotts there proved to be more organisation than at first appeared. The students' union COSAS had since 1983 produced a network of local 'youth congresses' such as the Soweto congress SOYCO or the Port Elizabeth congress PEYCO, influenced by the ANC and the Freedom Charter as their acronyms suggested. One of the key organisers was Daniel Montsisi who had been a prominent student leader in the Soweto uprising in 1976 before spending four years on Robben Island; and he saw the development of local congresses in the tradition of the ANC and the Youth League to which Mandela and Tambo belonged in the 'forties: 'we regarded ourselves broadly as a logical progression of that type of tradition,' he told Shaun Johnson. The organisers saw the youth as essential to the struggle, but not necessarily decisive. As Montsisi put it:

In the formation of street and defence committees, the youths are central. They are the first to be detained, the first to be shot. But this should not be confused with us thinking we are in the vanguard of the struggle. That role belongs to our working parents.†

As the schoolchildren became more militant, boycotting the schools and setting up their own committees and discipline, the older black

---

* Adam and Moodley, *op cit.* p. 114
† Shaun Johnson: the Youth in South Africa. Report for the David Davies Memorial Foundation, London, 1986

leadership of the UDF and the ANC were more anxious to harness and control this new power; and the parents, first in Soweto then across the nation, set up their own bodies. By the end of 1985 they had called the First National Education Conference to persuade the children to return to school, in return for an ultimatum to the government to meet their demands – including the unbanning of COSAS, reinstating sacked teachers and releasing detainees – within three months. For the time being the two black generations seemed to have reached some understanding; but as the death toll increased, and the feuds between rival political groups became more violent, the control was clearly tenuous. And the build-up to March 1986 became increasingly tense.

By the end of 1985 official figures stated that the police had killed 763 people over the year, of whom only three were white and 201 were children, while 2,571 had been shot and wounded.*

The most obvious contrast between this emergency and Sharpeville was the blacks' involvement with industry. Johannesburg was no longer primarily a city of mine-dumps and compounds: it was ringed with shining new factories, assembly plants, supermarkets and shopping centres – with black operators and checkers in place of whites. Many more blacks were now involved in the economic system, including trades unions which had been legalised six years before. And Botha now faced a basic contradiction between industry's need for formal unions with which to negotiate, and the determination of his security services to cut off the black leaders, including unions. 'The black trades unions were illegal in 1960, and they're now legal,' said Tambo. 'But the curious thing is that trades unionists are now being charged with high treason – because they've organised trades unions.'†

The black union leaders had already been flexing their muscles. 'The members of those unions are beginning to see what the government is doing,' said Cyril Ramaphosa of the mineworkers', the most powerful of them, in March 1985. 'The government has been promising for a number of years to make a number of changes, and the government hasn't lived up to its promises. So they are beginning now to feel that they should take things into their own hands.'‡ Ramaphosa knew that unions were the critical means of political organisation while the major parties were banned, and that they could produce more radical leaders. 'We have a very strong base,' he said a year later, 'maybe even much stronger, for instance,

---

* *Weekly Mail*, March 7, 1986
† Interview with author, July 1985
‡ Interview with ABC TV, March 20, 1985

than the ANC . . . We believe that the workers should take leadership
position because we would like to see a country that is going to be
ruled in the interests of the workers who produce the wealth of the
country.*

Ramaphosa had a trial of strength with the mine-owners in
August 1985, when his workers went on strike for higher wages. He
could claim some progress: the six great gold-mining houses had
been split as never before, with Anglo-American as usual on the
liberal wing and the Afrikaner-controlled Gencor and the British-
controlled Gold Fields on the extreme right. 'Gencor and Gold
Fields wish they had never opened the doors to unions,' Ramaphosa
said. 'They show that in their negotiations: though they can't afford
to press to abolish them.'† But the mine-owners were still able
to dismiss striking workers and the strike was broken. 'You can
commence a strike,' Ramaphosa said afterwards, 'but if the bosses
still have the right to dismiss your members, then you don't have
a strike anymore.'‡

As the emergency continued the unions became more associated
with the broader struggle for freedom. By November 1985 Ramaphosa was taking the lead in bringing black trades unionists together
to form a new confederation called COSATU, with the mine-workers'
vice-president Elijah Barayi as president. Barayi had been in the
ANC Youth League with Mandela and Tambo, which shaped his
political awareness; he took part in the defiance campaign in 1952;
and he saw COSATU as being 'part and parcel of the liberation
struggle'. He believed in socialism 'as practised by the Labour Party
in England' and wanted to nationalise the mines: 'Black people are
the people who are digging up gold and in return are paid peanuts.
Once we nationalise the whole industry, our belief is that everyone
will reap the fruits of his sweat and toil . . . This country is in crisis
because of capitalism. If we at least took the big firms, nationalised
them, then the government would look after its people and the
people would look after the government.' But he believed firmly in
the democratic system: 'I don't want a one-party state. I believe
that is a dictatorship of the worst kind.'§

The new confederation was launched at a meeting of 10,000
blacks in December in Durban, where the wave of strikes had begun
twelve years earlier. 'The wealth must be shared by all the people
in this country,' said Ramaphosa in his opening speech. 'It is
important for us to make our politics the politics of the oppressed

* Interview with Barry Streek, Africa Report, March 1986
† Telephone interview with author, August 1985
‡ Africa Report, March 1986
§ Interview with Philip Van Niekerk, Africa Report, March 1986

people of this country'. COSATU soon claimed half-a-million members of its affiliated unions, but there remained deep rivalries with other groupings split between political leaderships including AZACTU (the Azanian confederation of trade unions), the arm of the black consciousness group AZAPO and UWUSA, the Zulu unions linked to Buthelezi's Inkatha movement, while the ANC lamented that 'there are 560,000 workers organised in "white-dominated", racist trade unions, and only 14 percent of the total workforce is organised in any trade union.'* But the ANC rejoiced that 'a powerful new voice has been added to the politics of South Africa'. There were potential tensions between COSATU leaders and the ANC in exile; but Tambo knew that when the ANC was legalised the unions would be critical to its re-organisation.

Both government and businesses were confused by the politicisation of the unions. The government had expected to be able to infiltrate and monitor them, to clamp down before they became dangerous; the companies were caught between their need for leaders to negotiate with, and their dread of radical leadership. The mine-owners compared Ramaphosa with Arthur Scargill, the militant mine leader in Britain. 'The more radical elements are naturally drawn towards the power base of the unions,' said Robin Plumbridge of Gold Fields. 'It's awkward if they abuse their power.'

But the most immediate demonstration of black economic influence was the success of local consumer boycotts, which could exploit their purchasing power, pulling the strings of capitalism at the consumer end, while shareholders tugged at the investing end. Consumer boycotts were not new to South Africa: rural black families had boycotted potatoes in the late 'fifties in protest against farm jails; and there had recently been 'black Christmases' boycotting the shops. By early 1985 blacks were organising political boycotts in the Eastern Cape to persuade white shopkeepers to bring pressure on government, or to dissuade black and other shopkeepers from collaborating with the government.

One of the most influential was in the small coastal town of Kenton-on-Sea between Port Elizabeth and East London, where 2,000 blacks lived with one water-tap, no electricity or sewerage and a rubbish dump for the whites in the middle of their township. Just before the emergency they petitioned the local development board, and were faced by the police who tear-gassed them and arrested a hundred. They responded by boycotting white shops which had treated them badly, carefully excepting friendly shopkeepers. The boycott soon showed practical results: the white com-

* *Sechaba*, January 1986

munity formed a liaison committee to discuss the blacks' grievances, arranged for more water-taps, removed the rubbish dump. Then the emergency was declared, the police arrested four black members of the committee, beat them up and interrogated them as agitators.*

But the emergency further inspired the boycotters, particularly in the politicised Eastern Cape, near the big car-plants and other factories. In Port Elizabeth a debonair young black building worker Mkhuseli Jack emerged as the chief spokesman: he had been a student leader in the Soweto revolt and had been jailed many times since. He became prominent in the UDF, and became the 'loudspeaker' for consumer boycotts just before the emergency. He insisted that the boycotters must keep negotiating, using both carrots and sticks: 'If we just say we won't talk they'll be united against us.'† His committee had striking successes with white shops which agreed to their terms; and when the police detained him under the emergency the whites complained that they had no one with whom to negotiate.

The Port Elizabeth boycott was so damaging to white shops – forcing many to shut down – that the Chamber of Commerce complained to Pretoria that the emergency had wrecked their negotiations, and the mayor appealed in vain to President Botha to relax it. The movement spread to the Western Cape, including the prosperous town of Worcester: 'Why should we make Worcester rich,' asked Allan Boesak, 'when these people vote for the National Party and keep P W Botha in power?' As boycotts spread to the Transvaal, the Association of Chambers of Commerce, ASSOCOM, met to discuss the need for better communication. Raymond Ackerman, the retailing tycoon and champion of consumer sovereignty who ran the Pick 'n Pay supermarkets – who only a few years earlier had keenly supported the government – now formed a committee to 'press for reform and to promote dialogue' and emerged as a lifelong 'foe of apartheid'.

The boycotts had limitations; they never really worked in Soweto, which was too big and divided to be effectively monitored and enforced; and when the young 'comrades' tried coercion – for instance by forcing housewives to drink the oil they had bought from white shops – the older people turned against them. The movement was only really effective for remedying local grievances, and could not penetrate the more powerful financial interests. 'It has taken the struggle on to white doorsteps,' said the ANC magazine

* *See Financial Times*, October 29, 1985
† *Wall Street Journal*, April 28, 1985

Sechaba: 'It has not yet taken it into the inner corridors of power.'*
But the blacks had learnt to work the economic pulleys, like the
blacks in America, to achieve immediate results; and they had also
rapidly persuaded many big retailing companies that they must
campaign openly against the government if they wanted to keep
their black customers. Shopkeepers, supermarkets, cinemas and
retail chains became bolder in pressing for radical and rapid reforms,
all the more as recession bit into their business. The old Marxist
picture of a monolithic capitalism could not fit the whole spectrum
of different interests – from mining and engineering through manufacturing to retailing – each with their conflicting pressures from
black custom and unions on one side, and government patronage
on the other. Nor could immediate commercial interests altogether
explain the very different responses of companies to the crisis. For
most South African business was still controlled by a handful of
individual entrepreneurs, each with his own background, conscience
and perspective. It was personality and judgment, as much as
economic interests, which explained differences of behaviour. The
emergency was causing agonised rethinking by the more far-sighted
business leaders in all sectors, who were aware of their hateful image
among blacks, and most of all among the schoolboys who should
be their future workforce. They knew that they could not achieve
political stability without a settlement with the blacks; while opinion
polls were recording the growing hostility.

Chief Buthelezi looked more attractive to many businessmen,
particularly in Natal, as the violence increased. He insisted that
investment was a strategy *for* liberation and always gave a friendly
welcome to visiting businessmen. He explained the horrors of violence and the evils of the ANC, and after the ANC's special congress
in June he told American business visitors that its delegates had
been 'faceless nobodies' who were to blame for inciting blacks
against blacks. He remained ambivalent towards the ANC, praising
Mandela – with whom he had a friendly exchange of letters – while
denigrating Tambo. In September he ferociously attacked the ANC
to a crowd of 15,000 in KwaZulu, explaining how their so-called
armed struggle had been a dismal failure. 'The fundamental difference in approach between Inkatha and the ANC mission-in-exile
revolves around the use of violence.' He condemned both Botha
and Tambo for being out of touch: 'It is the people in the end who
will triumph and Inkatha is rooted in the people's power.'† But in

* Jean Middleton, 'The Consumer Boycott: A People's Weapon', *Sechaba*, April
1986
† Speech at Umlazi, September 28, 1985. *See also Clarion Call* (the official
magazine of the KwaZulu government, Ulundi), Vol, 13, 1985

the angry black townships round Johannesburg or Port Elizabeth, Buthelezi's Zulu traditions could not attract Xhosa or Basuto; and his Zulu *impi*s were practised in violence. 'He has left the nation,' said Dr Motlana of the UDF, 'and joined the tribe.'

The predicament of businessmen was much more fundamental. 'There can be no real change until business takes the side of freedom,' Winnie Mandela said to me in Johannesburg in August. 'In the past white businesses haven't used their clout because their profit margins were soaring with the help of influx control, decentralising and slave-wages,' said Percy Qoboza, the veteran editor of the black *City Press*. 'Now the tables are turned and apartheid is hurting them. I sense they feel helpless: they don't seem psychologically able to use their collective muscle.' Many businessmen privately agreed; but the gap between thinking and acting was as wide as ever, and they each looked to leadership from the other. There was special agonising among the Jewish community whose families had first come to South Africa to escape racial persecution in Tsarist Russia or Nazi Germany. As Mendel Kaplan put it, in his history of Jewish entrepreneurs:

> Businessmen as a group, until the second half of 1985, have been often mere spectators in the battle to remove, not only general discriminatory practices, but those specifically affecting the economy of which their companies are a part. If Jewish businessmen, in particular, fail to give leadership in the movement to abolish all discriminatory practices, they will be betraying their heritage in the country which gave the Jewish people their freedom and opportunities.*

What really hit businessmen was the state of the economy, and the collapsing currency. The rand had already been sloping downwards over the previous year, as foreign investors became more concerned about the political stability. The declaration of the emergency had been quickly followed by the Chase Manhattan's refusal to continue lending (*see* Chapter 2) which, with the French ban on investment, caused a massive loss of confidence. As the rand fell further, threatening any business with short-term loans in dollars, the businessmen looked forward hopefully to President Botha's speech to the National Party Congress on August 16 which was heralded as promising crucial reforms to reassure the bankers. But Botha at the last minute modified his speech, leaving out references to sharing political power with blacks and slamming the door on Mandela, whom he

---

* Kaplan, *op. cit.*, p. 389

untruthfully portrayed as a self-confessed communist. Nothing was left to placate the blacks – except a reference to pass-laws being 'outdated'. And Botha's main emphasis was on defying foreign pressure: 'Don't push us too far . . .'

The blacks were outraged: '*He* has pushed *us* too far,' said Winnie Mandela: '*He* has pushed the rest of the world too far. It's incredible – not even Hitler would have done that. That peculiar Afrikaner tribe, they get themselves into their corner and then ask people to negotiate to get them out of that corner.'*

But Botha's 'Rubicon' speech had also slammed the door on businessmen and bankers as it precipitated a new collapse of the currency, which went on falling for the next days; and a week after Botha's speech the stock-exchange was closed while the government re-imposed its emergency controls to prevent further capital flight (*see* page 34). The connection between politics and business now seemed total. 'I used to say that we should only be involved in politics when it directly affected our own financial interests,' the chairman of Barlow Rand, Mike Rosholt, said to me the day after the rand had collapsed, 'but now where can you draw the line?' Rosholt hoped that the economic crisis would concentrate minds in Pretoria, and was sure that businessmen must play a bolder role. 'When you think about it, compromises are part of our daily activity, every time we make a deal. We're more used to them than politicians.' And behind the scenes a group of business leaders, including Rosholt, had been seriously considering: might they possibly be able to do business with the ANC?

* Interview with author, August 1985

13

Tycoons and Revolutionaries

The longer the white minority regime persists in its racist policies, the greater the likelihood that black South African mythology will become overwhelmingly anti-capitalist and anti-Western.

Leonard Thompson, *The Political Mythology of Apartheid*,
New Haven, Yale University Press, 1985, p. 243

Since Harry Oppenheimer had retired as chairman of the Anglo-American Corporation in January 1983 there had been constant speculation about the character of the new leadership. Few people were very surprised at the choice of his successor, Gavin Relly, who came from the heart of the Anglo tradition: a former Rhodes Scholar, he had been private secretary to both Harry and his father Sir Ernest before climbing the Anglo ladder: he had run its Zambian mines at the time when President Kaunda had half-nationalised them – which shocked him much less than Oppenheimer – and he later ran its North American business from Toronto. He personified the 'Anglo style' which combined the manner of an English public school with being (as Relly put it) 'much tougher than one looks'.* He was more naturally conservative and much less politically experienced than Oppenheimer, but he was thrust into politics as a director of Anglo and as president of the SA Foundation. He thought that South African businessmen were more exposed to the international disapproval of apartheid than governments which were 'involved in the delicate egg dances of the diplomatic world', and he insisted that business was 'entitled to say when it thinks those politics are jeopardising its ability to create wealth'. He had his own doubts about capitalism: 'I am not keen on calling ours a capitalist society,' he said in 1985, 'because I think capitalism in certain circumstances is not very free. For instance, while Nazi Germany was a capitalist society it was never free in any proper sense.'†

Harry Oppenheimer still had an office in the Anglo building; his only son Nicholas, who became deputy chairman, was talked of as

* Interview with Alan Cowell, *New York Times*, November 18, 1985
† Interview with Hugh Murray, *Leadership* magazine, Johannesburg, 1985

Relly's successor, and the family firm, E Oppenheimer and Son, was still the largest single shareholder in Anglo. Harry still made some speeches round the world, and made no secret of his political worries: with the emergency he was totally disillusioned with Botha's promises to businessmen. Gavin Relly commissioned an immense volume weighing sixteen pounds full of flattering tributes to Oppenheimer and the Corporation,* but he made clear that he would not necessarily follow in his predecessor's footsteps: 'I don't intend to have to fill his boots. I intend to fill my own.'† He was less subtle and reflective than Oppenheimer: he had the bluff outdoors style of many Anglo executives; he held forth articulately, looking over his spectacles; he enjoyed robust argument and giving interviews, using phrases like 'I would judge that.' But he never had Oppenheimer's intellectual curiosity or love of listening, and did not pretend to. He was not deeply informed about black politics, and had never taken the ANC very seriously. It was all the more astonishing when, soon after the declaration of the emergency, he agreed to join a small group to fly up to Zambia to talk to Oliver Tambo.

Relly had a more awesome responsibility than the bankers: a huge industrial company could not simply cut its losses and pull out, as the bankers had done; it had a massive stake in the country's future, whatever its government. And Anglo now dominated the South African economy more than ever. One survey compiled in 1985 (fiercely disputed by Anglo) showed that it controlled, directly and indirectly, 54.2 percent of the Johannesburg stock exchange (which is said to represent 26 percent of South Africa's wealth), four times as much as its nearest contenders, Sanlam and SA Mutual. 'We're living in a country controlled by cartels and lobbyists,' wrote Robin McGregor, the author and publisher of *The Investor's Handbook* '– and a government only too keen to satisfy the lobbyists at the expense of 25 million people.'‡

Percentage of control over Johannesburg stock exchange

Anglo-American	54.1%	Rembrandt Group	4.4%
Sanlam	11.3%	Liberty Group	2.3%
SA Mutual	10.9%	Anglo-Vaal	2.1%

To many black radicals Anglo seemed to come close to Lenin's

* HFO: Some Personal Perspectives, 1985
† *New York Times, ibid.*
‡ *The Investor's Handbook*, Purdey Publishing (Box 47, McGregor, 6708, South Africa)

picture of 'monopoly capitalism', as Relly was fully aware. Would it not be better, I asked him, if it were broken up? 'But where would you start?' he replied. 'We've got a quarter of a million shareholders. We don't deal in price-fixing businesses. Gold doesn't rape the public. All our companies are very separate. The government knows that they would fiddle with Anglo at their peril – because there'd be no logic for preventing other fiddling.' But Relly was aware that Anglo and the other major corporations would have to be fundamentally changed to make them acceptable to any future black, or partly black, government. 'I don't stand by rigid paternalist capitalism; we need a change in the process of shareholding. But free enterprise should mean above all a freedom of choice.'*

The economic strength of Anglo was not easily translated into political power; and its semi-monopoly was a source of weakness as much as strength. It was always acutely vulnerable to Pretoria, whether through government contracts or broader political leverage; and it was reluctant to interfere with the autonomy of its hundreds of subsidiaries for fear of being accused of monopoly. A tragic example was its attitude to the country's most liberal newspaper, the *Rand Daily Mail*, which it controlled indirectly through the newspaper group SAAN. The *Mail* had a large black readership in Soweto, so that it formed (as Gavin Relly himself put it) 'a bridge between black and white thinking'. And Relly was personally concerned that white South Africans would 'get into a position where for lack of nitty-gritty investigation or comment by the press, we may come to be deluded as to the real nature of our society, and how it is developing.'† But the *Mail* was not popular with most businessmen or advertisers, who preferred the conventional Johannesburg *Star*, the traditional spokesman of the Chamber of Mines. By the 'eighties the *Mail* was losing several million dollars a year, and SAAN wanted to close it down: the journalists appealed to Oppenheimer and Relly, but in vain, and on April 30, 1985 it stopped publication, to be replaced the next day by *Business Day*, which was proclaimed as the 'national newspaper for decision-makers' and which had few black readers. To knock down the *Mail*'s bridge, just when the country was becoming rapidly polarised and businessmen were looking anxiously for contacts with blacks, raised more serious doubts as to whether South African businessmen were really acting in their own interests.

But as the wave of violence moved into the emergency, Relly was becoming more aware of the long-term dangers of Anglo's

* Interview with author, May 1986
† *Leadership, ibid.*

identification with Pretoria; and though he dreaded the 'African quagmire' he had seen in Zambia a peaceful transition to black rule. Already before the emergency there had been tentative moves to make contact with the ANC in exile from several businessmen, who included Ian Sims, the New Zealander who ran BP in Cape Town and Chris Ball, the chief executive of Barclays in Johannesburg. The most determined and open was Tony Bloom, the debonair young Harvard-trained lawyer who had taken over from his father – as the fourth generation of his family – to become chairman of the Premier Group in 1979. Premier's bakeries, stores and factories were increasingly dependent on black custom and thus concerned with their political image; but Bloom was also personally an intellectual, and one of the most courageous of the business leaders. Others outside business were also pressing for contacts with the ANC, including Hugh Murray, the entrepreneurial editor of *Leadership* magazine who had struck up a warm relationship with President Kaunda in Zambia, and believed that 'the ANC *is* a reality that South Africans will have to come to grips with – sooner or later'; and Harald Pakendorf, the adventurous young editor of the Afrikaner daily *Vaderland*, who had decided: 'it is only really the ANC which at the end of the day can be said to have a truly national following – if not for its methods at least for its ideals.' Pakendorf insisted that South Africa must 'grasp the nettle of the ANC, full well knowing that it may be dangerous, but not as dangerous as not doing it.'*

The South African Foundation, which was now much more independent from Pretoria, was also favouring contact with the ANC, and in January 1985 its man in London, David Willers, had already met two officials from the ANC in London, Solly Smith and Seretse Choabe. Willers assured them that South African businessmen were now committed to fundamental reforms, for reasons of self-interest, and preferred the ANC to be legalised: the Foundation would like to exchange views with the ANC and to find common ground; they were also 'anxious to try to avoid becoming a sabotage target of the ANC'. Solly Smith said that the ANC would be glad to have talks with anyone, provided they were not formal negotiations; and warned that if the ANC were to be undermined by more radical elements, the task of reconstruction would become much more difficult.

The revival in the reputation of the African National Congress had taken nearly all whites by surprise. It was still officially banned, unquoted in the press, and most of its leaders had been in jail for

* *Leadership*, 1985

twenty-two years; but Mandela had never been so famous. The power of the ANC, with their fragile organisation confronted by all Pretoria's military machine, seemed as mysterious as that of the Ayatollah Khomeini before the Iranian revolution, and in some ways more baffling; for it had no strong religious backing, and no network of mullahs and mosques. But it still represented the long tradition of black protest, martyrdom and freedom to which the young rebels now rallied. Many younger white businessmen were now seriously wondering whether they might not be dealing with an ANC government in their lifetime. 'Within the Republic,' wrote the historian of black politics, Tom Lodge, 'the conviction that the ANC constitutes the only viable alternative and successor to the incumbent administration is one that is beginning to affect not just the political responses of black people but those of whites as well.'*

In Lusaka, Oliver Tambo was still looking for international economic pressure to avert the need for greater violence; and he believed that businessmen could do far more to influence the Pretoria government. He was supported by his more left-wing colleagues, including the white communist Joe Slovo, and he took care to keep in touch with his contacts inside South Africa, to explain to them why he was talking to capitalists.

By early August a group of South African business leaders had agreed to take the bold step and to fly up to Lusaka. Originally they were to include not only Gavin Relly and Tony Bloom, but also Chris Ball of Barclays, Mike Rosholt, the chairman of the conglomerate Barlow Rand, and two influential Afrikaners: Anton Rupert of the Rembrandt tobacco group and Fred Du Plessis of Sanlam. But the first meeting on August 28 had to be postponed; then Ball had to attend a strategy meeting, and Rosholt explained he must go to his son's wedding. And when the plans were leaked Du Plessis and Rupert dropped out, fearing the anger of the president. But Botha did not try to stop the visit: 'He was cross, but not very cross,' said Relly. The foreign ministry in Pretoria even gave the businessmen's party a very superficial three-page briefing about the ANC.

On September 13, the little party flew up in an Anglo plane to Zambia: the businessmen Relly and Bloom, augmented at the last moment by Zach de Beer, the former Progressive MP who was now a director of Anglo, together with two newspaper editors, Pakendorf and Tertius Myburg of the Johannesburg *Sunday Times*. But Relly was far the most significant, as head of the dominant corporation;

* Tom Lodge, The Second Consultative Conference of the African National Congress, South African International, 1985

and he had agreed against the opinion of Oppenheimer, who did not conceal that he felt 'twitchy' about the excursion.

They met at the presidential hunting lodge of Mfuwe, the game park in Zambia, where Kaunda received them, and brought them together with the team from the ANC: Oliver Tambo, as President; the young director of information Thabo Mbeki, whose father Govan was still in prison with Mandela; the Indian Mac Maharaj, who had been on Robben Island; and Chris Hani. The blacks wore ties and neat suits, while the whites looked unkempt with open necks: 'If you'd been asked to say which were the businessmen, which were the revolutionaries,' said one of the whites, 'you'd have got it the wrong way round.' Kaunda spoke briefly, pointing out that they were all South Africans: he offered to leave them together, and was pressed to stay. Tambo insisted that they should not sit in two phalanxes facing each other, like opposing camps, but should be distributed round the room. He called Relly 'Gavin' and asked to be called Oliver. The atmosphere, everyone agreed, was soon extraordinarily friendly. 'It was one of the nicest days I've ever spent,' Relly said afterwards. 'A picnic among South Africans talking about their future together.' 'A more attractive and genial group would be hard to imagine,' said Bloom. 'It was a marvellous meeting,' said Tambo. They talked for six hours – continuing through lunch where Tambo said grace to the whites' astonishment – about the problems of violence, reconstruction, nationalisation and the country's economic future. Bloom was struck by the blacks' sense of patriotism after years of exile: they loved to talk about places and people in the Republic. He also thought they were highly intelligent leaders – 'streets ahead' of most black leaders inside South Africa – with whom there could be serious negotiations and compromise. He remained worried by the communist component and the ANC's links with the SACP, but he was struck by the lack of Marxist dogma: Sweden seemed to be their model, rather than Eastern Europe or Russia. The businessmen predictably asked about the threat of nationalisation, which was implicit in the ANC's Freedom Charter of thirty years earlier. Tambo insisted that some major corporations would have to be taken under state control: 'They represent tremendous wealth in the midst of unspeakable poverty.' He also asked the businessmen to stop supporting the state arms corporation, Armscor, and warned that the ANC would attack economic installations. But he adopted a very conciliatory approach, and talked about a future mixed economy in South Africa. When asked about the violence, Tambo said he personally abhorred it – 'I even take insects out of the bath' – but he and Thabo Mbeki explained that the intensification of the military struggle would inevitably mean that more civilians would die, though the ANC would not deliberately attack them. But Tambo insisted later that he had left them with no doubt that he would be 'compelled to allow violence' in the future.*

The whites left in a mood of some euphoria. Bloom believed it was a breakthrough and hoped for a follow-up. Hugh Murray insisted that there was 'considerable justification for further talks'. Gavin Relly was clearly moved by the goodwill. 'There are important areas in which one should be able to find fundamental agreement, starting with the recognition that we are all South Africans . . .', he said in London soon afterwards. 'All of us in that meeting wanted to see a new coherent society in South Africa based on demonstrable justice and a court-monitored bill of rights.'† And he later explained:

Predictably there remained great gaps between us. Businessmen do not embrace the prospects of nationalisation, either in practical or philosophical terms; they know as a matter of fact that economic thinking which derives from the shadowy, incompetent world of worn-out Marxism does not create wealth. On the other hand, who can deny that there are inequities in the generation and distribution of South Africa's wealth? A new society, reformed or revolutionary, would have to apply itself more diligently to the alleviation of deprivation in education, health and feeding.‡

The ANC still broadcast bloodthirsty threats against whites: On October 7 Radio Freedom from Addis Ababa said: 'We must attack them at their homes and holiday resorts just as we have been attacking black boot-lickers at their homes. This must happen to their white colleagues.' But Tambo soon afterwards explained in a broadcast on October 15 that business leaders could be an 'additional lever' in the ANC's struggle, even if they were motivated by their own self-interest: 'If they reach the conclusion that, indeed, the whole apartheid system is going to destroy their businesses, even the whole economy, at that point they will want to remove the apartheid system and will even join with forces which are set to destroy the system, provided they are sure that the system will not be replaced with something worse for their economy, for their pockets, for their profits.'

* *Financial Times*, September 14, 1985; *Weekly Mail*, January 17, 1986. *Also* author's interviews with Tambo, Relly, Bloom
† Interview with Jonathan Power, *International Herald Tribune*, September 23, 1985
‡ Article in the *Guardian*, London, October 7, 1985

Tambo was also ready to talk with international businessmen, all the more after his encounters in New York the previous March; and in October 1985 he was invited by a group of friends to visit London, not just to talk to the Anti-Apartheid Movement and the Labour Party – the traditional allies of the ANC – but to meet businessmen, bankers and other politicians. In the first part of his London visit Tambo briefly overlapped with Bishop Tutu; and the Commonwealth Secretary-General Sonny Ramphal gave a dinner for both at the resplendent Commonwealth headquarters at Marlborough House underneath the frescoes of the Duke of Marlborough's eighteenth-century victories. It was attended by Commonwealth diplomats, businessmen and churchmen, including Bishop Trevor Huddleston who had been the mentor of both guests of honour; but it was boycotted by the British government. Tambo talked warmly about his meeting with businessmen in Lusaka, where they were all South Africans together: but he warned of much harsher confrontations with apartheid government ahead. And he told the British guests: 'When you say that you don't want sanctions because it would hurt us most, you're not honest. You don't want to hurt your trade – which you think depends on apartheid.'

Later in October, at a small private gathering, Tambo met for the first time chairmen or directors of the biggest British companies investing in South Africa. Tambo began by saying that the meeting should have happened ten or twenty years earlier, since they both should have the same concern with a peaceful South Africa. He had welcomed the concern of American and South African businessmen; but the British were especially important with their huge investments, and he asked for their help in bringing pressure on Botha. They couldn't leave it to economic progress to break down apartheid. He was confident that the ANC were winning the fight for their rights – he would not be talking to them if he were not – but there would be much more violence, even a total catastrophe, unless international interests intervened. Every reform that Pretoria had made had been the result of international pressure. Already whites, including Afrikaners, were turning against apartheid as they began to feel the pinch: they would insist on a change of government as the pressure stepped up. Sanctions would never cause an 'economic wasteland' because the government would be changed long before that. A real wasteland would be produced if South Africa were left to itself.

The businessmen were reluctant to commit themselves, and they complained about the ANC's policy of nationalising the banks, mines and land in the Freedom Charter thirty-five years earlier. 'How can you expect us to help you, on behalf of our shareholders,' one chairman asked, 'if our only reward will be to be nationalised?' 'We do business in twenty African countries,' said another, 'often with the greatest difficulty. We have to be able to earn dividends. We're fed up with being told before independence "It'll be alright on the night." What guarantees can you give us?' 'But we are not committed to any dogma,' replied Tambo: 'we are committed to democracy, and we must wait for the people to decide what they want. Our chief concern is redistribution, in our country which has such great inequalities and concentrations of wealth.' Nationalisation had seemed the most obvious means; but there could be others, including perhaps a version of the American Sherman anti-trust act. He was impressed by the economic policies of Robert Mugabe in Zimbabwe (who though committed to extensive nationalisation had in fact stalled it and encouraged free enterprise.)

Tambo asked them to make clear their total opposition to apartheid, and to press the British government to a much stronger stand. 'I'm talking to you not as businessmen but as human beings.' He was puzzled that a nation which had fought at such cost to defeat the Nazis should have such reservations in defeating apartheid. 'You British were determined to destroy Hitler – which meant that much of Europe became a wasteland – but you destroyed him. We see the Pretoria regime as like the Nazis.' The businessmen had varying views. 'Isn't there a constructive way,' one of them asked the others, 'of showing that business is on the side of the blacks?' But most were wary. 'It's much harder for foreign companies to criticise the government than for the South Africans,' one of them told Tambo. 'We exert a lot of pressure behind the scenes, but we can't press too hard or they'll chuck us out.' It was a worrying argument, that multinationals had to be more subservient to tyranny than local companies, and it contradicted the Americans' insistence that multinationals had a special political responsibility. But the British were under much less domestic pressure from shareholders and dared not risk offending Pretoria by appearing to consort with the enemy. They were beginning to hedge their bets, but not to change sides. Tambo was disappointed, he said later, that they had shown no 'change of heart'.

But in the following days Tambo, who had so often visited London, was for the first time received into the conservative areas of the city: he gave a speech at Chatham House, dined privately with bankers and entrepreneurs, and was welcomed by the two biggest banks, Barclays and Standard. He had tea with Tory MPs and gave evidence to the House of Commons' Foreign Affairs Committee – to whom he explained once again the ANC's policy

on violence and reasserted that only sanctions could reduce the
bloodshed and that condemnations and denunciations of apartheid
meant nothing to Pretoria. 'However, they are very very concerned
now, since the position taken by the banks. In fact the withdrawal
of loans, the refusal to grant loans or to roll them over, has demon-
strated that sanctions can be effective. One of the consequences of
this has been that the business community in South Africa has now
been moved not by appeals but by the reality of the threat of
sanctions, of disinvestment, to take very firm positions against the
Botha regime.'

The British government – even junior officials – still had no
contact with Tambo or the ANC; but a few dissident Tory MPs,
headed by Hugh Dykes and Tim Rathbone, formed their own 'Talk
to Tambo' group and later invited a delegation from the ANC to a
forthright lunch. 'Why do you make it difficult for your friends by
blowing up cars with landmines?' asked the Tories. 'Why is this the
first time that Tories have talked to us in twenty years?' asked the
ANC.

In South Africa in the meantime the first euphoria after the
Lusaka meeting was soon evaporating, as President Botha began
to reassert his authority with a propaganda campaign against the
ANC, while bombings and explosions shocked white opinion. In
December a landmine exploded near Messina, close to the Zimbabwe frontier, killing six whites, followed by another near Stock-
port – the most serious acts of terrorism for eighteen months. At
Anglo-American, Gavin Relly was facing recriminations. Harry
Oppenheimer, still outspoken in retirement, remained twitchy
about the meeting, puzzled that the atmosphere was so friendly
even though Tambo had conceded nothing, particularly over
nationalisation; and in November he had told the American
Chamber of Commerce that businessmen should offer 'neither moral
support nor material support' for the ANC, since they want 'an
economic system that would destroy everything that we in this room
stand for'.* And Relly himself was beginning to backtrack. 'The
Lusaka meeting was really much more of a watershed than any of
the participants intended,' he said later. 'I've been blamed ever
since for opening the floodgates of international business to deal
with the ANC ... It was important to establish a relationship
between the wealth-producing sector and a new African economic
policy. But I don't think that we have a role to get the government
and the ANC together.'† When more bombs and land-mines were

* *New York Times*, November 18, 1985
† Interview with author, May 1986

exploding, Relly explained that Tambo had misled him, and not warned him about future atrocities. Even Hugh Murray, the journalist who helped to organise the meeting, had second thoughts, worried about the communists in the ANC and the bloodthirsty broadcasts: he still favoured more talks, but he thought that Tambo would have no real success until he stopped selling violence-related policies. 'The ANC is *not* about to seize power, no matter how it is hyped up . . .'*

By the end of the year the honeymoon was emphatically over, after a more gruesome act of terrorism which gave a warning of the black anger and chaos to come. Andrew Zondo was a schoolboy of fifteen when in 1983 (he later told the court) he was recruited into the ANC, and in exile at seventeen he joined the military wing Umkhonto. He had been appalled by the tear-gassing of black students by the police: 'From that day onwards whenever I look at a policeman I see him as an enemy.' Then in May 1983 he heard news of a South African air attack on Mozambique, which persuaded him that 'there was no chance to improve the life of blacks in South Africa except through violence'; and before Christmas 1985 he decided to take his own reprisals. With the help of an accomplice, Mr X, he planted a limpet-mine with a thirty-minute fuse in a refuse bin in the shopping centre of Amanzimtoti, the seaside town near Durban: intending (he explained) to give warning before it went off. But he could not find a free telephone, and the bomb went off, killing five Christmas shoppers. Zondo was caught and Mr X turned state witness at his trial, claiming that he and Zondo had been instructed by Umkhonto and the ANC; while Tambo later disclaimed knowledge, insisting that ANC strategy did not call for attacks in supermarkets, schools, or cinemas. But the Amanzimtoti deaths just before Christmas caused a wave of white indignation. The father of a child killed at Amanzimtoti, Kennie Smit, actually urged the government to begin talking to the ANC about peaceful co-existence; but the killings effectively sabotaged further businessmen's talks with the ANC over the following months. At a press conference in the New Year (which South Africans were given special permission to quote) Tambo warned that civilian casualties were unavoidable in escalating warfare and promised that the ANC would organise 'mass units' drawn from local populations; while he again asked business leaders to stop supporting the state arms corporation, Armscor. But most businessmen were now in no mood to listen. Ken Owen in *Business Day* in Johannesburg now said that 'the gap between the ANC and the SA government is simply too

* *Leadership* magazine, 1985

wide to be bridgeable,' and the *Star* said that Tambo 'has done incalculable harm to the cause of real reform in South Africa.'*

It was back to the classic deadlock: Relly and most business colleagues insisted that the continuing violence prevented future talks; while the ANC insisted that without violence no one would talk. 'It was *because* of the violence,' Tambo said, 'that Relly came to Lusaka.' The political pressures were now pulling both sides further apart, as extremists thrived on the confrontation: the ANC dreaded the emergence of a military state, while the businessmen foresaw a black anarchy ruled by a Khmer Rouge of ruthless schoolboys. But they both faced a common nightmare of a chaotic country in which no one could do business.

---

* *Business Day*, January 10, 1986. *Johannesburg Star*, January 10, 1986. *Weekly Mail*, January 17, 1986, *Sechaba*, August 1986

14

Multinational Twilight

A major challenge to business is quite simply to save the system of
capitalism from being fatally undermined by cynicism among blacks
that capitalism and white supremacy are in cahoots with one another.

Professor Hermann Giliomee, in a paper to management seminar
of Mobil Southern Africa, Cape Town, 1982

The businessmen's paradise of the 'seventies was now looking far
less alluring: the green bay tree was visibly wilting. Already in the
early 'eighties South African manufacturers were worried by the
declining competitiveness of their products and the poor economic
growth. In the decade up to 1982 South Africa's performance had
compared miserably with its major trading partners in the West:
its productivity, in terms of output per hour, had actually decreased
by 18 percent in the previous twelve years. Between 1980 and 1985
the gross domestic product had grown by an average of only 0.7
percent per year, compared to 3.6 percent in the 'seventies, 5.9
percent in the 'sixties and 4.4 percent in the 'fifties. South Africa
had a lower GDP per head than any of its major trading partners in
the West; and it had risen more slowly than any of them except
Switzerland.* It was becoming more like another African country.
  The political causes were clear. The School of Business Leadership in Cape Town had set up a 'Project Free Enterprise' which
produced two reports in 1984 and 1985: they found that black
workers had little confidence in their management, that some of
them were even actively sabotaging production, and that 'both
quality and productivity are irrelevant to workers who feel that they
do not participate in, or benefit from, the business system.' While
many more blacks had come into industry, few companies had
seriously attended to black advancement, which was seen 'as a
move of economic necessity rather than strategic vision'. Many
executives had continued to delay promoting blacks for fear of a
backlash among their white employees. Yet eventually, when they
had to promote blacks from economic necessity, 'in no instance

* Survey for SA Foundation by the Bureau for Market Research, *see SA
Foundation News*, July 1986

was any major white backlash experienced'. It was a devastating response to all those multinationals who deferred to the 'man on the spot'. As the report said: 'the business sector has made itself guilty of paying "lip service" for too long.'*

By the end of 1985 the political recession and falling demand were compounding the problems for exporting companies. The car industry, into which so much investment was flowing in the 'sixties, was now far too big: 'There is plant capacity in South Africa for about 600,000 cars,' said Walter Hasselkus the local managing director of BMW, which had so rashly chosen the Republic for its only plant outside West Germany: 'The market this year is about 200,000.' By December 1985 even BMW was pressing for political change: 'Multinational corporations know,' said Hasselkus, 'perhaps better than our friends in government do, how intense the Western world's impatience with South Africa has become. Let us create a political environment that takes the heat off foreign companies.' Pretoria was now proposing to subsidise exporting car companies and with this incentive BMW were having talks with General Motors about rationalising their production: but subsidies would inevitably increase the government's influence.†

The 'bubbling entrepreneurs' whom *The Economist* had admired in the 'sixties now looked less daring as more companies began to be cartelised round the two giants of government on one side and Anglo on the other. The economic crisis, with or without deliberate disinvestment or sanctions, was making the big South African groups relatively stronger, the foreigners weaker. The flow from local pension funds still provided money to invest in local industry and property, in a circle of self-sufficiency; but without foreign investment and lending, the prospects for growth were severely limited.

The one still-booming industry was defence, which provided through Armscor lucrative contracts in high-technology for many apparently peaceful industrial companies, making them increasingly dependent on Pretoria's patronage. The engineering conglomerate Barlow Rand (linked through share ownership with Anglo-American) appeared as a benign and liberalising company, under its civilised chairman Mike Rosholt; but through its subsidiaries, including C J Fuchs, Reunert and its half-share in British General Electric, Barlow's had secretly become a major producer of defence electronics and computers. Since 1980 Rosholt, together

* School of Business Leadership: Project Free Enterprise Final Report, Cape Town, 1986
† South African Report, December 6, 1985

with two other members of Barlow's board, Goss of SA Breweries and Cronje of Nedbank, had become a member of President Botha's new Defence Advisory Board – which placed him at the heart of the military-industrial complex, both profiting from it, and indebted to it.* It was hardly surprising if Rosholt had decided not, after all, to make contact with the banned ANC.

But no industrialist could now ignore the political hazards and the visible unworkability of apartheid. In January 1986, the Federated Chamber of Industries, the most far-sighted of the business lobbies, chaired by John Wilson of Shell, produced a Business Charter of Rights – after consultations with black groups including the ANC and the UDF – which came out with bold-sounding prescriptions including removing all discrimination, negotiating 'genuine political power-sharing by all South Africans up to the highest level' and 'full equal citizenship for all South Africans'. It was soon endorsed by the American Chamber of Commerce and later by Project Free Enterprise, which insisted that 'political and economic policy are totally interdependent'.† But the Charter was not specific about actual black votes, and there was some wry comedy behind the rush of condemnations of apartheid by business leaders who had so long lain low. As they commuted back to their all-white suburbs, voted for their all-white MPs and subsidised the white army and police, most businessmen were now revealing themselves as life-long enemies of apartheid in their annual reports, advertisements or charters: it was not difficult when even the State President had declared apartheid outdated. The word that had been so enthusiastically coined could be equally keenly discarded, leaving most of the structure and damage intact. And the charters were prepared to consider every reform except the one that political blacks were demanding: one man, one vote.

All the businessmen's worries about the future were multiplied by the projections of black population. A report by the Department of Health in 1984 had shown that black women were producing an average of 5.2 children, while white women produced an average of 2.08; and that at the present population growth rate the total South African population would be 47 million by 2000 and 79 million by 2020 – of whom 66 million would be black. The report warned that at this rate the balance between population and resources would be disturbed, 'seriously jeopardising stability and progress'. It was a forecast which seriously disturbed President

* Report on 'The Barlow Rand Connection' in the International Seminar on the UN Arms Embargo against South Africa, London, May 28, 1986
† Project Free Enterprise, p. 109

Botha; * but it worried investors and businessmen as much. For it implied that South Africa would belong still less to the first world, more to the third world – and especially to the rest of the continent, which now faced more serious population problems than Asia or Latin America. The nightmare of sinking into the 'African quagmire' was becoming real. The big banks, looking at the projections of social costs and revenues, were beginning to reckon that South Africa, even without apartheid, had a very uncertain economic future.

But now the mounting black anger, the costs of repression, bad economic management and the withdrawal of loans all made the future still less hopeful. It was hard to solve the population problem without major black participation and consent; some blacks in Soweto, kept at home during the emergency curfew, were talking about having more children to 'make soldiers'. By the year 2000, according to one survey, an extra 3.6 million jobs would be needed, merely to absorb new work-seekers; or 6.8 million if unemployment were to be eliminated.† No long-term investor could take a positive view of the country unless it made major political changes; yet changes would add still further to the economic burden. The economic problem was only partly of the government's making; but its politics prevented any solution.

The foreign multinationals found the prospect still less appetising; for it offered not only diminishing profits but increasing political protests at home. They could find themselves on a hiding to nothing; while the apartheid crisis, which caricatured so much of the West, could shine a harsh floodlight on their corporate characters.

The British companies still had far the biggest stake with between 40 and 45 percent of all the foreign investment‡ – though its value had halved in the two years of the falling rand. Watching the worsening profits and politics, the British chairmen were increasingly bewildered. Many of them now regretted their companies past enthusiasm for investing, and those with big interests in black Africa worried that they might miss some kind of black boat. But they seemed transfixed like rabbits in the headlights by the sheer size of their investments. They could not, like the American bankers, simply decide to withdraw: they had fixed plants on or under the ground which gave them an unavoidable stake in the country's future and pressed them to some kind of choice. They were hedging their bets, but they still dreaded having to antagonise the existing

* Leach, *op. cit.*, p. 241
† Survey commissioned by the SA Foundation. *See SA Foundation News*, July 1986
‡ British Industry in South Africa: BICSA, London, July 1986

Pretoria government: however awful it looked, the alternative could look far worse.

They all preferred not to choose, in their different ways. Unilever, the Anglo-Dutch multinational which had been worried about apartheid since the 'sixties (*see* page 88), still had a whole range of plants and products based on Durban; while together with its trading subsidiary the United Africa Company it had still bigger interests in black African states. Their chairman Sir Kenneth Durham not surprisingly opted for a very low profile in South Africa, and his successor in 1986 Michael Angus stayed still lower, hoping that blacks and protesting shareholders would not notice the extent of their involvement. Courtaulds had proportionately one of the biggest South African investments of all, and the big joint-venture in wood-pulp which they had begun with the government in the 'sixties was part of their international network. Their accounts showed 16 percent of their profits in 1985 coming from Africa (mostly South Africa), with a return on capital of 25 percent: they remained very wary of antagonising Pretoria and inclined to support Buthelezi rather than Tambo, partly because most of their plants were in Zulu territory.

Sir Alistair Frame, the Scots chairman of Rio Tinto-Zinc with its big copper mine at Palabora, was much more conservative than his predecessor Sir Mark Turner, and as mine-owners RTZ were less vulnerable to black opinion than manufacturers or retailers; while their political adviser David Watt, the former director of Chatham House, eloquently opposed any sanctions, both privately and as a columnist in the London *Times*. Lord Weinstock of General Electric, the British engineering giant, was deeply involved with Pretoria through contracts to build power-stations, while the collaboration of its subsidiary Marconi with Barlow Rand (*see* p. 202) involved it more deeply in the military-industrial complex. Weinstock's chairman, James Prior, who had been Minister for Northern Ireland, was worried about where to draw the line between terrorists and a legitimate opposition.

The two oil companies, Shell and BP, both felt especially exposed with their global visibility and their past record in the 'sixties as sanctions-breakers passing oil via South Africa to Rhodesia. BP's London director Patrick Gillam and its New Zealander chief executive Ian Sims in Cape Town had done something to improve black conditions, and had encouraged approaches to the ANC. But the company was inevitably compromised by its dealings with government; and its limitations were embarrassingly revealed when the paperback edition of the Commonwealth Report on South Africa (*see* next chapter) published a photograph showing a BP sign in a

service station above a notice saying 'Whites'. BP had to explain
that they had no control over the service station which used their
name under a ten-year franchise. Shell had its own vulnerability
after it was boycotted by anti-apartheid campaigners in America
and Europe, calling for it to disinvest; but its London chairman
Peter Holmes, who had previously run Shell in Nigeria, insisted
that it was improving black conditions in South Africa, while
the local chairman John Wilson became more publicly critical of
President Botha (*see* page 241) and closed Shell's offices on June
16, 'Soweto day'. But Shell remained suspect among many blacks,
and in September 1986 one of its personnel officers, Thomas
Nkadimeng – whose brother is a member of the ANC executive –
complained that he had been sacked for refusing to report to Shell
on subversive political activities in Soweto.* Shell denied the charge,
and insisted in an internal memo that personnel officers had merely
been asked to complete questionnaires to help explain the stresses
under which they lived.† But whatever the facts it was clear that
both the British oil companies would find themselves inevitably
more closely involved with security reports as the military build-up
continued.

The British chairmen remained frequently inhibited by their
tradition of leaving their subsidiaries to run themselves. While IBM
or GM wanted all their companies to follow a centralised corporate
policy, the British still liked to give maximum scope to their local
chief executive – usually a white South African subject to his
country's laws and customs, who could find himself in conflict with
headquarters, and even keeping secrets from them. Local managers
– as Project Free Enterprise had exposed – often exaggerated the
white backlash that would follow from bold instructions to defy
apartheid or promoting blacks; while high-minded statements about
equal opportunities could have little connection with the hierarchies
below. As one investigator into German companies in South Africa
found, the foreign firms 'put the foreigners into the highest positions,
and then put the white Afrikaners between them and the workers
and use these Boers as their front. It will always be a Boer who
sacks a black worker'.‡

The influential British trade association UKSATA, run by John
McQuiggan, was still close to the South African Embassy, and
enjoyed easy access to the Tory government. When in February
1986 Van Zyl Slabbert called on Lynda Chalker, the new Tory

* *New Nation*, Johannesburg, September 1986
† Shell management brief, September 19, 1986
‡ 'The Dilemma of Code Three', South African Council of Churches, 198,
p. 10

Minister for Africa, he was surprised to find her accompanied by McQuiggan who sounded more conservative than the Pretoria government. But by January 1986 some of its members wanted to defend their investments more robustly. Sir James Cleminson, the hunting-and-shooting chairman of the Confederation of British Industry, had recently visited South Africa; and the chairman of UKSATA, Neil Forster, who ran the British and Commonwealth shipping line, had close friends there. They called a meeting of eighteen companies and decided to form a new lobby called the British Industry Committee on South Africa or BICSA; and as its chairman they chose Sir Leslie Smith, a combative war-horse who had just retired after fifteen years as chairman of British Oxygen – whose South African subsidiary, though reduced, was still import-ant. Sir Leslie loved a political battle, and was soon thoroughly gung-ho; in March he wrote to all the main company chairmen asking them to support BICSA and suggesting that they should raise their profile and no longer keep their heads 'down below the parapet'. 'We must either believe our South African investments are worthwhile and constructive (for both sides) . . .' he said, 'or we should not be there': and he promised that BICSA would 'ensure that UK business interests remain paramount, and do not get con-fused with political issues'. Sir Leslie's letter worried some of the chairmen: were not 'detailed political issues' exactly what they *should* be getting involved with? And was it wise to commit themselves so totally against sanctions, when the blacks were clamouring for them? Eventually fifty companies including most of the biggest joined BICSA, contributing £2,500 each, while Sir Leslie appeared to pipe down about sanctions.

Sir Leslie and BICSA insisted that British companies were working vigorously against apartheid; but between the high-minded state-ments of directors in London and the practices on South African shop-floors there was often a wide gap – which emerged dramatically in the Rowntree Mackintosh chocolate company, whose Quaker roots were still evident in the two trusts which were its biggest shareholders, one of which, the Joseph Rowntree Charitable Trust, was specifically committed to 'promoting peaceful change and development' for blacks in Southern Africa. The company's South African subsidiary in East London, Wilson Rowntree, had a record of low wages and poor labour conditions in the early 'eighties, and left-wing groups in Britain began boycotting their bestselling chocolates, Kit-Kat. Then a security policeman gave evidence in a trial that Wilson Rowntree with other companies had arranged to call in the police if workers threatened to strike; and the Charitable Trust was still more concerned when Wilson Rowntree decided to join Sir Leslie Smith's BICSA and its anti-sanctions campaign. In July 1986 the trust's secretary Steven Burkeman went out to South Africa, and on his return publicly attacked the company's association with BICSA, warning that by apparently aligning itself with Pretoria it would 'make it very much more difficult to operate under majority rule'.

The American companies were beginning to see apartheid as a more fundamental challenge to their corporate reputations after the waves of shareholders' revolts and black protests: if they did not pull out, they felt obliged not just to oppose apartheid, but to be seen to do so. They were much more self-conscious than most Europeans about their corporate image and standing, and about the role of capitalism in the developing world. The South African crisis was now calling many bluffs, and it required them to show what they could really achieve behind the rhetoric of social responsibility.

Mobil still had a big stake in South Africa where it supplied 20 percent of the gasoline, and it was the most determined to present a high and noble profile, spurred on by its ebullient government relations officer Sal Marzullo. The profits from its oil refinery in Durban were falling with the recession and with competition from the state oil company SASOL, while its dependence on government was increasingly embarrassing, but it was committed to stay to the bitter end. 'If we left South Africa tomorrow,' said Allen Murray, its chairman in South Africa in February 1986, 'the South African government would take over our operation in fourteen seconds and then you know where our people would be.' He was pained that Mobil should be attacked by anti-apartheid activists: 'We don't disagree over what should happen in South Africa. We disagree over the methods; and suddenly we're the enemy.'

The chief executive of IBM in New York, John Akers, was also under heavy fire, with a highly visible business in South Africa including a brown skyscraper in the centre of Johannesburg and a large range of government computer contracts which were often suspected of helping the police state. Akers promised that IBM would stay as long as it had a chance to be profitable, but that looked less likely as Pretoria began to look to alternative computer systems and IBM laid off workers. And by May 1986 Akers was publicly more pessimistic about the slow pace of change.

The chairman of Citibank in New York, John Reed, was still more besieged, with demonstrators in Manhattan and sit-ins in Johannesburg. His local managing director David Hexter insisted that he was contributing to black advancement, and in May 1986 he announced a new programme to lend to black businesses. He claimed, to the annoyance of Barclays and Standard, that there was 'a sizeable market which is not being served'. But Citibank's headquarters in Park Avenue could not persuade their dissident depositors and shareholders that their presence was justified.

The biggest and most exposed American company was still General Motors – still more since Ford had merged with Anglo-American – and its chairman Roger Smith was continually vulnerable, all the more with a large black workforce in Michigan and the unavoidable presence of the Reverend Sullivan on his board. Smith was an unlikely political campaigner: within the corporation he was seen as a cold numbers man, preoccupied with increasing productivity and computerisation and with few social concerns. He was uncommanding in style, with a high-pitched voice: Ralph Nader, General Motor's arch-critic, called him 'the squeak that roars'.* General Motors in South Africa employed less than 1 percent of GM's global total of 750,000; and had made a loss for the last few years: it seemed odd that Smith should devote so much time to this awkward fraction. Like other chairmen he now felt challenged by the disinvestment campaigners to show that capitalism could work for blacks as well as whites, all the more through his commitment to Sullivan; and he refused to be pushed around by demonstrators. 'Remember that General Motors, like Pretoria, regards itself as a sovereign state,' as one Ford man explained. But Smith was already considering a dignified retreat.

Would the corporate protests move beyond public relations? The most showy way to oppose apartheid was the old Mobil way: to advertise. In the wake of the emergency and the visit to Lusaka, ninety-one business leaders inside South Africa published advertisements in the local papers on September 29, headed: 'THERE IS A BETTER WAY'. They explained they were 'deeply concerned about the current situation', and while rejecting violence they advocated accelerating reform by abolishing statutory race discrimination wherever it exists; negotiating with acknowledged black leaders about power sharing; granting full South African citizenship to all peoples; and restoring and entrenching the rule of law.

Behind the scenes Roger Smith was lobbying his colleagues, and three weeks later a clutch of chief executives advertised in American papers, including the *Wall Street Journal*, proclaiming a new business group, 'the US Corporate Council on South Africa': they reproduced part of the South African advertisement, adding 'Today, we add our voice to theirs', and pledging 'to play an active role in peacefully achieving their goals.' It was signed by two co-chairmen, Roger

* For a recent study of Smith's influence on General Motors *see* Ralph Nader & William Taylor, *The Big Boys*, New York, Pantheon Books, 1986, pp. 62–142

Smith of GM and Michael Blumenthal, the chairman of the Burroughs Corporation, also in Michigan; and they were supported by a steering committee of eight more chairmen and chief executives heavily involved in South Africa: John Akers of IBM, James Burke of Johnson & Johnson, Robert Hanson of Deere, Reuben Mark of Colgate-Palmolive, John Reed of Citibank, David Tappan of Fluor, Rawleigh Warner of Mobil and Howard Yergin of Caltex.

The Corporate Council began with a fanfare, promising to support South African businessmen against apartheid, and to protest directly to Pretoria. They supported the existing Sullivan group, and the Reverend welcomed them as 'the beginning of a very important initiative'; though some of the old Sullivan hands soon suspected that the chief executives, arriving in their private jets for high-level talks as if no one had thought about apartheid before, were on their own ego-trips, more concerned with shareholders than blacks: half the ten companies on the steering committee had been targeted as 'key investors in apartheid' by American church groups (*see* p. 172).

Ten biggest American employers in South Africa, 1985
(source: *New York Times*, December 2, 1985);

Ford Motor*	6,700
General Motors	4,900
Coca-Cola	4,800
Mobil	3,300
US Gypsum	2,600
Goodyear	2,500
Caltex	2,200
Allegheny	2,000
R J Reynolds	1,800
IBM	1,800

* Merged with Anglo-American's Amcar, of which it owns 42 per cent

---

After their first splash the tycoons became very secretive. On November 11 four of them – Smith, Blumenthal, Reed and Warner – flew to London to meet South African tycoons including Relly of Anglo and Rosholt of Barlow Rand; two weeks later five South Africans – Wim de Villiers from Gencor, Oppenheimer and Relly from Anglo-American, Fred du Plessis from Sanlam and Anton Rupert from Rembrandt – met President Botha in Pretoria to discuss reforms. They looked a formidable joint lobby of Afrikaners and English, but de Villiers insisted that there was no confrontation and soon afterwards the local chief executive of Burroughs, Mias van Vuuren, insisted that the Corporate Council was 'not seen by anyone as a pressure group on government'.* If not that, what was it?

The Council did have a secret strategy: to offer large sums in return for specific reforms. James Burke of Johnson & Johnson said that if there were the right reforms he was prepared to raise a hundred million dollars with other American businessmen for education 'on a dollar-to-dollar basis with the American government' which would then have to be matched by South Africans.† That offer was never tested; but several individual American corporations were soon offering their own funds for black education and welfare. Coca-Cola based in Atlanta, with Donald McHenry on its board, was especially anxious and set up its multi-million dollar fund. Mobil announced a $10 million foundation for black housing, small business and education: 'We believe there is only one way to answer the justifiable anger among blacks at the shortcomings in the education of their children,' said Mobil's local chairman George Racine. 'That is to improve teaching and the quality of education in one system.' Black education soon became the favourite cause for companies opposing sanctions; but unless it was firmly connected to black political groups it could easily become drawn into the traditional South African patterns.

Both British and American companies, like the diplomats, still preferred secretive discussions and seminars about apartheid on their home ground to any open activity and intervention out in the field. Apartheid became the hot topic in the conference industry, but most meetings were entirely with whites – in the old South African style. The most criticised gathering was in November 1985, at the Oxfordshire country house Ditchley Park, funded by both British and American trusts. The director Sir Reginald Hibbert set up a meeting about apartheid, to be chaired by Sir John Killick, an ex-ambassador who had been head of Dunlop South Africa; they invited South Africans, British and Americans, but no blacks at all. After some American guests fiercely protested, Cyrus Vance, the chairman of the American Ditchley committee, provided extra funds for last-minute black guests; but it remained a predominantly white occasion, to which the South African ambassador turned up unannounced. The black Americans, who included Donald

* South African Report, December 6, 1985
† *See* transcript of Slabbert's interview with Botha on November 25, 1985, published in February 1986

McHenry and Judge Higginbottom from Philadelphia, treated it as a fiasco; while the black South Africans (as Sir Reginald later described them) 'intervened like a sombre chorus reminding the conference in each session that, as far as they were concerned, there was as yet nothing about which to negotiate; the South African government's policies and actions at home and abroad were comprehensively repugnant to the black population of South Africa . . . There could be no doubt about the authenticity of their moving words.'*

The Corporate Council held more secret meetings, and in March 1986 chief executives met discreetly again at Leeds Castle, chaired by Edward Heath and convened by Leon Sullivan and Roger Smith. The South African tycoons were now much more cut off from the others. 'They had begun to see Sullivan as a kind of shield against Western criticism,' said one informant, 'but now for the first time they found themselves as adversaries, while the West were clearly distancing themselves. They became defensive.' There were now some South African blacks including the businessman Sam Motsuenyane (*see* page 231); but the whites fought shy of black politicians, let alone the ANC. 'But we don't even know,' complained Roger Smith, 'whether they're the goodies or the baddies.' They made no public statement afterwards, and when I met Sullivan on the plane back to Philadelphia he would only reveal: 'It was very penetrating. Very penetrating. That's all I can say. But remember the bottom line: *end apartheid.*' The Anti-Apartheid Movement in London called it 'an attempt by foreign business to determine the future of South Africa without reference to those who will be most affected'. Certainly the conferences in castles and country houses seemed very aloof from the critical question: how does it play in Soweto? They seemed much more preoccupied with their corporate images than with the real problem of political realignment.

There was one bold public showdown. The outspoken chief executive of General Motors in South Africa, Bob White, insisted that 'our involvement in politics has to move to another level' and announced that his company would pay the legal fees of any black employee who chose to use the 'whites only' bathing beaches outside Port Elizabeth. There was a brief tension: soldiers patrolled the beaches and the government told GM to 'keep its nose out of South Africa's business'. But when White publicly attacked the beach segregation as 'abhorrent' he was supported by local businesses; and by April 1986 the Port Elizabeth council had voted to desegregate its beaches. As so often, the white backlash proved only a flick.

* The *Ditchley Newsletter*, No. 15, January 1986

Sullivan himself was pressed to more open confrontation. In May 1986 he issued a sensational edict: he told the 192 American companies that had signed the Sullivan code that they must now adopt a 'stringent course of corporate civil disobedience to challenge actively all apartheid laws'. He asked them to 'assist blacks in the equal use of all private and public amenities, such as parks, beaches, hospitals, theatres, public transport, schools and housing'; and he warned them again that unless apartheid was completely dismantled by June 1987 he would endorse total economic sanctions. It was far more drastic than the 'Code of Conduct' which the European Community had revised in November 1985, which had been widely disregarded and inadequately monitored: and which the British government emphasised was 'not asking companies to act contrary to South African law'.*

Corporate Disobedience! It was a unique instruction to multinationals who had always insisted that they must obey the laws of each country; still more in South Africa where they had so often used the local law and customs as an excuse for their own segregation. Many of the Sullivan companies were appalled; yet a few local companies were already becoming more openly disobedient, not just with mixed lavatories and cafeteria, but by defying more basic segregation including the Group Areas Act. At Barclays Bank Chris Ball in Johannesburg had publicly boasted on a video how his bank had frequently broken apartheid laws; and by June 1986 the bank was breaking new ground by installing a black executive in the midst of the white suburb of Wendywood, and even throwing a barbecue for his neighbours. Social reforms which managers had always said were impossible were now seen as essential, as business became more desperate to divorce itself from apartheid. But time was rapidly running out; and while the white executives were contemplating more defiant acts against apartheid they were to be plunged into a new state of emergency which produced a still harsher confrontation, and made all those promises of discreet pressure and gradual improvements ring hollow.

* Code of Conduct for Companies with interests in South Africa. Command 9860, p. 3, HMSO, July 1986. *See also Weekly Mail*, September 12, 1986 for inadequate European definitions

15

The Road to Sanctions

It is time we in the West realize that we are contributing by default
to an inexorable movement toward genocide.

Robert McFarlane, *International Herald Tribune*, August 5, 1986

The Western governments in the meantime had taken up their
positions towards South Africa with a remarkable lack of concern
for their own companies' long-term interests. The British Foreign
Office officially explained in January 1986 that 'in essence the
government's policy towards South Africa is to further the considerable British interests in that country, and as part of this effort to
promote early and peaceful transition to a genuinely non-racial
democracy.'* But many of those considerable interests were becoming less sure that their government was really furthering them. While
American and British industrialists and bankers were beginning to
have talks with the ANC as well as with Buthelezi, both Reagan and
Thatcher refused to have any relations with Congress, and their
diplomats' contacts with other black political groups were fitful. Yet
the Western capitals were already being pressed towards sanctions
which would put an end to all hopes for expanding Western investment and 'constructive engagement'.

Both the American and British embassies in Pretoria remained
constantly anxious not to offend Afrikaners. The American ambassador Herman Nickel, who continued vocally to oppose sanctions and disinvestment, was aloof from the black world, although
the embassy had established an effective informal black network.
The British Embassy in Pretoria, under a conventional new ambassador Sir Patrick Moberly, was more preoccupied than ever with
avoiding rows with the government – it had not even invited Bishop
Tutu to the residence. It kept contact with black leaders only at
one remove through the consulate in Johannesburg and its advice
had played down the growing unrest as part of a cyclical trend. It
was a worrying failure of information. After the Iranian revolution

* For a discussion of British policy and its impact *see* Shaun Johnson, *British
Policy Towards South Africa*. David Davies Memorial Foundation. International
Relations, May 1986, p. 445

of 1979, which British diplomats and intelligence had so notably
failed to predict, the Foreign Office had tried to ensure that it had
better information about underground oppositions and revolutionary movements and had asked embassies in the Middle East to
provide special reports in the light of Iran. But in South Africa
the British still had very inadequate information about the black
opposition – much less than the American Embassy whose financial
interests were much smaller – while diplomats gave the same
explanation as in Iran: they could not offend the existing regime.

But it was the perceptions at the top which influenced and limited
the perceptions of diplomats and officials below, and which made
governments often less informed even than businessmen. In Washington President Reagan still showed a startling lack of knowledge
or interest and the White House often ignored the information and
analysis of the State Department, while George Shultz suffered from
the prevailing policy paralysis: appalled by the Afrikaner regime,
but more appalled by the thought of any likely black alternative.
Reagan was inclined to see white South Africans as embattled allies
threatened by guerillas and terrorists, comparing them either with
Israelis, with the Shah of Iran or with conservative regimes in
Central America. He always saw them in the East–West context,
as anti-communists against communists. 'Too often in the past we
Americans, acting out of anger and frustration and impatience have
turned our backs on flawed regimes, only to see disaster follow . . .',
he said in a major speech on July 22. 'What foreign power would
fill the vacuum if the ties with the West are broken?'

Reagan was happy to let Mrs Thatcher make much of the
running, and she too was concerned with the Soviet menace: 'To
me it is absolutely absurd,' she said in July 1986, 'that people should
be prepared to put increasing power into the hands of the Soviet
Union on the grounds that they disapprove of apartheid in South
Africa.' But she was also much more personally fired by the issue.
She had been to South Africa only once when she went out as
Minister of Education in 1972 to open an observatory and was
struck by the lack of apartheid in some areas: 'The first thing you
see when you get off at Johannesburg airport,' she told Hugo Young,
'is that you go into a hotel which is totally non-colour conscious.
You go into a dining room and there's all colours and backgrounds.'
She thought that Britain should have had more contact with South
Africa, not less: 'We would have influenced her more: she would
have been able to see that multiracial societies do work in other
countries.'* And her husband Denis had many South African

* Interview with Hugo Young, the *Guardian*, July 1986

business friends: in February 1986 at the height of the emergency he paid a visit to South Africa where he attended among other social events a dinner given for him by Mr Prime, the chief executive of a Durban car parts company with his colleagues.

She was totally sceptical about sanctions after the fiascos and hypocrisies over Rhodesia; and her scepticism was reinforced by successive South African visitors to Number 10 during 1985, including Chief Buthelezi, Helen Suzman and Harry Oppenheimer (who assured her that the blacks' support for the ANC was much exaggerated). Some diplomats expected that she might suddenly switch as she had switched over Rhodesia in 1979, accepting the need to negotiate with armed rebels. But her personal detestation of terrorism had, not surprisingly, increased since the IRA had tried to murder her and her cabinet in October 1984. She was determined that nobody in government, including the Foreign Office, should talk to the African National Congress. The resourceful South African ambassador in London, Denis Worrall, was determined to paint the ANC as a pariah like the PLO (though privately he thought it was important to be in touch with them); and his embassy was glad to disseminate the more bloodthirsty ANC propaganda and Marxist rhetoric from Radio Freedom in Ethiopia

Mrs Thatcher was convinced that she had a special influence on President Botha, based on forthright exchanges without humbug. She believed that she could influence the Afrikaner government towards peaceful and necessary reforms more effectively if she did not threaten or confront them; and she avoided any of the kind of moral rhetoric that she directed against the Soviet Union. But she was much less sensitive about her image with the blacks; and both sides in South Africa saw her as a fundamental ally of the government who would stand by them when the chips were down. The belief was already deep in the Afrikaner's thinking: in the words of Mrs Thatcher's predecessor as prime minister, Edward Heath – who had been through his own ordeals with Botha's predecessor, John Vorster:

The South African government believe, that when it comes to the crunch, whatever and whenever it is, they will always have the support of the American administration and the British government . . . because they believe that they can always use the Communist threat as the argument with which to handle Washington and Whitehall . . . The irony of the situation is that the longer South Africa continues its present policy, the more it drives its black population into Communist hands and the more it is encouraging the other black states in Africa to move towards a Communist outlook.*

Both Western leaders shared a loyalty to white South Africa and a dread of a black revolt; but they were up against very different political pressures. In Washington Capitol Hill, now effectively mobilised by the black caucus and liberal members of Congress, was pressing for bolder condemnation and intervention, particularly for sanctions; while members of parliament in London were much more muted, whether because of the effects of sanctions on unemployment, the gloomy record of black Africa, the fiascos of sanctions against Rhodesia, or the associations with black immigrants in Britain. After the declaration of the emergency, the Reagan administration had felt impelled to show its public disapproval; and Ambassador Nickel was recalled for several weeks. In September the European Community nations voted to withdraw their military attachés in protest; but the British government first refused to join in, until Mrs Thatcher climbed down reluctantly two weeks later complaining: 'It means we don't get as much information as we should otherwise.'†

Thatcher was now coming under heavy pressure for sanctions, not from parliament, but from the Commonwealth countries, particularly the black African states who felt impelled to show support for their black brothers who were now calling more vociferously for action. And the issue of sanctions came to a head at the two-yearly Commonwealth conference at Nassau in the Bahamas in October 1985. All the members except Britain were now pressing publicly for sanctions, led by Australia, Canada and India. It was true that the countries who were most ardent were often those which had least trade and investment, as Mrs Thatcher liked to remind them. And many of the black states close to South Africa which publicly clamoured for sanctions were privately fearful about the effects on their own economies. But this problem of dependence already existed: South Africa had already been exercising her own economic sanctions against any neighbours which caused trouble and harboured ANC refugees; and in January 1986 she tightened her stranglehold on Lesotho – the mountain kingdom surrounded by South Africa – and toppled Chief Jonathan's government after only two weeks' sanctions. As the Commonwealth stepped up its demands for sanctions, so Pretoria increased its threats to apply counter-sanctions against its neighbours – whether by cutting rail

* House of Commons, July 16, 1986
† Interview with Hugo Young, the *Guardian*, July 1986

and road links, by returning foreign workers or by military raids
and general destabilisation. But the threats were a tricky weapon;
for South Africa earned a large surplus from her trade with her
neighbours, and her own sanctions spotlighted her own political
domination through economic weaponry – which could strengthen
the argument for sanctions against herself.

The Western tycoons now watched apprehensively as the pressures mounted towards sanctions and disinvestment which would
negate all their arguments that greater investment would bring
greater freedom to blacks. While the Corporate Council and the
Sullivan Group in America were promising to improve black conditions and to push Pretoria towards dismantling apartheid, the
clamour for sanctions was undermining their claims.

At the Nassau conference the Commonwealth secretary-general
Sonny Ramphal tried to mobilise agreement and to bring pressure
on Britain, as he had successfully done in Lusaka six years earlier,
preparing the way for the Zimbabwe negotiations. But Mrs
Thatcher reacted to the traditional emotional rhetoric of the
Commonwealth with rising contempt. The other prime ministers
chose Rajiv Gandhi and Brian Mulroney from India and Canada
to lobby her personally, as two good-looking men representing
important countries; but with no success. Eventually the prime
ministers agreed on a 'Commonwealth Accord' which called on
Pretoria to dismantle apartheid, end the emergency, release Nelson
Mandela and unban the ANC. They settled only for minimal sanctions including a ban on Krugerrands, new government loans and
funding of trade missions, which Mrs Thatcher could rightly claim
were only 'a tiny little bit'. They agreed to appoint a Commonwealth
group of seven 'eminent persons' to 'encourage political dialogue in
South Africa with a view to establishing a non-racial and representative government'. If Pretoria had not made enough progress within
six months the Commonwealth would 'agree to the adoption of
further measures'.

The seven members included Dame Nita Barrow, a president of
the World Council of Churches; John Malecela, a former Tanzanian
minister; Sardar Swaran Singh, a former Indian minister; and
Archbishop Edward Scott, the Anglican primate from Canada. But
the most active were the two joint chairmen: Malcolm Fraser, the
former Australian prime minister who had taken up a noisy stand
against apartheid; and General Olusegun Obasanjo, the former
Nigerian head of state who enjoyed unusual respect in Europe and
America. For the British, the most important member was Mrs
Thatcher's own nominee Lord Barber, who was chairman of the
Standard Bank, one of South Africa's biggest creditors. He was

expected to be cautious; in the Conservative government in the early seventies he had shown little interest in black Africa, and over the last ten years he had regularly visited white South Africa, where he had business and other friends, without showing much concern with apartheid.

The eminent persons, or 'The Commonwealth Group' as they preferred to call themselves, were at first received with scepticism by almost everyone. Botha thought they were interfering, while Tambo feared they would indefinitely be played along by Pretoria, like the Western 'contact group' over Namibia, with too high a profile for any useful negotiation. But Mrs Thatcher persuaded President Botha to allow the group to travel freely in South Africa; Fraser and Obasanjo insisted that they must see Mandela in prison, to which Botha agreed; and Tambo decided to co-operate fully. For the next six months the eminent persons were to be seen as the chief hope of achieving a peaceful settlement in South Africa, not just by the Commonwealth but by the Americans, who saw Obasanjo as their special link.

On their first visit to South Africa in February and March none of the eminent persons, as they later said publicly, 'were prepared for the full reality of apartheid'; while they were surprised how deeply the black resistance had penetrated, even into remote country areas. Lord Barber, as he told ANC officials, changed his whole view of South Africa after seeing the other side. But the group also found, to their surprise, that there might be a genuine prospect of agreement between the government and the ANC; and that a peaceful settlement could conceivably be achieved after releasing Mandela. The group prepared a 'possible negotiating concept': Pretoria on one side would release Mandela, unban the ANC, allow them normal political activity, and pull out troops (though not police) from the townships; while the ANC would agree to suspend violence and begin negotiations.

They saw the personality of Mandela as the key to any settlement; and Botha on his side was well aware of the exasperating paradox that after twenty-four years in jail – far longer than Gandhi or Kenyatta – Mandela was more influential than ever, and could be more dangerous inside prison than outside. Pretoria was looking for a way to release him in the most casual way: after he had a prostate operation in December 1985 he had been kept in a separate hospital wing and allowed special privileges even though he was in good health, while the government encouraged speculation about his future. 'It was quite obvious that they must have planned to release him after the operation,' his wife Winnie said later. 'They wanted to destroy the myth surrounding this man, to let him out

in a position where he could not produce miracles . . . They were
testing people's reaction, preparing for his release. Now they've
overdone it. They're scared. They scare easy . . . The government
are now the prisoners, and the prisoners are now the jailors.'
By late February Botha had once again imposed conditions on
Mandela's release – that he would renounce violence. Mandela
could not agree to give up the only pressure which had had any
effect; nor could he agree to being released while the ANC was
banned. 'How could they have the *audacity* to impose conditions on
Mandela's release after he's spent a lifetime in jail?' his wife said.
'They're not ready for it. I can't imagine them doing it in the
present political climate, without moving an inch from twenty-four
years ago.'*

Mandela in jail personified the South African deadlock between
two forces which never met: against the military power of the state,
he held the power of an idea: liberation. Botha knew that if he died
in jail the fury in the townships could be unstoppable, and he
recognised that if Mandela were released he could restrain the
violence; but he dared not take the political risk, and continued to
build up his own myth of Mandela the arch-communist. On his
side Mandela still saw himself as a man of destiny: he was reading
new Afrikaans literature, to prepare himself to be the leader of all
South Africans, and he made clear to the Commonwealth group
that he would seek to reassure the white minority, and to restrain
black expectations. All the eminent persons were surprised by
Mandela's mellowness, good judgment and humour; perhaps most
of all Lord Barber, who exchanged jokes about his own escape from
a Russian prisoner-of-war camp about which he had written. 'Lord
Barber, send me a copy,' said Mandela. 'That could be very
useful. And to make sure that I get it, send it through the British
ambassador.'†

The Commonwealth Group were finding themselves ineluctably
pressed towards some form of sanctions. For Barber particularly it
was a depressing and difficult conclusion, denying all those hopes
that Western investment and business expansion would in themselves undermine apartheid. For the black states on the borders,
too, it was desperate recourse, for only massive aid could compensate
for the loss of trade and jobs with the South. But as South Africa
appeared to be heading for civil war there was little alternative,
short of military intervention, as a way to dissociate the West from
Pretoria; while black South Africans saw sanctions as a key signal

* Telephone interview with author, March 1986
† House of Lords, July 4, 1986

of support. By April Bishop Tutu had decided that he could no
longer hold off, and made a long emotional speech concluding: 'Our
children are dying. Our land is burning and bleeding. And so I call
on the international community to apply punitive sanctions against
this government to help us establish a new South Africa, non-racial,
democratic and just.' Tutu did not explain what kind of sanctions
but he hoped for 'something as painless as the run on the rand
which suddenly inspired the private sector to discover that they did
have tongues . . .' The State Department quickly replied that 'the
United States does not believe that punitive sanctions will help
promote change'; the Foreign Office said that 'Bishop Tutu has
advanced no evidence to show that international financial and trade
boycotts would help promote peaceful change'; the South African
businessmen explained once again that sanctions would damage
the blacks. But most black leaders now supported Tutu's call.

The eminent persons had left their 'negotiating concept' with the
South African government, who neither accepted nor rejected it for
two months. They thought that Pretoria was taking their ideas
seriously, after seeing them on twenty separate ocasions. Obasanjo
appeared to be specially trusted by the Botha government – including the defence minister Magnus Malan and the minister for the
constitution Chris Heunis – as a general who understood the problems of a divided country. President Botha had made clear that he
dreaded both sanctions and the escalating violence – which was
approaching a new danger on the tenth anniversary of Soweto on
June 16; while Pik Botha, who was in charge of the talks with the
group, sounded sympathetic. On their next visit in May the group
showed their negotiating concept to Mandela, who agreed that he
could accept it as a starting point, though he could not speak for
the ANC; they then showed it to the ANC and the UDF who asked for
ten days to consider it. They then flew to Cape Town for a key
meeting with the President's constitutional committee under Chris
Heunis. An hour beforehand they heard reports that South Africa
had raided three neighbouring countries, Zimbabwe, Zambia and
Botswana: it seemed a deliberate insult, particularly to Obasanjo
who had been nominated by Zambia and Zimbabwe. But they went
into the meeting, where the government told them that they must
insist on the ANC not just suspending violence but renouncing it for
all time, regardless of negotiations. The group all thought this was
'unrealistic and wholly unreasonable'; and South African business
leaders agreed with them. Obasanjo then urged that in the light of
the raids they should abandon their mission; and they flew back to
London hastily to compile their report. They had some disagreements: Barber at first wanted to produce his own minority report;

but after consulting with the Foreign Office and modifying some of the 'nasty words' he agreed to sign a unanimous report.

The report, when it was published in June, caused a new furore; for the eminent persons were much more critical and forthright than most politicians including Mrs Thatcher had expected. They concluded that the Pretoria government was 'not yet prepared to negotiate fundamental change, nor to countenance the creation of genuine democratic structures, nor to face the prospect of the end of white domination and white power in the foreseeable future'. They put some hope in financial pressures (though Gavin Relly and others had told them that their views had little impact on Pretoria). They insisted that local businessmen had 'potential for exerting pressures upon the Government to the benefit of the country as a whole'; they thought that businessmen were out of touch with black opinion, and could and should exert greater pressure on the Government. They were convinced that 'there can be no negotiated settlement in South Africa without the ANC; the breadth of its support is incontestable; and this support is growing'. In their final recommendations they carefully advocated 'measures' rather than sanctions; and the choice of measures was not for them, but for individual governments to recommend. But they left no doubt that some strong measures were essential: 'We are convinced that the South African government is concerned about the adoption of effective economic measures against it. If it comes to the conclusion that it would always remain protected from such measures, the process of change in South Africa is unlikely to increase in momentum and the descent into violence would be accelerated. In these circumstances, the cost in lives may have to be counted in millions.'*

Why had Pretoria decided so abruptly to reject the group's negotiating concept? There were varied explanations. Lord Barber said 'they simply could not bring themselves to take what seemed to them a leap into the unknown'.† Malcolm Fraser believed (as he told Mrs Thatcher) it was because the Commonwealth group had found important common ground between Mandela, Tambo and Buthelezi which therefore threatened Pretoria's policies of tribal separation and 'group rights':‡ and Obasanjo had the same impression. Sonny Ramphal thought that 'the Commonwealth group were doing too well for Pretoria's liking'. But the eminent persons were also conscious that: 'In recent weeks, the Government would appear to have moved consciously away from any realistic negotiat-

* *Mission to South Africa* (Eminent Persons Group), Penguin Books, 1986, p. 140
† House of Lords, *ibid.*
‡ *See* Speech to Royal Commonwealth Society, July 31, 1986

ing process'; and also that 'after more than eighteen months of persistent unrest, upheaval and killings unprecedented in the country's history, the government believes that it can contain the situation indefinitely by use of force.'* Behind the scenes the military in Pretoria were insisting that the government must show its true strength, both to the black rebels and to the right-wing Afrikaners. And the full extent of Pretoria's shift of policy was soon to become ominously clear as the government moved towards a showdown which faced business leaders with a more painful choice.

* *Mission to South Africa*, pp. 135, 138

16

The Boer Backlash

I wonder what it will be like
When we sit with Tambo
and tell him about the fall of the Boers

Song at youth rallies in the townships, 1986, (quoted by
Shaun Johnson, *The Youth in South Africa*)

How far could businessmen and bankers really influence President
Botha's policies in this crisis atmosphere? How far was he really in
control of the country? There were no simple answers, for his
behaviour was looking less and less consistent.

Certainly the emergency had revealed him with a visible loss of
authority: the businessmen's visit to Lusaka in September was due
as much to disillusion with Botha's policies as to any new-found
confidence in a black alternative. Only a year before he had been
acclaimed as the masterly architect of the new constitution and the
Nkomati Accord, the friend of European prime ministers. But since
the emergency he appeared to have been brought low by black
schoolboys; while South Africa, in the words of two Afrikaner
political scientists in January 1986, appeared to be 'stumbling from
one political upheaval to the next, inexorably sliding toward a civil
war'.*

Botha still saw himself as a courageous reformer who had
shrewdly kept his following through difficult manoeuvres; like a de
Gaulle or a Macmillan maintaining right-wing support while moving stealthily to the left. 'Under my leadership the whites have
accepted much in South Africa . . .' he told the opposition leader
Van Zyl Slabbert in November 1985. 'But I say that I represent
more than the whites. I am now conceited enough to say that I
represent the voice of more than 50 percent of the black people of
South Africa who do not want to throw the rights they have attained
into a pot and leave them there.'† He was determined to reassert
his authority after it had been by-passed by the meetings with the

* Deon Geldenhuys and Koos Van Wyk, 'South Africa in Crisis: A Comparison
of the Vorster and Botha Eras', *South Africa International*, January 1986
    † *See* transcript, published February 1986

ANC. He soon became much firmer in preventing liberal groups –
including Afrikaner students and churchmen – from making the
same journey to Lusaka, while his arguments were strengthened by
the new outbreaks of sabotage.

But in the meantime the flight of capital and the collapse of the
currency had been carrying their own message. Botha was being
blamed from the right as well as the left for having undermined
confidence, not just in the political system, but in the economy.
After the emergency Jaap Marais, the leader of the right-wing
Herstigte Nasionale Party, insisted that the economy had been
weakened by his dangerous concessions. Under Dr Verwoerd, he
argued:

> We had a very strong economy, we had a strong international
> position and had internal order. What more do you want in a
> country? Look at the chaotic situation the country is now in. We
> can't pay our debts, we are sitting with an inflation rate of 16%,
> people are going bankrupt at an unheard-of rate, unemployment
> is increasing. The basic cause of all this is that government started
> with equality. If equality succeeds, it must succeed at the level
> of the economy and if it fails there it will succeed nowhere.*

Botha was fully aware that South Africa desperately needed external
finance, and that only rapid concessions would appease the international financial community: and he went to great lengths to
reassure bankers – particularly Fritz Leutwiler – that bolder reforms
were on the way. By the end of 1985 he had been promising
businessmen that he would unveil new reforms at his opening of
parliament at the end of January; and with this expectation most
of them, including Anglo-American, had decided to avoid any
contacts with the ANC revolutionaries.

Botha's speech on January 31 – later known as 'Rubicon 2' – was
certainly far more conciliatory in tone than the first Rubicon speech
five months before: part of it might have been written specially for
the world's bankers. 'We accept unequivocally that the Republic of
South Africa is part of the international community. We have no
wish to isolate ourselves from the world, particularly not from Africa
of which we form an integral part. We accept that not all the
pressure is necessarily malicious . . . But I wish to make clear that
we do not need pressure to walk the road of reform and justice. We
do it out of conviction.'

* Interview with Willem de Klerk of Rapport, on SATV. *See South Africa International, ibid.*

Botha spelt out reforms more specifically than before, outlining a 'programme of action' which included restoring South African citizenship to all black South Africans including those in the home-lands; allowing freehold property rights to blacks; preparing to abolish influx control, to be replaced by a strategy of 'orderly urbanisation'; and replacing the hated pass-books with identity documents to be carried by all South Africans. He committed himself, however vaguely, to 'equal opportunity' and even 'equal education'; and 'all South Africans must be placed in a position where they can participate in government through their elected representatives . . .' He explained that: 'We have outgrown the outdated colonial system of paternalism as well as the outdated concept of apartheid.' And he proposed to establish a national statutory council, with himself as chairman, including leaders of black communities, to advise on constitutional structures for 'our multi-cultured society'.

The speech gave some immediate encouragement to the business community. Gavin Relly said it had 'brought South Africa back into the mainstream of western thinking'; and the rand soon climbed back to $0.45. But it represented a modernisation of apartheid, as the London *Financial Times* complained, not a dismantling of it; and it gave no indication of opening up to serious negotiations with blacks: even Buthelezi withdrew his support for a statutory council. Most blacks saw it as promising too little, too late. 'He has made promises that would have been considered treacherous if made by any of his predecessors,' said the black newspaper *The Sowetan*: 'If things were normal in South Africa he would have perhaps steered this country into better days. Things are far from normal. In fact we are poised on the type of precipice that only needs a push to land us in disaster. Taking a look at most of the prospective leaders who might succeed Botha, there is no hope for decisive change. This means South Africa needs a totally new government.' And Botha's liberal noises were soon drowned by contradictions. The minister of education, F W de Klerk, reasserted that education would remain segregated, which contradicted any claim that apart-heid was outdated; and when the foreign minister Pik Botha referred to the possibility of a future black president he was humiliated by his boss. President Botha, said Hennie Kotze, professor of political science at Stellenbosch, 'took the political initiative but lost it in the space of one week'.*

The businessmen were more than ever confused. Botha had let them down again; but they could not come to terms with the ANC,

* *The South Africa Foundation News*, March 1986

while the middle road appeared suddenly to be reaching a new
dead end. On February 7, Frederik Van Zyl Slabbert, the leader of
the white opposition party the PFP, abruptly resigned both his
leadership and his seat in parliament. It was a devastating blow,
for Slabbert appeared as a special kind of bridge. He was an
intellectual Afrikaner who had rebelled against the National Party,
yet still commanded some respect among his own people. He had
been a rugby hero; he was warm and open, with a boyish style and
a turned-up nose, and he seemed to personify the Afrikaner virtues
without the isolation or bitterness; even President Botha seemed to
see him as a kind of wayward son. Many saw him as the key to a
liberal future; while Slabbert on his side asked businessmen to
concern themselves more closely with politics:

> After all, businessmen have been politically involved or are
> politically involved in any other society. American politics
> couldn't survive if you didn't have your Democratic and Republi-
> can businessmen. In South Africa you have this pretence that
> businessmen are not involved in politics, but then secretly they
> funnel a lot of funds into the dominant party because the domi-
> nant party has the patronage and determines contracts and so
> on.*

Slabbert did not ask businessmen to take a very radical role. After
he had toured Europe and America in November 1985 President
Botha invited him for a long private talk (which Botha secretly
tape-recorded and later published); and Slabbert explained to him
that business people in the United States and Britain were not
really concerned about sanctions: 'They were concerned about
stability. What concerns them is the restoration of confidence and
especially how they saw their assets in this respect.' Botha on his
side complained about the contradictions of overseas businessmen:
'On the one hand they want stability and on the other they want
concessions. But they don't want an Africa situation, because if
they wanted that, why don't they invest in Zambia? Why don't they
invest in Mozambique, which we plead with them to do?' Slabbert
agreed about the hypocrisy of the critics ('If the average Australian
had to come here he would vote slightly to the right of the National
Party,') and told Botha how people overseas 'have suddenly become
aware of the dilemma of finding an alternative. It is something
which had not been there before and which I think one can exploit.'

---

* Interview with Professor David Welsh of Cape Town University, *Leadership*,
1985

The dialogue often sounded like two Afrikaners who were confident that they could get world business back on their side.

But Slabbert was becoming desperately disillusioned with his role as parliamentary leader of the opposition, and in his book *The Last White Parliament* he convincingly argued that it was becoming impossible to oppose a white system of government within the confines of an all-white assembly. He tried in February 1986 to persuade his white liberal colleagues to resign with him. But only one of them, Alex Boraine, agreed, and they left the other progressive MPs and their supporters in some acrimony. 'There is surely no precedent for the sudden resignation of an admired and trusted political leader,' said Harry Oppenheimer, his chief backer. He had 'gravely, and perhaps irreparably, damaged his own credibility in public life.' The Johannesburg *Business Day* angrily rebutted Slabbert's claim that the business community had let him down. 'He was above all the political creature of Big Business,' said the influential columnist Ken Owen. 'He was helped into politics by Big Business, sustained in it, supported and sponsored by Big Business.'

The Progressive MPs quickly elected a new leader Colin Eglin, a more professional politician who lacked Slabbert's charisma but held his colleagues together, while Slabbert himself looked to a more radical role. When he was leader he had not shown much interest in the black opposition. He had visited Lusaka to talk to the ANC after the businessmen's visit, but did not seem very impressed. As he told Botha: 'The trouble with the ANC is that it is a myth – no, not a myth – it is a romantic image to those abroad . . . I told them in Lusaka that if they were really in control of the situation, why didn't they call a moratorium on violence for six weeks and say "We will show you?"' . . . the ANC should not be held up as an organisation which is so powerful that they can handle the unrest.' He sounded equally unimpressed by Buthelezi: 'His big problem is that should Mandela die in jail he will become the Muzorewa of South Africa and he is well aware of it . . . He must be locked into an initiative.' (When Botha later released the transcript, Buthelezi was furious at being described like 'an uppity Kaffir' and Slabbert apologised; but Tambo was less touchy and explained that he understood that Slabbert needed to pacify Botha.)

Immediately Slabbert had resigned, the ANC in Lusaka welcomed the news fulsomely: 'An act of vision has made this February day a moment of pride for all the people in South Africa,' said the secretary-general Alfred Nzo. And other black leaders including the black consciousness party AZAPO and the United Democratic Front agreed. Slabbert reciprocated by having long talks with the ANC's publicity director Thabo Mbeki in London. But the ANC made it clear that they saw his role as working on white opinion, not black; and Slabbert's influence among Afrikaners had diminished after his resignation, while some of the more left-wing nationalists, 'the New Nats', had a more effective power-base. When Slabbert visited America again in April he was made aware, as he put it, that 'My trouble is, I'm not black.' He and Boraine remained active as intelligent brokers establishing links with black politicians. But the traditional role of the white liberal as the spokesman or lobbyist for blacks was now rapidly dwindling. The ANC and other black leaders appreciated white allies; but they knew that in the end they would strike the real bargains with the heart of Afrikanerdom, with the Broederbond or even the right-wing parties.

The English-speaking businessmen were now faced with a starker choice, between the government or the ANC; and they still looked anxiously to Pretoria for signs of economic pressures to liberate the government. Much now depended on the handful of prominent Afrikaner businessmen who had a major influence in Pretoria. Would they be prepared to retreat into a siege economy, or would they seek some reconciliation with the West?

Many liberals still put hopes on Anton Rupert, still at seventy the head of the Rembrandt tobacco group which now had most of its investments in other industries ranging from banks through life assurance to clinics. Rupert often represented Afrikaner paternalism in its most attractive and visionary form: he had actively encouraged black small businesses, helped to develop industries in Lesotho and believed genuinely in industrial partnership between whites and blacks. Through his cigarettes and his art-collecting he was also an international figure, a friend and admirer of David Rockefeller and a frequent visitor to New York, London and Germany. He saw his own country's problems as part of the world's. 'South Africa finds itself in the van of a crisis which Europe will eventually also have to face,' he said in 1985. 'The world should have more sympathy with South Africa because we are in the forefront of the unemployment problem.' He warned that black unemployment had doubled in the previous year, with job opportunities constantly disappearing; and he went on tactfully to suggest to his government that part of the blame lay in over-regulation. But while Rupert talked much about the common patriotism of all races, his visionary world seemed to exclude the real world of police, bombings and detentions. He said that apartheid was dead and the corpse must be buried, and he appealed to Botha to take bold action, but he did not specify the details. He resented any international interference, and after he

had angry disagreements with President Botha he was concerned
not to offend him further. He remained stubbornly optimistic, and
liked to repeat the observation that the Chinese symbol for crisis
also meant opportunity. He still saw white South Africans as playing
a unique role in Africa. 'We are sometimes cursed but we are
always respected,' he said in his annual report after the emergency
in August 1985. 'Southern Africa is waiting on us. If we succeed in
our task we shall command respect from the world and, like a
magnet, attract much-needed capital. Does this appear to be a flight
of fancy? May I then remind you that "He who does not believe in
miracles is not a realist".'*

The more conventional Afrikaner tycoon was Fred du Plessis, the
head of the conglomerate Sanlam which, based on life insurance,
had extended itself through property, banking and industry. Osten-
sibly, he firmly rejected the policy of closing Afrikaner ranks and
moving towards isolation, an option which he called 'slow stag-
nation and death'; he insisted that a growth rate of 4 percent was
essential to produce enough new jobs for the growing population,
and that this was impossible without foreign participation. And he
now denounced the past policies of apartheid which had misused
South Africa's mixture of peoples: 'We used that very diversity to
force the population into tight little compartments of self-interest –
racial, linguistic, cultural and tribal.' But du Plessis too remained
a true Afrikaner. As President of the SA Foundation he was exposed
to criticism from the world's businessmen including Roger Smith's
Corporate Council, but he could discount most of it as uninformed.
He described in March 1986 how the foreign businessmen at one
meeting had 'enumerated a few changes that would ease their
situation in South Africa and they were then dumbfounded to
be told that most of their stated requirements had already been
embodied in official policies'. He conceded that there has been 'a
hardening of attitudes towards South Africa in business circles
abroad', but he looked to foreign governments, particularly the
British government, which showed more 'realism and understanding' than the businessmen, and welcomed Mrs Thatcher's opposition to sanctions. And as the Afrikaners felt more embattled, du
Plessis was inclined to agree with Botha on the need for stronger
action against black rebels, whatever the international cost.

Rupert and du Plessis, like most other Afrikaner businessmen and
President Botha himself, put much of their hope on the emergence of
a black middle-class of small businessmen or professionals to counter

---

* Rembrandt Group: Chairman's address, August 29, 1985. *See also* speech on
'Free Enterprise in Africa' to the South Africa Club, London, April 16, 1986

the radicalism of the ANC and provide a bridge with the black world. But as the crisis continued the black businessmen were also being rapidly radicalised. Their moderate chief spokesman was Sam Motsuenyane, chairman of the African Bank and president of the National African Federated Chamber of Commerce (NAFCOC) who had been hopeful about President Botha's reforms; but even he was now very disillusioned. In July 1985, after the emergency had been declared, he led a business delegation to see the foreign minister Pik Botha, to press for Mandela's release and for dialogue with the ANC: but he was bitterly disappointed by Botha's 'Rubicon' speech – 'a major political and economic disaster' – which ignored all his proposals; and in 1985 he and other businessmen paid a visit to see Tambo in Lusaka, from which they came back encouraged that the ANC foresaw a major role for free enterprise. The black businessmen were visibly distancing themselves from their Afrikaner counterparts: when Fred du Plessis opened the annual meeting of NAFCOC in July 1986 he explained, somewhat disingenuously, that the Afrikaner's business success did not depend on their political power; but Motsuenyane quickly replied that the blacks' position was quite different: 'The Afrikaner has never been deprived of the right to vote in his own country.'*

The younger Afrikaner businessmen felt more inclined to mix with the wider white community as the common danger gave them a common purpose, while Afrikaners felt more concerned to embrace the free-enterprise ethic, partly to counter the 'communist onslaught', partly from a greater sense of their own opportunity. 'As Afrikaner business people became more numerous and more successful,' wrote Leonard Thompson, 'they became committed to the market economy, and consequently less dependent on political patronage and less tied to the rigid racial ideology of the past.'†
And in political calculations the arithmetic suggested that President Botha or his successor could only preserve their leadership in parliament by appealing to more English-speaking voters to compensate for the loss of the Afrikaner right-wing – surrendering some of the exclusiveness of Afrikanerdom in exchange for the broader white support. 'The real question is whether the Afrikaners can hold on to their monopoly of power,' said the Afrikaans journalist Stanley Uys in November 1985. 'Whether they can continue to exclude the English-speaking population from any role in the decisions. So long as they maintain that monopoly, they won't be able to make any real concessions to the blacks.'‡

* Barry Streek in *Weekly Mail*, July 18, 1986
† Thompson, *op. cit.*, p. 191–2
‡ Interview with author November 19, 1985

But though Botha periodically wooed English-speaking voters
and businessmen he showed little desire to open up the citadel of
Afrikanerdom which had provided such rich rewards for his people
over forty years. This white tribe, insulated by political power and
patronage, was more exclusive than any of the black tribes whose
separateness it sought to encourage; and Afrikaners talked about
their ethnicity with a mystique which European nations, like the
Dutch and English, had long ago abandoned. The special hold
of their Afrikaans culture was evident even in Breyten Breytenbach, the dissident Afrikaans poet and painter who had broken
out to marry a Vietnamese princess, lived in exile in Paris and then
joined the underground group Okhela, loosely linked with the
ANC. When he secretly returned to South Africa to establish an
underground resistance, he was betrayed and served seven
years in jail, surrounded by brutal Afrikaner warders. He vowed
that 'Nothing can ever bridge the gap between the Afrikaner
tribe and myself'; and when he was moved from Pretoria jail
'I swore then – as I still swear today – that never will I freely
set foot again in Pretoria. Let that bloated village of civil servants
and barbarians be erased from the face of the earth.'* Yet nine
years afterwards in April 1986 Breytenbach returned to Pretoria
to receive a literary prize, where he warned his Afrikaner
audience: 'We are culturally incapable of initiating, accompany-
ing or accommodating the imminent transformation of our
society. Our rottenness is unique and our self-destruction will
certainly also be unrepeatable.'†

By March 1985 all President Botha's authority and Afrikaner
pride were being challenged by the mounting international pressure, and the confrontation with black rebels at home. In the black
townships the 'comrades' and street committees were taking the
initiative, and moderate black leaders were increasingly under
pressure. Even Winnie Mandela, who was a heroine to the young
black activists in spite of her relative restraint, had suddenly burst
out with a call to take necklaces and matches into the white suburbs.
The ANC leaders were appalled, knowing that she would be said to
represent Mandela's own views, which she did not: she was persuaded to keep quiet for the following weeks, and then effectively
withdrew her previous call: 'I wasn't advocating violence: I was
saying that the time would come when people shall be called upon
to defend themselves . . . The panicking racists say I advocated

* Breyten Breytenbach, *The True Confessions of an Albino Terrorist*, London, Faber
and Faber, 1984, p. 255
† Johannesburg *Sunday Times*, April 13, 1986

violence. I have not done so yet.'* But her outburst had been an ugly warning of horrors ahead.

The main political battleground remained the black schools. As the three-month ultimatum by parents in December came close to expiring the government had appeared conciliatory. They lifted the state of emergency, and the minister of education Gerrit Viljoen appealed for black children to go back to school. At the end of March 1,500 parents, teachers and pupils attended a second National Education Conference in Durban, and decided to advocate a return to school, while also planning major demonstrations on May Day and June 16, the anniversary of Soweto. The parents' generation appeared to be regaining their control; and an important keynote address, carefully prepared by a committee, was delivered by Zwelakhe Sisulu, the son of the ANC veteran Walter Sisulu who was now editor of the black paper *New Nation*. It explained how:

In any struggle it is extremely important to recognise the critical moment, the time when decisive action can propel that struggle into a new phase. It is also important to understand that this moment does not last for ever – that, if we fail to take action, that moment is lost. This particular moment has several important features.
* The State has lost the initiative to the people. It is no longer in control of events.
* The masses recognise that the moment is decisive and are calling for action.
* People are united around a set of fundamental demands and are prepared to take action on these demands.
Having said this, I want to strike a note of caution. It is important that we don't mistake the moment or understand it to be something it is not. We are not poised for the immediate transfer of power to the people. The belief that this is so could lead to serious errors and defeats. We are, however, poised to enter a phase which could lead to the transfer of power. What we are seeking to do is to shift the balance of forces in our favour decisively . . .

The balance did seem to be shifting. The black activists in the UDF and elsewhere were building up their 'alternative structures' which mocked the government's own hierarchies, and their most striking victory came on May Day when they organised their first successful one-day strike: in Port Elizabeth and most of the Eastern Cape

* Speech at Orlando Stadium, May 1986

nearly 100 percent of the workers stayed away, and even in the gold-mines the workers went out on strike: Anglo-American reported 83 percent absent.* May Day had become a highly politicised festival: in Soweto 20,000 blacks attended a rally of the trades union group COSATU, while in Durban Buthelezi's party Inkatha launched its own United Workers Union of South Africa (UWUSA) at a rally of 60,000 Zulus. It was the first time black South Africans had made their own calendar.

The government were now being threatened not only by black school-children, but by right-wing Afrikaners who were rapidly becoming highly-publicised, through their extreme group the Afrikaanner Weerstandsbeweging (AWB) led by the ex-policeman Eugene Terre'Blanche. On May 22, when the foreign minister Pik Botha was scheduled to speak at Pietersburg in the Northern Transvaal, Terre'Blanche successfully took over the meeting with his 'storm falcons' waving their flags with the emblems of the three-armed Swastika. The AWB's own political policies were puerile: its 'programme of principles' was openly anti-semitic and anti-capitalist, blaming Jewish capitalists and Anglo-American for allowing blacks to flow into the cities and promising to free Afrikaners from 'spiritual and economic enslavement by Anglo-Jewish money'. The actual following of the AWB was much exaggerated by its publicity and melodrama; but it clearly had many supporters among the Afrikaner police who refrained from moving against the invaders, and it was appearing ominously like the paramilitary wing of the conservative party under Andries Treurnicht: when several Afrikaner right-wing groups assembled at the Voortrekker monument in June, Terre'Blanche was the most acclaimed speaker.† It provided a pretext if not a reason for Botha to take bolder action against black rebels.

By the beginning of June the political tension was mounting rapidly as the tenth anniversary of Soweto approached. The government had put forward two new bills, the Public Safety Amendment Bill and the Internal Security Amendment Bill, to enable the Minister of Law and Order to declare 'unrest areas' and to give the police special powers including ordering detention without trial for 180 days – thus making a state of emergency virtually unnecessary. But the bills were opposed not only by the Progressive Federal Party but also by the Indian and coloured MPs elected under the new constitution, who insisted on sending the bills back to the standing committee – thus delaying their passing until after June

* *Weekly Mail*, May 2, 1986
† *See* Patrick Laurence in *Weekly Mail*, June 6, 1986

16. As the critical date came closer the minister for law and order, Louis Le Grange, was pressing for emergency powers; and Botha himself was increasingly impatient of international pressure and the threat of sanctions.

On June 12 Botha declared his second, and much more far-reaching, state of emergency which would precipitate a more fundamental crisis, and would drive a deeper wedge between South African businessmen and their Western counterparts.

17

Crackdown

We are tired of having to govern South Africa under the threat of sanctions.

President Botha

No factory or mine can work without us. No city can function without us. Nothing in this country can work without blacks. We are no longer simply hewers of wood and drawers of water.

Chief Buthelezi in his address at Jabulani Amphitheatre,
Soweto, June 29, 1986

In its centenary year Johannesburg showed all the outward signs of triumphant permanence and prosperity since its wild beginnings as a mining camp in 1886. The city centre was scarcely recognisable from the bleak grid of rectangles where I had worked thirty years before; and only a few corrugated rooves and gingerbread balconies still jostled next to the sheer office towers. A many-faceted mirror-building, shining like a giant diamond, had sprung up on the site of the old Indian markets along Diagonal Street, to provide yet another building for the Anglo-American Corporation. A cylindrical glass tower had risen up next to the stone law courts, containing the newest luxury hotel, the Johannesburg Sun. The names of the world's multinationals glittered from the tops of the tower-blocks.

Banners and posters now advertised the 'city with a heart of gold', 'our strength is our people'; and a romantic television serial had just been launched to commemorate the centenary. 'On this site was to rise one of the greatest cities in Africa . . . a city of the future, with so little time to look back.' Johannesburg had prepared for a programme of celebrations, and a rush of tourists. But the plans and slogans – 'a hundred cheers for a hundred years' – had gone sour in the course of the year: the black Community Support Committee had warned the sponsors that they would 'incur the wrath of the black people', and proposed their own slogan 'a hundred years of oppression'. The business sponsors had admitted defeat. The white woman selling centenary souvenirs at the kiosk near the town hall told me she had not sold enough in one day to pay for her bus-fare.

And on Monday June 16, 1986, the blacks were celebrating their own anniversary – ten years after the Soweto uprising. The government said it would be a 'normal working day', but the city centre was as empty as if it had been visited by a plague: the station and bus-termini, which usually teemed with black commuters, were deserted. Only a few white people were walking the streets and some were actually *carrying* their own parcels out of the Johannesburg post office, watched by a group of blacks sitting on the steps. There was no reliable news since the State of Emergency had been declared four days before: the newspapers gave bare reports from the government, the radio provided cheery items including a romantic travel talk by Laurens van der Post. No one could go in and out of Soweto, or knew how many people had been imprisoned. In a black newspaper office the journalists told me that a four-year-old girl in Soweto had been shot in the back, and a whole church congregation arrested: it was not till the end of the week that both reports were confirmed. Rumours reverberated about the success or failure of the one-day strike: the government radio news ('brought to you with the compliments of Nissan South Africa'), insisted that most blacks had gone to work against all the evidence of the streets. By the next morning it was clear that for the second time in the year the blacks had shown they could assert their own sanction: to withdraw their labour. Anglo-American had already made a virtue of necessity, following the Premier Group by declaring it a half-holiday: 'South Africa's calendar of public holidays,' announced Gavin Relly, 'no longer reflects the full spectrum of national sentiment.'

The only centre of activity was the brown stone cathedral which had seen so many protests in the forty years of apartheid. Before midday it filled up with all races, including some familiar faces of liberals, academics and do-gooders but only two prominent businessmen – both of them Jewish. The service opened with a reading froim Isaiah, beginning: 'Shout without restraint,' and continued with hymns. Then Bishop Tutu delivered his sermon, insisting that he would never agree not to mix religion with politics, and warning that the emergency was 'grossly insensitive and highly provocative'. He asked 'why are we allowing this country to be destroyed?' and ended with his arms stretched out to heaven while the cameras whirred. As the service ended a black woman in red began singing the ANC anthem – Nkosi Sikelele Africa – holding out her clenched fist, while half the congregation joined in.

From their glittering new buildings and suburban estates, the Johannesburg tycoons now surveyed the most testing political crisis of their city's lifetime. The second emergency which President Botha had declared on June 12 was far more rigorous than his first one eleven months earlier; and he was determined to rally the business community behind him in an atmosphere of crisis. At each previous crisis – 1952, 1960, 1976, 1985 – radical politicians and journalists had always tended to exaggerate the extremity of the repression, leaving no words to describe the next turn of the screw. This crackdown was undoubtedly more thorough and efficient than anything before: it gave far greater freedom to the police to arrest, detain and interrogate whoever they wished, with unprecedented censorship to prevent any reporting of their actions. (After I wrote a report on detainees for the London *Observer*, I was informed that the minister of home affairs had withdrawn my exemption from a visa.) It was not until two months later that the government revealed that 8,500 people had been detained under the regulations (which many lawyers still thought was only half the full number). And only in August, when the courts found that censorship had been illegally imposed, could a few glimpses of police activity be revealed behind the censors' blanks – though in the words of the *Weekly Mail*: 'The black lines camouflaged only those few areas not already covered by a mass of other legislation affecting reporting on prisons, police and the Defence Force.' This was one report which emerged uncensored in August, about the township of Zwelethemba near Worcester in the Cape which had been the scene of earlier consumer boycotts (*See* Chapter 12); it provided a glimpse of the new kind of military apartheid which was being enforced in the midst of an advanced industrial system.

> Zwelethemba is a township virtually under siege; a South African Defence Force camp is pitched on its borders, and within walking distance is a police station, hastily erected during the last State of Emergency. Searchlights from towers that encircle the township span the streets nightly, frequently coming to rest on the front doors of known activists or anyone else suspected by the police. A 7 pm to 7 am curfew imposed the weekend the current emergency began is still in force.*

The major battleground was once again the schools, where new regulations forced pupils to re-register and to carry special identity cards, and forbade them to take part in any non-educational activities in the school buildings, while soldiers and police were sent into schools to enforce order. There were accounts of security forces beating the schoolchildren, taking them out of class, and even acting

* *Weekly Mail*, Johannesburg, August 22, 1986

as teachers to provide their own version of history and geography; there was one report of a whole class being arrested and detained. The new generation of schoolchildren was growing up alongside the police state in its most literal everyday form: their chief daily experience of whites was of uniformed men carrying guns and sjamboks. The children retaliated with school boycotts in some areas, sometimes attending with their own underground schools. They were still in the vanguard of the revolt, with older politicians on every side trying to mobilise and control them. While the ANC and the UDF were trying to keep them within their parents' discipline, Chief Buthelezi furiously attacked the ANC in exile for exploiting the children, at a massed 'prayer meeting' which he addressed in Soweto, with police protection at the height of the emergency:

> Our children will yet be turned into cannon fodder unparalleled in the history of mankind if we continue to allow others to employ our anger as though it was their property . . . Nowhere in the history of the world have young people of school-going age achieved the liberation of their country on their own . . . Those who sit in exile and use our young folk as storm troopers as they seek personal glorification, or the glorification of narrow sectional interests, must be rejected by every black South African.*

But there was little sign that the schoolchildren needed any encouragement from outside to spur them against the police. The real danger as the emergency bit harder was that they would accept no allegiance, that their fury could not be contained, and that the internal feuds between warring black factions would descend into anarchy.

There was no doubt that the government was determined to use the new emergency to smash the networks of political groups, particularly youth groups and offshoots of COSAS which were linked to the UDF, that had grown up to challenge their power in the previous two years; and the police were clearly encouraging the growing tensions between the UDF and its rival AZAPO. Nearly half the detainees were youth leaders, and the security forces had clearly been closely watching the new 'alternative structures': there were suspicions that they had deliberately allowed them to flourish over the previous year, in order to identify their leadership and then cut them down.

The UDF kept up a bold front, and the ANC was certainly more famous than ever. 'For the government to say that the ANC is banned

---

* Speech at Jabulani Amphitheatre, June 29, 1986

is laughable. You know it and we know it.' Zwelakhe Sisulu, the
resilient editor of *New Nation* told the Afrikaans journal *Die Suid
Afrikaan* in June before he was himself detained. Several key black
leaders evaded arrest. On the third anniversary of the UDF in August
1986 its publicity secretary Murphy Morobe, who had been in and
out of hiding for a year, reappeared to maintain that 'the UDF has
not only survived the most severe repression but has grown into a
mass movement . . . our organisations are stronger and deeper than
before and are thus better able to replace activists detained, killed
or forced into exile.' And by early October the leaders of the UDF,
together with COSATU and the National Education Crisis Committee,
all emerged from hiding to announce a 'momentous' campaign
for 'national unity against apartheid and the emergency'. The
government responded a week later by forbidding the UDF to receive
funds from abroad, which had been contributing half its finances.*
But the resistance groups had undoubtedly taken a battering: as
Shaun Johnson, having interviewed a wide range of young black
leaders, described them in July 1986:

> Today youth organisations are in disarray. Leaders are incarcer-
> ated, others are underground and unable to supervise day-to-day
> organisational business, meetings are impossible, and there is a
> distinct air of directionlessness and despair. I do not believe that
> the Emergency can destroy the complex, deeply entrenched youth
> structures. But it can certainly set back what was seen to be a
> linear process of growth.†

The businessmen in Johannesburg faced the two extremes of black
fury and white repression with still greater bewilderment. Most of
them, I found, agreed that the state of emergency was necessary:
they had dreaded a new outburst of violence on June 16, and many
believed the government's warnings that the ANC had prepared a
national revolt. The declaration of the emergency had been followed
by a local boom and a flurry of economic activity stimulated by the
finance minister Barend du Plessis with a new package. At the
Reserve Bank Governor de Kock was able to revive the value of the
rand, partly by massive selling of dollars; and he explained that:
'When investors realised that South Africa was not on the verge of
revolution – no matter how serious the situation was – it was natural
that both the financial and commercial rand should appreciate.'

* *Weekly Mail*, August 22, 1986, October 3, 1986, *Financial Times*, October 10,
1986
  † Shaun Johnson, *ibid.*

The censorship contributed to the boom. 'The sparseness of news,' said Max Borkum, the former chairman of the stock exchange, 'has helped to give people euphoria.' Exchange controls had helped to bolster the domestic economy. As businessmen said: 'We are rand-locked.' The government used the mini-boom to show that business appreciated a tough, decisive stand, and by the end of the first week of the emergency de Kock was claiming that South Africa was now 'on top of the debt crisis'.

But the mini-boom, most businessmen agreed, was full of illusions. Capital was still leaking out of the country, whether through Swiss banks which were laundering rand or through South African companies doing their own disinvesting through their subsidiaries abroad. Estate agents reported that 10 percent of all property in city-centres was empty – even though Indians and others were now allowed to buy properties in some white areas. Unemployment was hitting not only blacks but whites; and under a government relief scheme 250 whites were now working in Johannesburg's city parks, digging ditches for $2 a day. Nor did de Kock's optimism stand up for long. Two months after the emergency began he revealed in the Reserve Bank's annual report that the gross domestic product (adjusted for inflation) had grown by only 1 percent in 1984–5, and in 1986 it would not be more than 2 percent – compared to an average of 4.9 percent in the long heyday between 1946 and 1974; and he admitted that economic recovery had been slowed by 'domestic lack of confidence and foreigners' strongly negative perceptions of South Africa's political stability and economic prospects'.

The businessmen – particularly the retailers and manufacturers – knew they would have in the end to gain the consent of the black workers and customers. Boycotts and mini-strikes still continued despite the regulations, and the middle-class black employees came under much greater pressure from radicals in the townships. And Botha's policies showed no real consistency or reassurance: his oscillations between reform and repression provided the most dangerous combination, first raising black expectations, then dashing them and provoking resistance: it looked almost like a deliberate formula for revolution. Five years earlier Botha had yielded to the pressure of industrialists to allow black unions: now his police had arrested most of their leaders, in the middle of crucial wage negotiations. Even without their leaders, the unions could still keep some shop-workers away, in protest against the detentions.

Some businessmen did publicly oppose Botha's crackdown. The Federated Chamber of Industries, presided over by John Wilson of Shell, made a statement which 'strongly disapproved of the state of emergency and the further detention and disassociated itself from

the strategy of political repression and economic isolationism to
which the South African government is apparently committed'.
Many business members of the Chamber angrily dissented from
the statement, and President Botha wrote a furious private reply to
Wilson saying it was 'quite ridiculous' and that the government
was already committed to negotiation and conciliation.

> Kindly do not trouble me with your points of view if you are not
> prepared to take the trouble of familiarising yourself with mine.
> Unless you too come to grips with the realities of the security
> situation in this country and act accordingly you are bound to
> pay a heavy price. This is not a threat – it is a considered warning.
> Instead of criticising the government in the most irresponsible
> fashion you should be helping it. That is your duty as a South
> African . . .

'But with whom is government negotiating these reforms?' Wilson
asked in an article just afterwards: 'The identifiable black leaders
are specifically excluded from the negotiation process . . .'* Botha,
after his earlier conciliatory talks, was now spelling out much more
brutally his attitude to foreign investors, insisting that they must
knuckle down or get out. And in spite of his protests, John Wilson
had rashly insisted just after the crackdown that Shell would continue to invest heavily in South Africa with 'the full backing of its
international shareholders'.†

A few businessmen went further. Tony Bloom of the Premier
Group and Chris Ball of Barclays took part in a candid radio
discussion with two leading members of the ANC, Thabo Mbeki and
Mac Maharaj, and later lunched with Oliver Tambo (*see* Chapter
1). They were fiercely attacked for talking to terrorists while more
bombs were going off, and the government-controlled *Citizen* called
it a 'Blooming shame'. Gavin Relly of Anglo-American was now
lying lower, well aware of his company's vulnerability in the current
political mood. 'With the rise of the right-wing in white politics,'
wrote *The Citizen* with a nasty implied threat, 'the last thing Anglo
should want is a revival of the Hoggenheimer canard which was
fortunately buried several decades ago.'‡ Most companies preferred
generalised protest to specific actions, and many multinationals and
others joined to sponsor yet another advertisement, prepared by J
Walter Thompson, showing black and white hands stretching

* *Business Day*, Johannesburg, July 4, 1986
† *Sunday Tribune*, Durban, July 20, 1986
‡ *The Citizen*, June 3, 1986

towards each other. It said 'Instead of a State of Emergency, let's declare a State of Urgency to remove all discriminatory legislation without delay . . .' and asked the government to free political detainees and negotiate with acknowledged leaders about power sharing. But Afrikaner businessmen were notably absent from the signatories.

Faced with the choice of decisive police repression and an uncertain black mob, most businessmen were more concerned with their short-term security than their longer-term survival. They put some hope once again in President Botha; and as sanctions loomed closer they were pressed to rally more closely behind the government to defeat them. Botha was again promising a major new speech, this time at a special Federal Congress of the National Party in Durban in August; and the world leaders, including Thatcher and Reagan, were again assured that if they would refrain from provocative pressure Botha would push through his own reforms. But the Congress was preceded by a mood of defiance encouraged by the apparent effectiveness of the emergency and by the internal mini-boom.

The Johannesburg stock market was now hitting record levels while gold and platinum prices were pressing upwards, partly *because* of the South African crisis: the prospect of chaos and catastrophe could be good news for many speculators in a country with so many key minerals in short supply; and the platinum price had already shot up in anticipation of cut-backs and sanctions. Just before the Congress de Kock had announced that the higher gold price would ensure that South Africa would have a surplus on the current-account balance of payment of over four billion rand.

Botha's speech proved yet another anti-climax for the world, and revealed much more clearly that the basic structure of apartheid would still remain intact. He produced two new proposals: that major black townships such as Soweto could be given a special status as autonomous city-states, which he compared to Europe's city-states like Monaco; and that South Africa could join in high-level talks with the major Western nations to discuss stability in Southern Africa. His minister for constitutional affairs, Chris Heunis, discussed a new Council of State which would bring together homelands and the city-states with parliament. But Botha insisted that apartheid would prevail in residential areas and in schools, that he would not negotiate with the ANC or make any concessions to world opinion: 'Granting concessions under conditions bordering on blackmail merely encourages the raising of demands.' And he ended his speech by reasserting the mystical role of the Afrikaners to lead the subcontinent: 'I look at the constellations in the sky at night and what are the words I see written there? Southern Africa for Christendom.'

His speech totally contradicted the beliefs of Western leaders – most of all Mrs Thatcher – who had insisted that the Afrikaner government, if left to itself, would dismantle apartheid and genuinely begin to share power with black leaders. The government emphasised that reforms would continue, but within the context of strict control of the black movements: and the emergency now appeared, as Allister Sparks of the *Washington Post* described it, as 'a desperate attempt to stem those forces and get the logs back in place while the limited reforms are completed'.* President Reagan rushed in to welcome the idea of talks about apartheid – which gave a new fillip to Botha at the Congress – but the State Department quickly back-tracked, explaining that the meeting would 'focus on regional issues, rather than apartheid'; while the British Foreign Office was now more forthright, insisting that Mandela must be released and the ANC unbanned: 'We are disappointed that President Botha showed no signs of taking the quantum leap forward which is so clearly necessary.'

More riots and repression followed the Congress, with growing evidence that the army as well as the police were using systematic torture to try to cow all opposition. The security forces, with the help of censorship, were beginning to give the impression of order and calm. But behind Botha's show of strength the reports from the townships suggested that they were moving still further out of control; Soweto remained a battleground as the government tried to enforce the payment of rents; and the white director of housing, Del Kevan, had her house in a white suburb bombed with a limpet-mine after which she resigned. The more leaders were detained, the less the prospect of limiting and controlling the violence. Some members of the ANC, which had called to render South Africa ungovernable eighteen months before, were beginning to worry that it might become ungovernable by anyone.

And even the communists, the persistent advocates of revolution, were becoming more concerned about the potential loss of control. Six weeks after the emergency the South African Communist Party – now coming more into the open – celebrated its sixty-fifth anniversary in the Conway Hall, the traditional meeting-place of the Left in London. In the packed hall tough stewards frisked everyone: old-style British communists, young anti-apartheid idealists, South African exiles of all colours. A black choir in red shirts sang the old Congress songs, punctuated with the names of Mandela, Tambo,

* *Observer*, August 16, 1986

Slovo. Round the hall hung photographs of the martyrs – Bram Fischer, Ruth First, Moses Kotane. On the platform, above pictures of Lenin and Marx, the red flag was draped alongside the black, green and gold flag of the ANC; and the chairman of the SACP, Joe Slovo, sat with the Secretary-General of the ANC, Alfred Nzo.

The British communists seemed exhilarated by the prospect of a real revolution complete with the kind of heroes, martyrs and complete commitment which had long faded in Europe. 'The dreams which inspired the founders of the party are about to be realised,' said the secretary of the British Communist Party, Gordon McLennan. But the South Africans were more guarded. The ANC pledged friendship with the Communists and Alfred Nzo said 'Our banners flutter together at the head of the columns'; but he took care to explain that 'The ANC will defend the right of anyone who chooses to belong to the SACP, or to any party of their choice, so long as they are not a vehicle for racism or fascism'; and he recalled how Churchill, Roosevelt and de Gaulle emerged as giants during the Second World War when they fought the forces of Nazism.

The key speech was by Comrade Joe Slovo, the chairman of the South African Communist Party who was also on the ANC executive: a lawyer from Lithuanian Jewish parents – like so many successful compatriots – he had practised as a lawyer in Johannesburg before he went into exile for twenty-five years, where his wife Ruth First was killed by a letter bomb. He still sported a blazer, South African style, and a throaty South African accent. He paid tribute to the Party 'which brought into existence the first modern national liberation movement in Africa'. He was convinced that the factors for revolutionary advance were now coming together: the rulers could not rule in the old way, the people were discovering people's power, the ANC were in the vanguard. 'The South African masses are on the move as never before: we vow to help them finish the job.' But his speech was muted, theoretical and cautious. He described how South African communists had to work out their own indigenous theory of revolution; and how they could never be separated from the ANC – which 'has no competition as the alternative power in our land'. He explained that the SACP, unlike Congress, owed its allegiance solely to the working people: 'The road which was taken when the liberation flag eventually flew in Pretoria would depend on the correlation of class forces which came to power.' After they had achieved majority rule there would still for some time be a role for private property and a mixed economy, including 'managers and business people of goodwill'. He explained that: 'Enough experiences have been accumulated of disastrous great leaps forward to teach us to be wary of baking slogans rather than

baking bread during the transition phase.' And he warned against
the 'Pol Pot philosophy' which thought you could 'pole-vault into
socialism and communism the day after the overthrow of white
rule . . .'

Many members of the ANC were surprised by Slovo's caution,
and his lack of a practical programme. 'He was trying to calm down
the young hotheads,' one ANC veteran said after the meeting. 'It
looks as if the ANC has swallowed the SACP,' said another. I asked
Slovo afterwards how far his speech represented new thinking.
'Well, it represents thinking. We've been catapulted into a new
situation. We've been used to being an agitational opposition, not
an alternative power. Now we've been forced to formulate our
approach.' How close did he see the possibility of chaos? He replied:

> A lot of the future depends on Pretoria: if the government digs
> in its heels, chaos may make negotiation impossible, and a bloody
> struggle would leave a lot of historical debts to be paid. Of course
> the so-called chaos has already caused the crisis, which is a
> positive happening: but there are manifestations which we don't
> like, as the kids begin to say: what can we do today? I've never
> believed that it's the job of a revolutionary to make a revolution:
> only to lead it. There are lots of situations which have no control.
> I've never relished the escalation of violence: we didn't go into it
> with any *élan*, but because it was the only option, the last option:
> and we want to get out of it as soon as possible.

While President Botha continued to blame the communist onslaught
for any resistance, many communists were already dreading an
anarchy in the black townships which could go far beyond their
influence: most of the 'comrades' who set the necklaces on fire owed
no allegiance to the ANC or the SACP. The old Afrikaner mythology
of the fight against communism was beginning to lose its relevance
to the rest of the world; and as America and Europe began finally
to move towards sanctions the Afrikaners were having to re-think
their old assumption that the West would always support them in
the final anti-communist crusade; and some were beginning to see
American capitalists as an enemy more threatening than Soviet
communists.

18

The End of a Road

I would be more impressed with those who made no bones about the
reason they remain in South Africa and said honestly: 'We are
concerned for our profits' instead of the baloney that the businesses
are there for our benefit. We don't want you there. Please do us a
favor: Get out and come back when we have a democratic and just
South Africa.

Bishop Tutu, *New York Times*, June 16, 1986

Botha's crackdown had defied world opinion, and the issue of
apartheid and sanctions exploded across America and Western
Europe. South Africa was now more than ever the caricature of the
world's problems, reviving dormant fears about race and chaos and
bringing back the old arguments about poverty and inequality and
the conflict between business and morality. But the clamour for
sanctions also showed all the difficulties of taking effective steps.
South Africa's gold and precious metals were still interlocked with
the world's money and high-technology industries: half the continent depended on its exports and trade. How could you isolate and
cut out a malignant growth in the midst of the world's intricate
trading system? And what happens after disinvestment?

The chiefs of the multinational corporations – with General
Motors, IBM and Shell in the forefront – watched their own justifica-
tions and diplomacy being overtaken by the public outcry which
was pushing their governments towards the sanctions that would
undermine their investments. Sanctions also drove a wedge through
the Western political world. The two key leaders, Ronald Reagan
and Margaret Thatcher, still passionately opposed them, and still
hoped that the apartheid problem would solve itself. But both were
now under much heavier bombardment until slowly and reluctantly
they were compelled to change course.

After Botha's crackdown Mrs Thatcher still resisted pressure
from the European Community, the Commonwealth and growing
numbers of conservatives. Parliament held an emergency debate,
and the British government undertook to work actively 'for effective
measures which will help achieve a peaceful solution in South

Africa'. Soon afterwards the twelve prime ministers of the European Community held a summit which called again for the release of Mandela and the unbanning of the ANC, and agreed to send out the British Foreign Secretary Sir Geoffrey Howe for a final attempt at dialogue before imposing sanctions. Sir Geoffrey reluctantly agreed on his unpromising mission, explaining that apartheid was 'not Christian, not civilised and certainly not in the interests of the West that it should survive'. But Mrs Thatcher seemed determined to undermine Howe's leverage on Botha by attacking the immorality of sanctions in a succession of interviews. Nearly all black leaders, including Mandela, Tambo and the churchmen Tutu and Boesak, refused to see Howe, insisting that his visit was merely a delaying tactic against sanctions: Botha eventually agreed to see him, but then himself slammed the door, and Howe returned empty-handed. He had been sent (said the Tory MP Robert Adley) 'up the creek without a paddle and then brought home without a canoe'.

The House of Commons was now much more vocal. Denis Healey, the shadow foreign secretary who had just visited South Africa, called for comprehensive mandatory sanctions to bring the issue to a head; and Ted Heath also supported the call for sanctions, while warning that effective action would require a naval blockade. But most of the Conservative Party was still resolutely opposed. The Foreign Affairs Committee of all-party MPs produced a rush report based on their hearings which had begun with Tambo a year earlier. They could not agree whether wider sanctions would strengthen or weaken the government: they believed that after a while they 'would be likely to bite very hard, and no South African government would be able to ignore their effect in the framing of its policies'. But they were pessimistic about the chances of peaceful negotiation to a democratic system. In all the debates most politicians shunned the basic issue of black majority rule, and it was left to a diplomat, Lord Moran, to voice the real fears of conservatives:

> There can be no half-way house in South Africa. Either you must have a white dominated society or you must have one man, one vote, which would lead to black majority rule and, in due course no doubt, a one-party regime, soon to come in Zimbabwe . . . I think one man, one vote would necessitate the departure of most of the 3 million whites, many of them to this country . . .'*

It was still the Commonwealth more than parliament that made trouble for Thatcher; and after Botha had so decisively rebuffed the

* House of Lords, July 4, 1986

eminent persons they were on the warpath for sanctions. Malcolm Fraser from Australia insisted that sanctions were essential to bring South Africa not to its knees but to its senses: he agreed they might only have a 50 percent chance of success; but said the alternative was the total destruction of Western interests in South Africa. General Obasanjo burst out publicly against Thatcher's 'misguided tribal loyalty'; and Brian Mulroney of Canada and Bob Hawke of Australia joined forces with the black states. British conservatives and white South Africans quickly pointed out that Canada and Australia would suffer little, and might gain something from imposing sanctions; but Mulroney and Hawke both argued that the British were too preoccupied by the short-term to see their long-term interests ahead.

Through July, while the South African police were mopping up the black resistance, the sanctions issue reverberated through Britain with furious rhetoric on both sides. It easily lost touch with any serious consideration for the interests of either business or blacks; and South Africa became darkly related to immigration and race riots in Britain: 'Do you want another Brixton?' The attacks on sanctions soon overspilled into attacks against the Commonwealth, on its secretary-general Sonny Ramphal, and eventually on the Queen herself, who was accused of supporting the Commonwealth against Mrs Thatcher – an assumption which even briefly threatened to cause a constitutional crisis.

But while politicians insisted that sanctions were against Britain's commercial interests, many businessmen were now much less sure that they wanted to be part of an anti-sanctions crusade. Their spokesman at BICSA Sir Leslie Smith charged into the fray, mustering a posse of companies to make a statement against sanctions which was widely publicised in South Africa, protesting that they 'would retard rather than accelerate the process of change'. But sixteen of the fifty member-companies including the biggest banks, Barclays and Standard, refused to sign it, and many members with interests in black Africa, including Unilever and both oil companies, were now acutely embarrassed. Sir Leslie then tried to produce an agreed policy about South Africa which was passed from one company to the next like a hot potato, and was eventually issued with minimum publicity and contorted prose. It neither supported nor criticised sanctions: while condemning punitive pressures, it 'understood the frustrations' which had led the Commonwealth to call for sanctions, and was 'certainly not opposesd to further pressures which support those working for non-violent change from within'.* But many companies, again including Barclays and Standard, now wanted a

* British Industry in South Africa, BICSA, July 1986

bolder identification with black aspirations and were discreetly in favour of limited sanctions: Barclays were even privately suggesting sanctions against South African airlines.

The United States Congress was now a much more militant force for sanctions than the British parliament; and few American companies tried to oppose them. The House of Representatives had already passed a drastic bill for sanctions which had taken Washington and Pretoria by surprise; and Reagan's contradictory speech of July 22 (*see* page 14) which gave such succour to Botha, only provoked the Senators to stiffen their terms. They were led by two Republicans: Richard Lugar from Indiana, who was very conscious of the articulate black community in Indianapolis; and Nancy Kassebaum from Kansas, who chaired the Africa sub-committee, whose conservatism had turned to frustration. Both were influenced by Senator Kennedy, who provided a forum for Obasanjo and Fraser. In mid-August Lugar proposed his full sanctions bill, which included banning steel, airlines and government bank ac-counts, which was followed by a historic debate re-examining both American policy and the role of big business. Lugar gave credit to American companies' achievements: how Sullivan had established the first code of conduct, how Kelloggs corn flakes had first recognised a black union, how American companies had operated the first non-racial charities. But he insisted that his proposed sanctions were essential to combat apartheid. Senator Kennedy described the Americans' shame 'that our country is implicated in the terrible system that blights South Africa. Our corporations have benefited from the apartheid economy, and our government has, for many years, indulged the leaders of apartheid'. Senator Proxmire invoked the Declaration of Independence to insist that when governments suppress the people '. . . it is their right, it is their duty to throw off such government.' Senator Weicker remembered how '. . . When I first came to the US in 1970 everybody recognised that apartheid was wrong, but everyone said it would go away – let nature take its course . . . But the cancer did not go away. It has spread. It is worse today than it was in 1970.' And he urged Senators not to repeat the mistakes of the 'thirties when 'We chose to wait, and we chose not to act . . . The laws of Nazi Germany *vis-à-vis* Jews are identical to the laws of South Africa *vis-à-vis* black South Africans.'

The conservative senators counter-attacked with their own ideol-ogy, led by Jesse Helms from North Carolina who wanted an amendment that the United States would not negotiate with the African National Congress unless they abandoned violence and committed themselves to free and democratic government. He warned that the ANC was 'a Communist front controlled by the

South African Communist Party, which itself is under the control of the Communist Party of the Soviet Union'. He came out with biographies of ANC leaders prepared by the CIA (but looking very similar to Pretoria's own reports*) which its director William Casey had especially de-classified; and his views were supported by Senator Denton from Alabama, who had held hearings on terrorism in 1982 and who compared South Africa to Vietnam, Cambodia, Iran and Nicaragua. But Helms was rebutted by Weicker who quoted the report of the eminent persons and Mandela's own statement in 1964 that 'the creed of the ANC is and always has been African nationalism'. After some bargaining Lugar and Helms agreed to a modified amendment, calling on both government and the ANC to renounce violence, but maintaining the package of sanctions, which went through by sixty-seven to thirty-one.

The Senate was now openly confronting the White House, and their two courses were set for the biggest collision on foreign policy of Reagan's presidency. In September Reagan was determined to veto the sanctions bill, and hoped that he could bring enough Senators over to his side – with the help of promises of aid and a black ambassador to Pretoria – to reduce the two-thirds majority. But most of the House and the Senate were now adamant; and at the beginning of October the two houses of Congress finally voted on the bill. The South African foreign minister Pik Botha telephoned senators during the debate to warn them that Pretoria would retaliate against American farmers: and Chief Buthelezi called them more discreetly to insist that sanctions would hurt the blacks. But Pretoria's intervention only rallied most of the Senators, and on October 2 the Senate voted by seventy-eight to twenty-one to pass 'The Comprehensive Anti-Apartheid Act of 1986'. It was almost a complete alternative foreign policy: it spelt out conditions to both sides, calling for Pretoria to release Mandela and for the ANC to condemn 'necklacing'. But its overriding purpose was to impose sanctions which would be stepped up if Pretoria made no substantial progress in twelve months towards a non-racial democracy.

The European governments had also stumbled towards sanctions, more reluctantly and less convincingly. At the Commonwealth meeting in early August Mrs Thatcher had already agreed to go along with the other Europeans, and she was glad to shift the burden of opposing fuller sanctions to Helmut Kohl in West Germany – who wanted to continue importing South African coal and who was pressurised by a pro-Pretoria lobby including Franz-Josef Strauss

* Compare the CIA notes published in the debate of August 14, 1986 with 'Talking to the ANC' published by the government in Pretoria earlier in 1986.

in Bavaria. In the final meeting of the twelve European nations in
September, the Germans and the Portuguese defeated the proposals
for coal sanctions; but the rest of the package went ahead, including
bans on steel and on new investment, but not on airlines. The
European sanctions were less comprehensive than the American;
and both sides of the Atlantic had shown deep divisions. Yet the
agreement to impose sanctions, however divided and incomplete,
represented a complete break with earlier policies over the last forty
years of apartheid.

It also marked a tragic admission: that investment and economic
improvement would not in themselves lead to peaceful change and
the achievement of black rights. It was the end of that long road of
the love-affair between South Africa and Western capitalism, which
had begun in earnest a century before with the discovery of gold in
Johannesburg. The recriminations would continue. Christians and
Marxists would blame the corporations for having built up apartheid; Western industrialists would insist that their commercial
interests were against any colour bar, and many would argue that
they were now resisting apartheid as far as they could. Certainly
the demands for disinvestment had produced some spectacular
improvements in black wages and conditions from companies which
were justifying their presence. But the heroic confrontations with
apartheid which they advertised abroad were a long way from
blacks' own day-to-day perceptions of white companies, whether
they were confronting an Afrikaner *baas* on the shopfloor, or observ-
ing the white executives retreating back to their white suburbs. And
few businessmen would willingly give up a life-style which combined
nineteenth-century servants and leisure together with twentieth-
century comforts and technology.

As South Africa began moving closer to civil war the attempts by
the multinationals to take on apartheid – whether by desegregating
washrooms and canteens, promoting black executives, funding
black education or even practising civil disobedience – were looking
more trivial compared to the build-up of the military and police
machine, which itself owed much to Western technology, and which
was now demanding a mounting tribute of obedience, taxes and
intelligence from the industrialists. Multinational managers would
be compelled to provide fuels, equipment and personnel to help the
army and police beat down the black resistance, and they would
have to keep military secrets even from their own headquarters in
London or New York; while the country-wide network of Joint
Management Centres bound them still closer to Pretoria.

The governments' moves towards sanctions were soon followed
by a dramatic exodus – at least on the surface – of American

corporations. Already over two years the numbers of American companies in South Africa had gone down from 325 to 265; and the retreat included Procter and Gamble and Coca-Cola (though it still sold its syrup). At General Motors, Roger Smith had become increasingly uneasy since visiting South Africa in April 1986, as a member of George Shultz's advisory committee: 'Something happened to that government there that changed their mind,' he said later, 'and they are not doing what I hoped they would. Maybe the world did it to them: maybe the siege mentality has set in.' GM was also, Smith said, 'struggling desperately' against the declining car-sales; and he was keeping the local company under constant review. Then on October 21 he announced that GM was finally pulling out, after six decades in South Africa: it had been losing money for several years, he explained, and 'we have been disappointed in the pace of ending apartheid.' The very next day the chairman of IBM John Akers followed suit, blaming the 'deteriorating political and economic situation'. The withdrawal of the two giants – the biggest in the world by sales and market capitalisation respectively – knocked on the head any lingering belief in Washington that corporations could be the main agents of change against apartheid: though the State Department spokesman Charles Redman complained that the withdrawals would weaken American influence, and would hurt black workers.

The disinvestments were not quite what they looked. Both GM and IBM were selling out to local South African managers, to whom they would lend the money to buy the subsidiary, and for whom they would still supply their technology; and they would even put in some more capital before new American investment was banned after November 12. 'They're not cutting us off so much as they are cutting us loose,' said a local IBM executive; and IBM had taken similar steps to cease investing in India and Nigeria. 'All our customers will continue to get the service excellence which is associated only with IBM products,' said an advertisement just afterwards. General Motors later explained that they would 'maintain close ties' with the company, and the new chief executive Robert Price was a GM man who had run the South African subsidiary before. The American headquarters could be thankful: they would soon have no assets, no employees and no visible presence in the country, so that they could avoid the world's criticisms, while still profiting from sales under their agreements. They would come closer to the Japanese, who had never invested in South Africa but profited from selling cars or computers.

There was some gloating in Pretoria about the innocuousness of the disinvestment, and some recrimination among anti-apartheid campaigners: 'These companies are not withdrawing from South Africa,' wrote Duncan Innes in the *Weekly Mail* 'they are simply changing the form of their involvement in this country.' Yet the disinvestments remained very serious blows to South Africa: the repayment of the loans would cause a further drain of capital; the multinationals now had much less permanent stake in the country's future; and they could not be relied on to pass on their technology for long. The loss of support from those magic initials IBM and GM was a more visible symbol of the break with the West than any government sanctions.

The exit of General Motors turned out to be much less neat than Roger Smith had hoped, leaving a wake of bitterness. Three thousand workers promptly went on strike in protest against the 'secret and mysterious dealings', insisting on safeguards and benefits under the new owners, thus delaying the introduction of a new car, the Opel Monza. When GM fired some of them and hired more workers from the great pool of unemployed the strikers angrily picketed them, allegedly threatening them with necklaces, until police dispersed them with dogs. After three weeks of striking the management issued an ultimatum, and most strikers returned sullenly to work. The black union federation COSATU insisted that the strike had been against the non-consultation, not against disinvestment itself: and GM was a special case since the future of its South African plants was very uncertain anyway. But the anger over GM's precipitate departure caused some gloating among the opponents of disinvestment who had warned that it would cause loss of jobs; and it put the politicised black union leaders – who wanted both to stop Western support from Pretoria and to safeguard jobs – in a more extreme quandary. It gave a new poignancy to the old saying: 'if there's one thing worse than being exploited by a multinational corporation, it's *not* being exploited by a multinational corporation.'

American capital would remain deeply involved in South Africa's future, even if it preferred not to be – whether through past investments and responsibilities, through the interdependence with the rest of Africa, or through the indispensable precious metals and gold. Disinvestment was the end of one road, but it now raised more acutely the question of the American role in the post-apartheid era, and whether Western capitalism could come to terms with a future black government, and vice versa. Without pressures from Pretoria, the American multinationals now felt freer to make contact with black leaders, including the African National Congress. Could the multinationals change sides, as Gulf-Chevron had swiftly jumped when Angola had become independent, or as Mobil had switched in Rhodesia

–Zimbabwe? Or would the aftermath of South Africa's civil war be so bitter and destructive as to exclude even the oil companies, despite all their skills at surviving? Much of the answer would depend on whether the multinationals could exercise their own long-term diplomacy, and follow up disinvestment with more positive steps to associate themselves with a future black majority.

The most far-reaching of all disinvestments came from Britain, when the chairman of Barclays Sir Tim Bevan, after visiting Johannesburg, announced on November 24 that Barclays was selling out the whole of its 40 per cent interest in its South African subsidiary Barclays National to Anglo-American, together with De Beers and the Insurance group Southern Life. Sir Tim still publicly insisted that it was primarily a commercial decision that 'it was not the job of businessmen to get involved in politics', and that the bank was neither for nor against sanctions. The directors had in fact decided to sell out at a board meeting the previous May, largely because they had been losing business from protesting depositors in Britain: the anti-apartheid campaigners and students in Britain could rightly claim a victory after sixteen years of campaigning. Barclays' disinvestment, like General Motors', caused no immediate economic damage: the London board had to sell its 40 percent interest for about £82 million, at the low exchange rate of the financial rand; the new owners would be glad to maintain the profitable network of branches, still keeping a 'working relationship' with London; and the London board was still saddled with its billion dollars of South African debt. But the Barclays withdrawal, following its decision a year earlier to stop all lending – and coming in the same week as the disinvestment by two more North American groups, Kodak and Bata shoes – was the most significant of all the West's gestures of its dissociation from apartheid policies. For it marked a withdrawal not so much of technology or management but of confidence and credit, in the literal sense of trust, which is the bankers' life blood: it discouraged other foreign corporations, including Barclays' many clients; and it left the remaining British companies, including the rival bank Standard, more exposed to attack. The argument continued about the political impact: Chris Ball of BarNat was worried that it 'would remove the leverage of foreigners' and that 'creeping strangulation' would only change perceptions slowly. But if Western capitalists had wished to show that they had finally written off Pretoria, they could hardly have made it plainer, after sixty years of investment and lending, than by selling their stake in the biggest bank in the country.

Most of the British multinationals remained. A few companies including the Prudential and Hill Samuel cut back their involvement, but the biggest insisted that they would not follow the

Americans, and could improve conditions by staying. Shell remained the ANC's chosen scapegoat, and was increasingly worried: 'Shell is the only company having to handle an international campaign against it,' said John Wilson in an anguished address to his staff in August. He admitted that businessmen had been naïve in trusting Botha, and 'were oblivious of the extent to which cooperation between the state and business in fact repressed black aspirations'.* He saw more trouble ahead: 'Shell's position is not comfortable. The threat of disinvestment is real.' In October the Dutch senior managing director of the Shell group, Lo van Wachem, responded to pressure by condemning Pretoria's policies, in a much-publicised letter to senior executives round the world: he gave a gloomy view of South Africa's future and said that Pretoria's concept of change was 'far removed from the aspirations of the majority'. He denied that business by itself could induce Pretoria to change, while still insisting that Shell must stay, to help prepare black South Africans for the end of apartheid. Yet Shell's position, like that of other European companies, remained suspect to blacks; and the ANC and the UDF still saw them as the allies of Pretoria's military clampdown: for while Shell clearly saw the dangers ahead, they were not able effectively to identify themselves with 'the aspirations of the majority'.

President Botha was stepping up his pressures on companies to rally behind the government, and in November 1986 he summoned his third major meeting in seven years with South African business leaders. Some dissidents were not invited, including Chris Ball of Barclays National and (until the last minute) John Wilson of Shell. Others, including Gavin Relly and Tony Bloom, arranged to be out of the country. But most companies were represented, including Anglo by Zach de Beer, who was encouraged by a report by the President's Economic Advisory Council which acknowledged that 'further reforms in the economic and political fields are largely complementary'. Several speakers at the conference reiterated the need for political reform – but carefully not spelling out specific needs such as the release of Mandela. President Botha, who opened the conference with an appeal for 'realistic idealism', was able to conclude that the meeting was 'full of goodwill'. But the uncritical presence of the businessmen, with no fundamental reforms in sight, was inevitably seen by blacks as a return to the traditional alliance between business and apartheid.

Many liberal white South Africans remained baffled that the West

* Keynote address to Senior Staff Conference, Cape Sun Hotel, August 4–5, 1986

could impose sanctions and thereby set back blacks' economic prospects. Dr Bethlehem, the respected economist of Johannesburg Consolidated Investments, had reckoned in September 1986 that sanctions would drastically reduce the blacks' share of the national income, from a projected 36 percent to 20 percent by the year 2000:

> For the black section of the population it would be a massive sacrifice in foregone opportunity, not only in economic terms but also in political terms, for the political leverage of a black community whose income comprised nearly 36% of all income earned in South Africa would be very much greater than the leverage of a community whose income share was less than 20%.*

It was true that sanctions were the bluntest of blunt weapons, which would hit many others beyond its target. But they were also, as Senator Lugar explained, one of the very few ways in which foreign nations could intervene, short of war.

They certainly came as a shock to Pretoria, in spite of the long forewarnings. For forty years the Afrikaners had dismissed most Western rhetoric against apartheid, with good reasson, as mere posturing; they had remained confident that the West would back them up against the communist onslaught when the chips were down. Now for the first time the Western rhetoric had been backed up by governments as well as by bankers and corporations, in an unmistakeable dissociation.

But more significant than sanctions was the West's shift of policy towards the African National Congress. In September 1986 Sir Geoffrey Howe talked for the first time to Oliver Tambo, following his junior minister Lynda Chalker, in a two-hour discussion at his country house. They had the usual argument about violence; but Sir Geoffrey emphasised that he wanted to keep in touch with the ANC, which in turn welcomed the British government's acceptance that they were central to any South African solution. In the meantime, George Shultz in Washington planned to receive Tambo in the New Year. Pretoria responded to these new openings with angry outbursts; not surprisingly, for they marked the defeat of their strategy to portray the ANC as the tools of Moscow, and to isolate them as pariahs and terrorists like the PLO; while they were a victory of the ANC in *their* strategy to isolate Pretoria. The West's talks with the ANC added the critical political dimension to sanctions: for they indicated that the West was not only withdrawing support from the South African government, but beginning to change sides.

* Sanctions and the Process of Adjustment, JCI, September 12, 1986

Could these half-hearted sanctions have any real effect? South Africa was theoretically acutely vulnerable as an industrial state heavily dependent on trade; but its interlocks with the world system also made it hard to hurt it without hurting others – or the whole system. Gold still provided half South Africa's trade; and the neatest sanction would deliberately depress the price of gold. *The Economist* on July 19 recommended with apparent seriousness that the central banks should threaten to start selling their gold unless Mandela was released – a suggestion which Senator Orrin Hatch took up in Washington. But it was never politically plausible: it needed the support of conservative central bankers, and it would also hit other gold-producers in North America and Australia. And gold was up to its old tricks: as the world economy looked more uncertain the gold-price began to move up, providing a fillip to Pretoria's finances which looked like temporarily compensating for sanctions. Some black politicians were now dreading that the worse their repression the higher the gold price would climb, in eager anticipation of riots, strikes and shut-downs which would reduce the supply.

Arms had been the first target for sanctions; but the UN embargo of weapons since 1977 had often been breached. It was not true, as Pretoria often boasted, that the embargoes had made South Africa virtually self-sufficient in weaponry; the intricate technology of advanced weapons systems now included many crucial components for which there were serious shortages, particularly in electronics; a confidential government report in 1985 had warned that 'any move towards disinvestment from South Africa would have a particularly severe effect on the electronics industry'.* But the profits to be made from selling components to Pretoria were irresistible to middle-men and suppliers: the French who had theoretically obeyed the arms embargo were still supplying spare parts for Mirage planes, while the new South African-made fighter the Cheetah which Botha launched in 1986 was based heavily on French and Israeli technology and components. Only if Western governments began monitoring the arms embargo much more rigorously could they prevent key components getting through.

An oil embargo had been proposed by anti-apartheid campaigners since the early 'sixties; for South Africa had no oil of her own, and the oil-from-coal plants of SASOL could not keep pace with the growing consumption. An embargo by OPEC became more effective after the fall of the Shah of Iran in 1979, who had been Pretoria's loyal ally; and South Africa had to pay high premiums

---

* Gavin Cawthra, *Brutal Force*, London, International Defence and Aid Fund, 1986, p. 102

to buy oil through Oman, Brunei and other embargo-breakers. By 1983 (President Botha revealed three years later) South Africa sometimes had only enough oil for a week; and the premiums over ten years had cost 22 billion rand.* But the oil glut after 1985, like the climbing gold price, came to Pretoria's rescue, making producers more desperate to sell surplus oil; and in early 1986, when the oil-price collapsed, South Africa rapidly replenished her stockpile of oil which was stored in disused mines and elsewhere. Oil tankers continued to arrive at South African ports, many of them commissioned by the embargo-breaking companies Transworld in Rotterdam and Marimpex in Hamburg: the Shipping Research Bureau in Amsterdam, which monitored the oil embargo, identified eighty-three tankers delivering crude oil during 1983 and 1984, including seventeen from Brunei, thirteen from Saudi Arabia and thirteen from Oman. The European Community agreed in September 1985 to cease oil imports to South Africa, but did little to implement the ban.† A serious oil embargo still appeared the most obvious stranglehold on Pretoria; but Western governments were still far from having the will or the means to enforce it.

A ban on airlines flying to and from South Africa had a special attraction to sanctioneers, including Andrew Young who had advocated it for many years. It would have an immediate psychological impact on white South Africans – even if they could still fly to Europe via neighbouring states – while leaving blacks relatively unscathed. The enlarged airports in Zimbabwe or Botswana would become vital to South Africans, thus providing potential hostages against Pretoria's reprisals, while airlines could begin to connect up an alternative air traffic system for the sub-continent. But international airlines – which always see themselves as the special champions of free trade and free movement – strongly resisted any disruption. British Airways, the biggest foreign carrier, had some worries about their dependence on South African airports, and in July 1986 they applied for landing-rights in Botswana. But they were loth to loosen their long-established links; their daily flights to and from South Africa brought in almost a fifth of their total profits – all the more welcome when transatlantic traffic had fallen and BA was about to be privatised – and their combative chairman Lord King had firmly lobbied Mrs Thatcher to resist airline sanctions. Both BA and Lufthansa insisted that if they stopped flying to Johannesburg, Swissair and El Al would gladly take over their

* Speech at Vereeniging, April 25, 1986
† *See* Newsletter on the Oil Embargo, February 1986 and September 1986. Shipping Research Bureau, P.O. Box 11898, Amsterdam

business; but when American sanctions prevented South African Airways from flying to New York Lufthansa added an extra flight to Frankfurt.

It was the Swiss, who belonged to neither the UN, nor the European Community nor NATO, who were portrayed as the weak link in nearly every chain of sanctions: determined that their money must be neutral and secret, prepared to lend, to swap gold or to get capital out of the country with equal impartiality; and the more threatening the sanctions, the greater the profits to be made out of breaking them. But the Swiss, together with the Taiwanese, the Israelis and other identifiable sanctions-breakers, were also convenient scapegoats and excuses for other Europeans to cheat. In Britain officials of the Department of Trade zealously briefed businessmen how to compete with the Swiss in evading sanctions, with the slogan 'one man's sanctions is another man's opportunity': while the Swiss ambassador in Pretoria was privately assuring the black opposition that his country would not increase its trade.

As the Western governments voted for sanctions, Pretoria prepared its own extensive sanctions-busting machinery, with a department of experts – many of them with experience from Rhodesia twenty years before – working with industrialists and importers. Sanctions-busting became part of the new patriotism, to which businessmen had to show their loyalty. But this did not mean they would be ineffectual, nor did Pretoria think so. As the bills were going through they lobbied furiously against them, and Pik Botha made a much-publicised tour to find new trading links in the Far East – where he was well received by Taiwan but got short shrift from Japan. Pretoria would certainly be able to circumvent most sanctions, but at great extra cost; and in the meantime the ban on new investment and the bankers' own sanctions underlined the most serious fact: that there was little prospect of more foreign capital on which to build future growth.

The crucial question about sanctions was not economic but psychological and political: how would white South Africans react to the West's signal? The first impact would certainly provide a challenge and stimulus, to prove themselves and defy the world – as in Rhodesia twenty years earlier. But the sequel would be less exhilarating: for whatever the success of the sanctions-busters, apartheid was already hitting many whites' pockets, and some of their jobs; and the future looked much more dismal. However successful the repression of blacks, it could not generate a lasting internal economic recovery, while the armed forces and police would become a still larger drain on the economy.

It was true that white South Africans had inherited from international investors a remarkably dynamic economic system, which was close to self-sufficiency in many areas. But could they maintain and develop that system, with more and more black consumers as well as factory-workers, while denying them political and human rights and turning the townships into armed camps? Or would the imperatives of industry inevitably press the society towards more individual freedom? There was no lack of depressing precedents, in Nazi Germany, in parts of Latin America or in Eastern Europe, for industrial expansion thriving on minimal rights; and Asia had its own mutations of Western capitalism, like Korea's, which could prosper without genuine democracy. But there was no real parallel for a racial minority in an advanced industrial state depending for their prosperity on an overwhelming majority which was rallying against them. Even before the crackdown white industrialists were already worried in their own factories by the alienation, the lack of incentives and the industrial sabotage which was slowing their productivity. Botha's policy of recognising black unions while stamping out their political role presented a more fundamental contradiction than existed, for instance, in Poland: for apartheid had pressed the black workers into a much more distinctive solidarity, which identified blackness with alienation from the state.

Many Afrikaners were now depicting themselves as 'a first world inside a third world' and liked to believe that their white islands could survive securely and prosperously, while drawing their labour and servants from townships which could be fenced-off in their own separate world of anarchy, repression and black-on-black violence. But could these white bastions remain immune from black-on-white violence, when their factories and homes depended on them? The Afrikaners still clung to the mythology of their tribe, in the midst of their industrialisation: and many conservatives abroad liked to admire the toughness of this 'white tribe of Africa' and to predict that, in a continent of tribes, the strongest would win. But South Africa's unique industrial development had already forged a much more integrated economic system than anywhere in Africa, which was drawing both blacks and whites away from their tribes; and no amount of fencing off could remove their basic interdependence.

Certainly the immediate future must still depend on the decisions of the most powerful tribe. Are the Afrikaners really prepared to pay the price of their economic growth and Western security to defend their own tribal stronghold? Do they have the cohesion – which the Southern States in the civil war ultimately lacked – to sustain a second civil war in defence of their privilege? They had proudly clung to their mythology since the Boer War, and many Westerners including Mrs Thatcher saw them as stubborn to the

last. But myths are never a clear guide to future behaviour; and
even the 'Iron Lady' is outwardly most defiant when she is about to
give way. The Afrikaners had never really been tested since 1902.
They had never had to choose between economic expansion and
white domination because they had comfortably got both: 'The ox
wagon was also a bandwagon,' as Conor Cruise O'Brien put it.*
Through the 'sixties the multinationals had been glad to help extend
both the economic and the military state. However much Western
governments had huffed and puffed against apartheid they had
always played in with yet more delaying tactics from Pretoria, while
their military and intelligence teams had encouraged the Afrikaners
to believe that they stood together against the communist menace.

But Western bankers and governments had now brought home
the choice between apartheid and prosperity, to the point where
whites as well as blacks were being put out of jobs. Verwoerd's
'grand apartheid' may always have been an intellectual sham,
which dressed up domination with religious and anthropological
trappings; but while it was accompanied by spectacular economic
growth in the 'sixties it could convince Afrikaner intellectuals and
even some Westerners. It was its economic failure in the 'seventies
that began to discredit that apartheid theory: and it was not the
political theorists, but the bankers and the blacks between them
who pushed Botha into declaring apartheid outdated and abolishing
the pass-laws. Botha's policies now had no real consistency: at the
end of 1985 he had come very close to releasing Mandela under
pressure from Western governments and bankers; six months later
he switched 180 degrees, slammed the door on Mandela and
declared a more ruthless emergency. With such changeability
no one could confidently claim that the Afrikaners were immune
to pressure: their government was visibly confused, indecisive
and inconsistent, their reforms prompted by international demands.

The theological basis for apartheid was itself crumbling under
both internal and external pressure. In October 1986 the Dutch
Reformed Church, which still claimed 38 percent of South Africa's
whites among its members, reached a muddled compromise by
which they would admit all races to membership, while still not
merging with black or coloured reformed churches; and they also
accepted a policy document announcing 'racism is a sin, which no
person may defend or practice' – which effectively undermined the
religious basis for all past apartheid laws.

The whites no longer have any grand design to maintain white

* *Atlantic Monthly*, March 1986

supremacy over a fast-growing black majority, no new blueprints to replace the tattered schemes for tribal homelands; while Botha has discredited his own tri-cameral parliament by overruling it to declare the emergency. Pretoria still clings to the strategy of dividing black tribes, which enables Afrikaners to argue that there is no real black majority; but the revolts within the homelands and the defections of their leaders are already undermining those assumptions. The Afrikaners' special language of power-sharing, group rights and consultation looks more obviously bogus as the government becomes more desperately pragmatic, determined to maintain its power with brute force like any other police state.

For the younger generation of Afrikaners – and of all white South Africans – the long-term future under sanctions must be bleak: slow economic growth, if any, which cannot keep pace with the rising black population and costs of defence; factories which depend on markets abroad, which are increasingly denied to them; an expectation and pride which had been nurtured on widening horizons and rapid development, now facing contraction; and above all a degeneration into a brutal civil war. Pretoria's current counter-attack against the black resistance may well produce for a time a new appearance of white calm and black divisiveness, with the help of mass detentions, unleashing black vigilante and encouraging tribal conflicts: but the government can offer no convincing scenario of how they can gain any long-term black consent. Without it, military priorities will take over from economic incentives, while whites will face much greater personal dangers and strains. The argument will continue as to whether the Afrikaners will be stubborn to the end; whether (in the Boer War terminology) they will be 'hands-uppers' or 'bitter-enders'. But as the choices become harsher, mythologies will clash with realities. It is quite true that the Afrikaners, unlike the French in Algeria, have nowhere else to go; but for that reason, they will in the end – like the whites in the Deep South – face the realities of compromise, as the French colonists never did.

In the light of past history it is absurd for Western governments or companies to expect Pretoria to make reforms by itself, to dismantle the structure of apartheid. The context and assumptions which Pretoria has set distort all the perspectives inside South Africa, where the roads only meet off the map and the communities look less and less like a single nation. The South African union seventy-eight years ago now looks like a dangerous experiment which has reached the point of explosion and semi-civil war which can tear the country apart. And as Keppel-Jones warned forty years ago, just before the apartheid government came to power: 'The salvation of this country can lie only in a reversal of historic

tendencies so thorough as to constitute a revolution.'* The interest
of the West must lie in making that revolution as bloodless and
manageable as possible: in preserving the continuity of human
rights, the respect for the law and civilised values; and in making
their own links with a future non-racial or black government.

To achieve that, Western governments must follow their own
road-map and ignore Pretoria's dead end. Western businessmen
and diplomats talk about the precipice and the abyss, but prefer
not to contemplate how they might cross over them: with all their
protestation against apartheid, they try to avoid the question of
'one man, one vote', or who will hold power in the end. Yet the
character of the future black government, and its relationships with
Western governments and corporations, will depend crucially on
the nature of the transition, and on the bridges that the West can
build across the ravine. The longer the West refuses to face up to
a future black majority, the more anti-Western it is likely to be.
The complaints that the black opposition is communist can all too
easily be self-fulfilling, if the West refuses to provide its own support;
but the evidence inside South Africa suggests that it is home-grown
nationalism and anti-capitalism which present a much greater force
than external communism.

The Western corporations must be decisive actors in this drama,
as much as governments. Their interests are crucially threatened;
their behaviour, more than their governments', will determine black
attitudes to the West; and they can act more decisively and quickly
than governments (as Kissinger said).† Many more American
companies will certainly disinvest, rather than endure attacks at
home for the sake of an unpromising future inside South Africa;
and disinvestment is preferable to the kind of passive playing-in
with Pretoria which has accompanied so much investment over the
forty years of apartheid, and which has so damaged the relations
between blacks and business. But disinvestment is in itself a purely
negative policy, which all too easily leads to a general writing-off
of the future of Southern Africa, white or black. There remains, I
believe, a potentially crucial role for Western corporations which
choose to stay – provided they face up to the long-term implications
and responsibilities, as actors not spectators in the drama. This
narrative has, I hope, shown how often in the past corporations
have undermined their own future by assuming political impotence,
and not daring to pursue their own long-term interests, whether by
publicly dissociating themselves from apartheid, by educating and

* *See* p. 62
† *See* p. 21

promoting their black employees, or by breaking down internal segregation, for fear of reprisals or a white backlash which are often illusory. Today the necessity to take a political role is far more urgent. To safeguard their own future the corporations will have to distance themselves from the short-term pressures which push them towards Pretoria, and look ahead to a future black government. If they are to convince blacks that they are on their side they will have to make a much more decisive commitment to their community and political groups: they cannot merely provide 'neutral support' in the form of black education, housing or welfare – which will always be compromised by the constraints of the apartheid system.

Within South Africa the military-political offensive and the polarisation on both sides will lead to a still more ferocious confrontation, which will make it harder for companies to change sides. The peaceful movements for black rights, including consumer boycotts of shops and protests of labour unions, become more difficult as their leaders are detained and the young activists call for more ruthless action. The government is once again determined, as it was in 1960 and 1977, to show that it can achieve what Britain and France failed to achieve in their colonies in the fifties (with very few exceptions such as Malaya); to permanently crush the opposition with their counter-revolutionary offensive and to make the ANC more ineffective than the PLO. The severity of the emergency laws and the effective clampdown on news may well give the appearance of success for some time in military and police terms. But the government's military obsession continues to distort its thinking, as it did in previous crises. No military strategy, as General Malan used to admit, can ever succeed without capturing 'hearts and minds': and it is not only black hearts and minds that have become more rebellious, but those of many administrators, theologians and business executives who cannot contemplate a permanent military solution.

The context of the conflict is now rapidly extending to the neighbouring countries as Pretoria takes reprisals against them: while the two ex-Portuguese states, Angola and Mozambique, are rent by civil wars in which the rebels are supported by South Africa; and the death of President Machel has brought a new danger that Mozambique will be split in two. No one should underestimate Pretoria's scope for destabilizing the whole region, thus both extending their influence and appearing to prove their point that blacks are incapable of self-government. But the wider conflict presents an opportunity as well as a danger for the western governments and corporations: for the solution to many deadlocks can be found by changing the context (as Jean Monnet insisted when he overcame the deadlock between France and Germany in 1950 by taking the first steps towards a European Community). The western nations can only begin to resolve the South African deadlock, and to intervene effectively to reach a peaceful solution, in the wider context of the surrounding states which are beyond the reach of the apartheid system: and they will have to pick up this challenge in the most positive way. For the front-line states will become the real bases of opposition, through which the West can maintain its presence and continuity untainted by Pretoria; and they will desperately need to build up their alternative infrastructure of air, rail and roads links independent of Pretoria's control, if they are not to become dragged further into the South African disaster. Only by providing support in this wider region can the western governments and companies break away more completely from the fatal associations with apartheid which have so seriously damaged their future prospects of maintaining their influence in a black South Africa.

Index

Choabe, Seretse, 192
Christian Institute, 111
Chrysler, 87, 90, 102
Church Commissioners, 174
Churchill, Lord Randolph, 48, 51
CIA (Central Intelligence Agency), 81,
     82n, 251
Ciba-Geigy, 152
Cillie, Judge, 111
Cillie, Piet, 66
Citibank, 29, 31, 35, 129, 139–40, 173,
     208, 209, 210
Citicorp, 171
Citizen, 242
City Press, 143, 187
Civil Rights Commission, 166
Clark, Senator Dick, 126–8
Clausen, Tom, 129
Cleminson, Sir James, 207
Coca-Cola, 27, 210, 211, 253
Code of Conduct, 213
Coetzee, General, 147
Cole, Lord, 88
Colgate Palmolive, 65, 210
Collins, Canon, 106, 148
Colonial Office, 47
Comintern, 72–3
Commentary, 13
Commonwealth, 11–13, 15, 62, 67, 87,
     90, 153, 196, 217, 218, 219, 247,
     248, 249, 251
'Commonwealth Accord', 218
'Commonwealth Group', ('Eminent
     Persons'), 11, 13, 25, 218–19,
     221–3, 249, 251
Commonwealth Report on South
     Africa, 205
Community Support Committee, 236
'Comprehensive Anti-Apartheid Act,
     The', 251
Confederation of British Industries, 89,
     100, 207
Congo, 79, 114
Consolidated Goldfields, 14, 25–6, 49,
     51, 55, 102, 124
Control Data, 142, 172
'Corner House', 49, 92
Cosas, 159, 177, 181, 239
COSATU, 183–4, 234, 240
Council for Christian Social Action,
     120
Council for Economic Priorities, 120
Council of Foreign Relations, 166

Courtaulds, 26, 88, 94, 123, 124–5, 205
Crocker, Chester, 19, 32, 143, 144, 153
Cronje, Frans, 152, 203
Crosland, Anthony, 89
Cunningham, Alex, 127
Curtis, Lionel, 52

Davidson, Basil, 84
Davidson, Ian, 175–6
Davies, John, 89
Davy, 94
De Beer, Zach, 22, 23, 193, 256
De Beers Consolidated Mines, 22, 35,
     46–9 *passim*, 56, 57, 69, 72, 95
De Broe, Williams, 115
De Kiewiet, C. W., 53, 63, 69, 74, 84
De Klerk, F. W., 226
De Kock, Gerhard, 32–40 *passim*,
     154–5, 240, 241, 243
De Larosiere, 35
De Tocqueville, 150
De Villiers, Wim, 92, 210, 211
Deere, 210
Defence Advisory Board, 203
Delmas, 19
Denton, Senator, 251
Department of Health, 203
Deutsche Bank, 139
Devon, Transvaal, 100
Diedrichs, Dr Nico, 61
Diggs, Charles, 165
Diggs, Max, 165
Discount House of SA, 94
Ditchley Park, 137, 211
Drum, 7, 19, 179
Du Plessis, Barend, 33, 34, 36, 38, 240
Du Plessis, Fred, 22, 193, 210, 230, 231
Dube, Dr John, 71
Duncan, Sir Val, 123
Dunkelsbuhler, 55
Dunlop South Africa, 211
Durban, 18, 46, 81, 100, 107, 161, 183,
     205, 208, 234, 243
Durham, Sir Kenneth, 205
Dutch Reformed Church, 156, 261
Dykes, Hugh, 198

East London, 107
Eastern Cape, 69, 76, 77, 160, 185, 233
Eastman Kodak, 172
Eckstein, Hermann, 49
Economist, The, 91, 118, 124, 153, 202,
     258

Swissair, 259
Syfret's Trust, 102

Tambo, Adelaide, 148
Tambo, Oliver, 7, 77, 114, 158, 179,
   181, 183, 205
   admired in townships, 18
   and Amanzimtoti killings, 197
   and America, 148
   meets American companies, 165–6
   and ANC, 69
   and ANC's ideology, 162
   and ANC's new slogans, 159
   background, 75
   talks with bankers, 24–5, 30, 43, 166
   and black consciousness, 112
   and black unions, 182
   talks with British and American
      ministers, 27
   talks to businessmen, 24–5, 165–6,
      194–7, 231, 242
   and Buthelezi, 145, 186
   Christianity, 106
   and Commonwealth Group, 219, 222
   and disinvestment, 139, 159
   and Howe, 27, 255–6
   at Kabwe, 160, 161
   lack of communication with other
      leaders, 45
   law work, 75, 76
   Leutwiler refuses to meet, 40
   meets London bankers and MPs,
      197–8
   on martial law, 178
   and 'necklaces', 20
   meets Relly, 190
   and Pretoria bombing (1983), 147
   talks to David Rockefeller, 30
   and sanctions, 26, 198
   seeks help, 83
   comment on SA arms programme,
      102
   on trades unions, 182
   treason trial, 78
Tanzania, 80, 83, 92, 112, 139
Tappan, David, 210
Tar Baby Option, 118
Tate & Lyle, 123
Terre'Blanche, Eugene, 234
Texaco, 172
Thatcher, Denis, 12, 138, 153, 215–16
Thatcher, Margaret, 19

view of Afrikaners, 12, 15–16, 138,
   174, 260
view of ANC, 138, 214, 216
and apartheid, 244, 247
and bankers' withdrawal, 31
relationship with Botha, 153–4, 216
and Commonwealth, 218, 247, 248,
   249
and Commonwealth Group, 11, 219,
   222
and Mandela, 41
opinion of conditions in SA, 12–13
and sanctions, 12, 13, 14, 15, 31, 171,
   216, 217, 230, 247, 248, 251, 258
and 'Soviet menace', 215
and terrorism, 12, 216
Themba, Can, 74, 80
Thomas Barlow, 102
Thomas, Franklin, 163, 164
Thompson, Julian Ogilvie, 22
Thompson, J. Walter, 242–3
Thompson, Leonard, 133, 189, 231
Thorn EMI, 174
Time, 122, 140
Times, The, 205
Tongaat Group, 146
'Torch Commando', 57
TransAfrica, 164–5
Transkei, 75, 104, 112
Transvaal, 46, 50–54 *passim*, 70, 185
Transvaal, Eastern, 179
Transvaal, Northern, 88
Transvaal Chamber of Industries, 115
Transworld, 259
Treason Cage, The (Sampson), 7
Treasury, 67
Treurnicht, Andreas, 109, 150, 234
Trollope, Anthony, 47, 69
Trust Bank, 22, 36, 92
Tshombe, Moise, 114
Tucker, Bob, 23
TUCSA, 107, 135
Tuke, Sir Anthony, 130, 139
Turfloop University, 136
Turner, Louis, 88
Turner, Sir Mark, 205
Tutu, Bishop Desmond, 14, 18, 158,
   167, 177, 179, 214
   and American involvement, 168
   on apartheid, 141
   and bankers, 38, 41
   on businessmen, 247
   on civil rights, 164

and Howe, 248
London visit, 196
Nobel Peace Prize, 158, 166
calls for sanctions, 220–21
on State of Emergency, 178, 237
tours America, 167–8, 172

UAL, 94, 102
Uitenhage, 160, 169
UK-South African Trade Association
(UKSATA), 89, 90, 100, 124, 138,
174–5, 206, 207
Umkhonto we Sizwe, 81, 83, 106, 112,
147, 199
Ungar, Sanford, 137
Unilever, 88–9, 122, 123, 124, 125, 205,
249
Union Acceptances, 94
Union Bank of Switzerland, 37, 138
Union Carbide, 90, 141
Union Corporation, 93
United Africa Company, 205
United Democratic Front (UDF), 19,
157–8, 159, 167, 169, 179, 185,
203, 221, 228, 239, 240, 255
United Nations, 35, 70, 73, 89, 100,
101, 106, 113, 126, 129, 138, 258
United Party, 61, 63, 132
United Workers Union of South Africa
(UWUSA), 234
University of South Africa, 97
Urban Foundation, 23, 115, 116, 173
US Chamber of Commerce, 126
US Corporate Council on South Africa,
209–11, 212, 218, 230
US Gypsum, 210
Uwusa, 184
Uys, Stanley, 104, 231

'Vaal Triangle', 159
Vaderland, 192
Van den Bergh, Hendrik, 61, 90, 132
Van der Post, Laurens, 12, 98, 237
Van Eck, H. J., 62
Van Vuuren, Mias, 211
Van Wachem, Lo, 256
Van Wyk, Chris, 22, 36
Vance, Cyrus, 125, 211
Verwoerd, Dr Hendrik
and apartheid, 64–6, 97, 104–5, 178,
262
assassination, 90

attempted assassination of, 79, 80,
113
and Botha, 132
forced out of Commonwealth, 153
creation of republic, 67
Viljoen, Gerrit, 233
Vojta, George, 129
Volk, Het, 53
Volkskas, 61
Volkswagen, 76, 160
Voorbrand tobacco company, 98
Voortrekkerhoogte, 147
Vorster, (Balthazar) John, 84, 100,
101, 104, 106, 107, 115, 127, 134,
137, 216
attitude to blacks, 90
and businessmen, 90–91, 133
and Buthelezi, 114
imprisoned as supporter of Hitler,
61, 90
and 'Muldergate' scandal, 132

Waddell, Gordon, 22, 14, 151
Wall Street Journal, 30–31, 170–71, 209
Walters, Sir Peter, 173
Warner, Rawleigh, 173, 210
Washington Post, 121, 244
Wassenaar, Andries, 98–9
Watt, David, 205
Weekly Mail, 238, 254
Weicker, Senator Lowell, 165, 250, 251
Weinstock, Lord, 205
Wernher, Harold, 53
Wernher, Julius, 49, 53, 55, 92
Wernher, Lady Zia, 53
Western Cape, 185
Wheatcroft, Geoffrey, 48
When Smuts Goes (Keppel-Jones), 62
White, Bob, 212
Wiehahn, Professor Nic, 134
Wiehahn report, 134–5
Wilking, Louis, 169
Willers, David, 192
Williams, Ruth, 63
Wilson, Francis, 97
Wilson, Harold, 100, 101, 108
Wilson, John, 134, 203, 206, 241, 242,
256
Wilson Rowntree, 123, 207
Wisner, Frank, 153
Witwatersrand
see 'Rand'
Wolfson, Isaac, 86